THINK LIKE A CEO AND GET RICH

THINK LIKE A CEO AND GET RICH

How an Everyday Couple Retired in Just Seven Years
and Started Living the Life They Truly Wanted

Tyrone Shephard

Library and Archives Canada Cataloguing in Publication

Shephard, Tyrone,
       Think like a CEO and get rich : how an everyday couple retired in just seven years and started living the life they truly wanted / Tyrone Shephard.

ISBN 978-0-9952717-0-8 (paperback)
ISBN 978-0-9952717-2-2 (ePDF)
ISBN 978-0-9952717-1-5 (eMobi)
ISBN 978-0-9952717-3-9 (ePub)

This book is designed to provide accurate and authoritative information on the subject of personal finance. While all of the stories and anecdotes described in the book are based on true experiences, some names are pseudonyms, and some situations have been changed slightly for educational purposes and to protect each individual's privacy. The opinions and ideas expressed herein are solely those of the author. The author and publisher are not engaged in rendering legal, accounting, tax, insurance, financial, investment or other professional advice or services in this publication. This publication is not intended to provide a basis for action in particular circumstances without consideration by a competent professional. The strategies outlined in this book may not be suitable for every individual, and are not guaranteed or warrantied to produce any particular results. Furthermore, any examples presented are intended only as illustrations.

The author and publisher assume no responsibility for errors or omissions and expressly disclaim any responsibility for any liability, loss or risk, personal or otherwise, which is incurred as a consequence, directly or indirectly, of the use and application of any of the contents of this book.

Published by
Tyrone Shephard
PO Box 64552, Coquitlam, British Columbia, V3J 7V7
Canada
www.moneysuckingmaggots.com
moneysuckingmaggots@gmail.com

To my children, Daniella and Alexander.

And to everybody else who dreams of achieving financial freedom and living the life they truly want.

Table of Contents

Acknowledgements

To everybody who has helped me to write this book, I say a sincere – THANK YOU.

In particular, I'd like to thank my brother, Kyle Shephard, and my good friends Chau Vo and Mark Chabot, Vice President and Wealth Advisor for RBC Dominion Securities Inc., for their valuable knowledge and input.

To my wife, Analia, thank you for supporting me through all the crazy escapades of the last decade. The journey to financial freedom, the numerous career changes, and all the other adventures, would not have been possible without your love and support. I am blessed to have found you.

Why This Book Was Written

This book is an account of how my wife and I were able to achieve financial freedom in our mid-thirties. The strategies we used are not revolutionary or difficult to implement, nonetheless, they are strategies that are rarely used by most individuals today.

These strategies are, however, used by the CEOs of the largest, most successful corporations on earth and have been used extensively by some of the most successful CEOs and business leaders of the past two centuries. If you learn these strategies and start thinking like these powerful CEOs, you will get rich.

My hope is that this book enables others to realize that achieving financial freedom and living the life they truly want is a goal that is well within their grasp.

INTRODUCTION

Financial Freedom

"Can we really afford to do this?" asked my wife.

I had already quit my job two years ago when I was thirty-six years-old, and now, at thirty-five years-old, my wife was on the verge of doing the same.

What's more, we were also just a few short weeks away from dropping everything and spending the next year or two in Spain. We weren't going to Spain for any sort of job opportunities. In fact, we had no jobs lined up at all.

"People at work keep asking me how we can afford to do this," she continued.

My wife's friends at work weren't the only ones wondering how my wife and I were able to afford this little escapade. I don't think my wife's parents believed we were quitting our jobs and moving to another country until we actually boarded the plane. Likewise, my brother, a well-paid doctor in Seattle, was in a state of shock over how we could afford to keep our house in Greater Vancouver and still be able to pay for this little adventure.

To be honest, dropping everything and moving to Spain wasn't exactly what I had pictured for us either when, ten years earlier, we had first come up with a plan to try and rapidly grow our wealth and retire much quicker than most.

Up until that point, I had spent most of my life in school. And after many years of university, not to mention two post-graduate degrees, I had accumulated a lot of knowledge but very little wealth.

Now, ten years later, all that had changed. At thirty-eight and thirty-five years-old, my wife and I had now achieved a level of financial freedom that many people our age only dreamed of. We had a net worth that far exceeded $1 million, and we could support our lifestyle using the income generated from our investments alone.

In short, we were no longer dependent on our employment income to live the lives we truly wanted. We had achieved financial freedom. We could work if we wanted to work, but we didn't need to work. Given all of this, we had decided that dropping everything and taking a year off in Spain was what we truly wanted.

How did we accomplish this relatively rapid increase in wealth? We did it by thinking and acting like the business leaders and CEOs of some of the largest, most successful businesses of our time.

CHAPTER ONE

Think Like a CEO

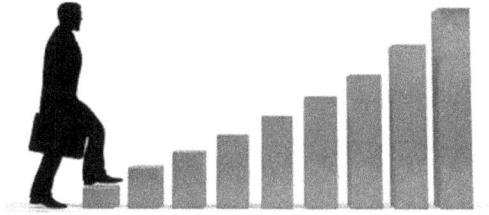

The year was 2005. I had just finished my MBA, and I had recently started working in downtown Toronto for a large multinational pharmaceutical company.

My parents, who had always lamented the importance of going to university and getting a good job, couldn't have been prouder. All those years of hard work and schooling had finally paid off. I would now be able to settle down, spend the rest of my life at work and, hopefully, save enough money for a comfortable retirement sometime in my late sixties.

There was one small problem. I wasn't happy. I would say that after less than a year on the job, I was mostly indifferent. I would also say that the idea of spending the rest of my life stuck in the rat-race and retiring many decades later was a pretty depressing thought.

I would work late most evenings, take work home with me at the end of the day, and take even more work home with me on the weekends. I also seemed to be perpetually glued to my phone or my computer. And if I wasn't working, I was commuting.

On a good day, it would take me about an hour to get to work. On a bad day, it would take me closer to an hour and a half. If it snowed, make it two hours.

Moving from the suburbs to live in downtown Toronto and succumbing to Toronto's soul crushing real estate prices wasn't much of a better option.

My new, somewhat disenchanted life seemed to revolve around going to work or being at work. The work I did was okay, but the thought of being stuck in a job every day for the rest of my life was not.

Not too long after I came to this gloomy conclusion, I attended a presentation designed to inform new employees about the company's pension plan.

The cheerful presenter seemed to merrily put up slide after slide, showing all the different ways employees could contribute to the company's pension plan, and discussed what type of payout these contributions would lead to sometime in the *very* distant future. As with most meetings, many people seemed to sit there blissfully unaware of anything that happy woman was saying.

For me, however, those slides started adding to the uneasy feeling that had already been building in my stomach over the past few months. Sitting there, looking up at those slides, was a rude awakening to the fact that unless I did something about it, I would be stuck working like this for the next forty years.

Visions of Bill Murray dropping a toaster into his bathtub began to enter my head. Dropping a toaster into the bathtub was what Bill Murray's character, Phil, did in the movie *Groundhog Day* in an attempt to kill himself so that he could escape the monotonous, unhappy existence he somehow ended up stuck in when he was forced to magically wake up every morning and relive the same unhappy day of his life, over and over again.

For Phil, dropping a toaster into his bath didn't work. Just like most people who are unhappy in their jobs, Phil simply ended up waking up again the next morning, exactly as he did every morning, stuck in his own personal purgatory.

I remember deciding at that moment that this would not be my fate. I decided right then and there to put my financial freedom into my own hands. I also decided that I would achieve financial freedom far quicker than the forty years shown on those slides.

I had taken plenty of business courses in my life, and I was about to start putting this knowledge to good use. My business knowledge would now not only be used for my company's financial well-being; it would be used, far more importantly, for my own financial well-being.

I started pursing the goal of financial freedom in the same way that a great CEO pursues the goal of growing a company's profits. And just like a great CEO, I was determined to succeed.

Think Like a Great CEO

Great CEOs are relentless in their pursuit to continuously increase their company's profits. The cold hard truth is that increasing profits each year is the only option that many of these CEOs have.

Besides the fact that their paycheque and their future employment depend on these increased profits, their company's very existence could be in jeopardy if these CEOs are unable to deliver on this endeavour. Without consistent profit growth, a corporation's share price will inevitably tumble. And if the share price tumbles, a large corporation could lose hundreds of millions or even billions of dollars.

As a result of this unyielding pursuit of profits, the CEOs of the largest, most successful corporations in the world are able to increase their company's profits each and every year. In doing so, they enable their corporations to pay out handsome returns to their company's shareholders.

In fact, at the time of writing this, some large corporations such as Colgate-Palmolive, Johnson and Johnson, Proctor and Gamble, 3M, and The Coca-Cola Company, have paid out increasing dividends (a sum of money paid out at regular intervals to a company's shareholders) for over fifty years.

What's more, many of these corporations are very likely to continue with these increasing dividend payouts for years to come.

What types of strategies do the CEOs of these successful companies employ to achieve this type of success? More importantly, can you use these strategies to grow your own wealth?

Employing the same strategies that these successful CEOs use will not only help you to grow your own wealth, it will help you to grow it at a rate much quicker than traditionally thought possible.

Let's list these strategies now, and then spend the rest of the chapter introducing them in more detail.

Strategies Used by Successful CEOs

1. Have a business plan.
2. Concentrate on core competencies and get your money working for you.
3. Relentlessly cut costs and control expenses.
4. Strengthen your financial acumen.
5. Take the money you earn and invest it to make more money.
6. Manage risk.
7. Use the power of leverage.
8. Minimize taxes.

Every successful CEO in the world uses these eight strategies to build a company's wealth. You need to start doing the same.

Unlike the corporations mentioned above, however, you will not use these eight strategies to produce consumer products such as toothpaste, soap, or colas; you will use these strategies to create a portfolio of income producing investments.

Income producing investments will be the core components of your *financial freedom fund* (a portfolio of investments that will lead to your financial freedom). These income producing investments will provide you with a never-ending stream of income and, what's more, they will eventually lead to your financial freedom.

Your financial freedom fund is your own personal business and, congratulations, you are the CEO. It is the most important business that you will ever be a part of. Just like a successful CEO, be diligent in the application of the strategies mentioned above and be relentless in the pursuit of financial freedom. If you do this, you too will succeed at creating a never-ending stream of rising income.

Have a Business Plan

Successful CEOs don't rely on luck to generate wealth. They have well thought-out strategies and they have well thought-out business plans that *ensure* they create wealth.

Furthermore, great CEOs excel at executing these plans. There's no point in coming up with a great business plan if you are not going to execute it. As we will see in chapter 2, business magnate John D. Rockefeller used this strategy to become one of the richest people the world has ever seen.

You need to adopt a similar approach with your financial freedom fund. You need to come up with a strategy for becoming financially free, and you need to come up with a well thought-out business plan to guide you. And most important of all, you need to execute this plan.

Many people devote years studying and training for their profession but devote no time at all towards managing their money. This cannot be you. Everything starts with a plan. That being said, it's amazing how many smart people there are out there that have no plan at all for managing their money. Even more surprising is the fact that many people don't seem to be bothered by this.

This is unfortunate. If many people were to devote a fraction of the time they spend working for others, to instead working for themselves and coming up with a well thought-out plan to manage their own finances, they could probably retire many years earlier.

> *"Vision without execution is just hallucination."*
> - Henry Ford.

A plan by itself, however, won't lead to financial freedom. You also need to execute this plan. As billionaire business leader and legendary inventor Henry Ford once said, "Vision without execution is just hallucination." If you want your financial freedom to become a reality, you need to have a plan and you need to execute it.

Concentrate on Core Competencies

The CEOs of successful businesses ensure that their companies spend years learning, training, and becoming good at whatever it is they do. Along the way, these companies develop a certain set of skills and amass a certain amount of resources that offer them a competitive advantage in the marketplace. These skills and resources, taken together, are referred to as a company's *core competencies*.

Great CEOs make sure their companies develop and take advantage of as many profitable core competencies as possible. Then they use the money generated from these core competencies to make even more money. You need to do the same.

You need to develop some sought after core competencies that enable you to earn as much money as possible. Then you need to use this money to make even more money.

Have a Cash Cow and Get Your Money Working for You

Successful CEOs also ensure that their companies use their core competencies to create reliable sources of steady income. These reliable sources of steady income are often referred to as *cash cows*.

Once established, these cash cows require very little work to maintain and reward their owners with a perennial source of income. Better still, CEOs take the perennial income generated by their cash cows and invest it to generate more income.

You need to do the same. Your job is your cash cow and you need to take some of the money it generates and invest it. Make no mistake about it; the more money you can squeeze out of your job, the quicker you will be able to achieve financial freedom.

Just like successful CEOs, concentrate on developing core competencies, make as much money as you can from them, and then use this money to earn even more money.

Keep in mind, however, that having a good-paying job doesn't necessarily mean that only well-paid professionals, such as doctors or lawyers, are able to achieve financial freedom.

The majority of the people that I know with high-paying jobs never obtain any sort of financial freedom. They have higher paying jobs, but they never get any of their money working for them. They simply spend all of their employment income on bigger houses, newer cars, eating out, and more expensive vacations. They don't reach financial freedom any quicker than the rest of the world; they just spend more money than the rest of the world.

Even if you have a salary that is below average, it will still be possible for you to obtain financial freedom quicker than most. To do so, however, not only will you need to concentrate on your core competencies, you will also need to relentlessly cut costs, control expenses, and live below your means. As we will see in chapter 3, this is the secret to success for many of the millionaires in America.

Relentlessly Cut Costs and Control Expenses

The CEOs of all successful companies relentlessly cut costs. Not only that, these CEOs never stop looking for ways to do so!

If these CEOs can find a way to cut costs, they do it. Whether it is having fewer employees, finding cheaper raw materials, or finding a cheaper space to rent, they do it. And no expenses are left unexplored. Successful CEOs are lean mean profit making machines. Here too, you need to follow their lead.

Costs are financial freedom sucking maggots. Large recurring costs latch onto your financial freedom fund and perpetually suck money away from it. Find a cheaper place to live, start doing more things yourself, and become more frugal. Whatever it is you can do to lower costs, do it. And start doing it right now.

Having the fortitude to minimize your daily living expenses will allow you to maximize the amount of income you have left over to invest. And having income left over to invest will be absolutely essential to achieving any sort of financial freedom quickly.

After all, how can you ever get your money working for you if you spend it all every time you get it?

While others may choose to spend their money frivolously, your best chance for achieving financial freedom quicker than most will be to live below your means, save your money, and invest it. Remember, the sooner you get your money working for you, the sooner you'll stop working for it.

Sam Walton, the legendary founder of Walmart, made cost cutting a way of life for his company and for himself. We'll hear more about his story in chapter 4 and see how it led to Walmart becoming one of the largest retailers in the world and to Sam Walton becoming one of the richest men in America.

Strengthen Your Financial Acumen and Think Outside the Box

Financial acumen is the ability to make good financial decisions. It is one of the key drivers of success for businesses and it will be one of the key drivers of success for you.

No successful CEO would ever make an important financial decision without first putting in a great deal of thought and analysis. You must adopt this way of thinking, too.

Whenever you have a large decision to make that will affect your finances, like buying a house, you need to make sure you consider this decision carefully. Do not take these types of large financial decisions lightly. Consider them carefully and analyze how they will affect your financial freedom fund. Evaluate all your options and then make the decisions that will enable you to reach financial freedom sooner, not later.

From this day forward, start thinking about and evaluating the financial consequences of all your decisions. Always consider as many options as you can and always try and choose the ones that save or generate the most money. Business magnate and legendary inventor Henry Ford was famous for coming up with ingenious ways to save or generate more money. We'll go over his story in chapter 5 to see how he became one of the wealthiest individuals of all time.

In addition to financial acumen, great CEOs succeed because they think outside the box. Businesses thrive on innovation, and innovative businesses use their ideas to earn even more money. You need to do the same. And when it comes to achieving financial freedom, you also need to consider doing things differently than most.

Sometimes the best options for achieving financial freedom will take you off the beaten path. And sometimes the best options will lead you away from the herd. Don't worry about it. **Following the herd is not going to lead you to financial freedom.**

Take the Money You Earn and Invest It to Make More Money

All successful CEOs take some of the money their companies earn and invest it to make more money. Automotive companies take some of their earnings and use them to develop new models of cars. Mining companies take some of their earnings and use them to discover new mines. Whether it is a new mine or a new model of car, these CEOs are essentially investing in their future cash cows.

Successful CEOs don't squander their money; they invest it to make more money. You need to do the same.

Even if you do get a good-paying job and cut costs, you will never achieve financial freedom by stuffing that large pile of dollars you save under your mattress. Instead, you need to invest all those dollars. You need to invest them and get them working for you.

I guarantee you these dollars will be the best little employees you ever have. They won't complain, they won't go on vacation, and they won't take sick days. All they will do is work. They will work day and night to make you more and more money. Make a pledge right now to spend less of your money on financial freedom sucking maggots and to invest more of your money in income producing investments.

Does this mean you should take all of your savings and invest it in your friend's new business idea that he *guarantees* will make you both rich? No. While this type of investment may sometimes workout, more often than not, it doesn't.

The safest most effective way for you to grow your wealth while keeping the reliable income coming in from your day job is to invest your savings in a combination of stocks, bonds, and real estate. And your number one investment option should be the stock market. In chapter 8 we will see the story of how a janitor from Vermont was able to generate over $8 million dollars by following this strategy.

History has proven that, over the long-term, the stock market always go up. Even if there are ups and downs along the way, sometime in the future, the stock market will eventually end up higher.

In fact, the compound annual growth rate (CAGR) of the Standard & Poor's 500 (S&P 500), an American stock market index composed of 500 of the largest companies listed on the New York Stock Exchange (NYSE) or the National Association of Securities Dealers Automated Quotations (NASDAQ) exchange, in the period between Jan 1, 2004 to Jan 1, 2015, has been roughly 8% per year (assuming reinvestment of dividends). Even with the financial crisis in 2008, if you had invested in the S&P 500 over this time period, you would have earned an average return of 8% per year. The CAGR generated by the S&P 500 over the thirty year period between Jan 1, 1985 to Jan 1, 2015 is even more impressive and works out to be 11.4% per year (again, assuming reinvestment of all dividends).

Is this growth going to stop? Not likely. The S&P 500 has been growing for centuries. The idea that the corporations that make up this index are going to somehow suddenly stop making more money is not realistic.

Historically speaking, corporate earnings in the U.S. have grown at an average rate of about 4.7 % per year, and as I write this, the S&P 500 has a dividend yield of 2.2%. Put these two metrics together and you would expect a minimum growth rate of roughly 7% per year.

A long-term CAGR of 7% on any investments made in the stock market is the assumption made for all the stock market investments discussed throughout this book.

Referring to the graph below, it can be seen that the S&P 500 went from a value of 17 at the beginning of 1950 to a value of about 2,000 at the start of 2015. This means a $1,000 investment in the S&P 500 at the start of 1950 would be worth roughly $123,500 at the start of 2015. This is in spite of all the recessions and financial crises experienced along the way. Moreover, if you had invested $1,000 at the start of 1950 and then reinvested all the dividends you had received, you would have been looking at an even bigger return, somewhere in the neighborhood of $1.1 million.

S&P 500 (1950 - 2015)

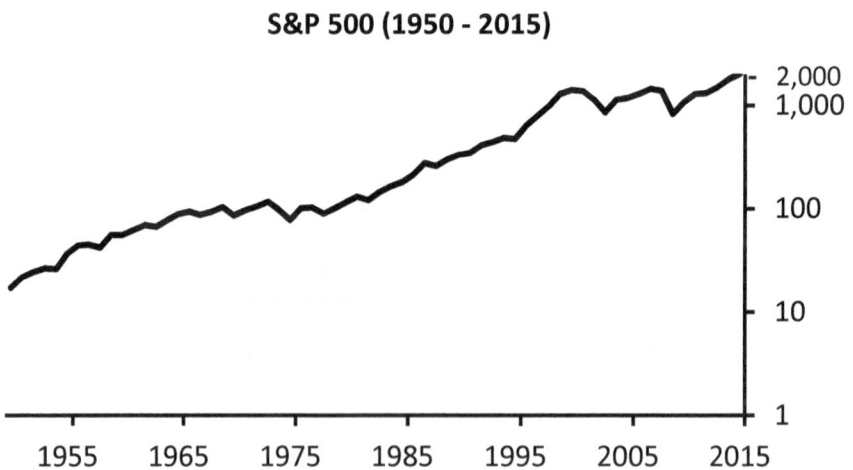

Manage Risk

Not only do great CEOs excel at making money; they also excel at managing risk. They don't speculate, they invest in diversified lines of business that have a history of earning money. And they don't ignore large risks, they get insurance. You need to follow their lead and do the same.

The CEO of a pharmaceutical company wouldn't dream of investing any money towards developing a new medication without ensuring beforehand that this investment would generate an appropriate return. You need to do the same. Successful CEOs invest their money, they don't speculate. Neither should you.

Don't throw your money away on companies that may or may not make money someday. Instead, invest in companies with a proven history of increasing their earnings. Furthermore, invest using proven strategies such as index investing and dividend investing (see chapter 7).

The CEOs of the largest, most successful corporations are also able to manage risk by ensuring that their companies are properly diversified. These CEOs make sure their companies receive multiple streams of income from many different products in many different countries. Johnson and Johnson, Colgate-Palmolive, 3M, and Proctor and Gamble, all produce thousands of different products and sell these products in over one-hundred countries.

In chapter 11 we will hear how legendary business leader and investor Sir John Templeton pioneered diversification in the investment industry and became a billionaire many times over. Once again, be like these successful CEOs and diversify your investments over many industries and many countries. Do not put all your eggs in one basket; you just might drop the basket.

Finally, successful CEOs know that it only takes one unlikely catastrophe to spell financial disaster. Knowing this, they do everything they can to prepare for and manage as many risks as possible. They put money aside for a rainy day, and they get insurance. You need to do the same.

Use the Power of Leverage

The CEO of every successful corporation uses leverage. Corporations borrow money to make money. And if you want to achieve financial freedom sooner rather than later, you need to consider using this strategy as well.

Through the power of leverage, the CEOs of the most successful corporations in the world have their debt work for them. In the process, they dramatically increase their company's rate of return. In chapter 9 we will explore how Warren Buffett's company, Berkshire Hathaway, has used leverage for decades to generate returns that far exceed those of the stock market index.

Whether it's the CEO of an Oil and Gas company borrowing millions of dollars to find a productive oil well that will eventually make this company hundreds of millions of dollars, or the CEO of a large consumer products company borrowing money to expand the company's operations into another country and make even more money, the most successful corporations in the world borrow money to make money. Few individual investors ever do. It might be something, however, that individual investors may want to consider.

For the average person, even if you do get a well-paying job, cut costs, and invest your money wisely, it may still take you many decades to achieve financial freedom.

The graph at the top of the next page shows the expected growth in savings for an investor who invests $5,000 per year from the age of twenty-five to the age of sixty-five. The graph assumes a CAGR of 7% per year.

Growth of Savings Account

(Assumes $5,000 contribution per year and 7% CAGR)

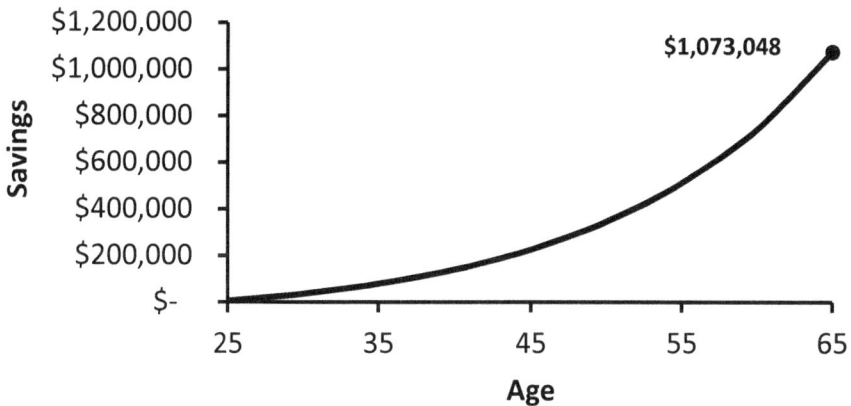

This graph shows that even if an investor starts investing at twenty-five years of age, it will still take that investor roughly forty years to become a millionaire.

If forty years seems too long to you, and despite cutting your costs, you still only have a little left over to invest each year, then using a little bit of leverage might be your best option.

Before you borrow anything to invest, however, make sure you know the risks. While borrowing to invest can lead to financial freedom in a shorter time period, it is also inherently more risky (see chapter 9).

Borrowing a reasonable amount at a low interest rate and investing it properly in a diversified portfolio that properly manages risk, targets reasonable long-term returns, and receives favourable tax consequences, is a good strategy.

Borrowing much more than you can afford to lose, selling all your holdings at the first sign of trouble, or trying to play the day trading game with a few risky stocks, is a recipe for disaster.

Minimize Taxes

The CEOs of large corporations do everything in their power to minimize taxes. In chapter 10 we will hear how IKEA founder and billionaire, Ingvar Kamprad, has saved his company and himself over $1 billion dollars by following tax minimization strategies.

Successful CEOs don't evade taxes, but they do minimize them. They set up their businesses in the most tax favourable locations, they take advantage of every tax credit and tax deduction they can get their hands on, and they control the timing of their income and deductions so that their taxes are kept to a minimum. You need to do the same.

The simple act of investing in a tax-free retirement savings account (TFSA in Canada or Roth 401(k) or Roth IRA in the U.S.), for example, could potentially save you hundreds of thousands of dollars over the course of your working life.

These tax-free retirement savings accounts, available to most people in Canada and the U.S., enable their owners to grow their savings tax-free and then withdraw these savings tax-free at a later date.

The table on the next page illustrates the potential savings that can be achieved by using these types of accounts. The table shows the difference in savings that result from an initial investment of $10,000 that is made either inside or outside of a tax-free retirement saving account. The table assumes that this $10,000 investment is allowed to grow and compound at a CAGR of 7% over a timeframe of thirty years.

Growth of $10,000 Investment (7% CAGR and 30% Tax Bracket)

Years of Growth	Inside Tax-Free Saving Account	Outside Tax-Free Saving Account
0 Years	$ 10,000	$ 10,000
10 Years	$ 19,672	$ 16,134
20 years	$ 38,697	$ 26,032
30 years	$ 76,123	$ 42,001

After thirty years, the $10,000 investment made inside the tax-free retirement savings account will have grown and compounded annually (tax-free) to roughly $76,123. In comparison, assuming profits were realized as income and taxes were paid on these profits each year, the same $10,000 investment made outside the tax-free retirement saving account would have only resulted in total savings of $42,001. This one tax strategy alone, for this one $10,000 investment, saves over $34,000 in taxes. Just imagine all the tax savings that can be realized if you use many different tax strategies for many different investments. Unfortunately, many people don't.

The Choice Is Yours

The eight strategies discussed above have been helping the CEOs of large companies generate wealth for centuries. They will help you to become wealthy too. How quickly you obtain your financial freedom, however, will be up to you.

"Knowing is not enough; we must apply. Willing is not enough; we must do."

- Johann Wolfgang von Goethe

If you want to obtain financial freedom much quicker than most, you will need to be quite stringent in your adoption of these strategies. As Johann Wolfgang von Goethe says, "Knowing is not enough; we must apply. Willing is not enough; we must do."

You will need to have a well thought-out business plan that details exactly how you plan to achieve your wealth (an example of one is shown in chapter 2), concentrate on building some well sought after core competencies that can lead to a good paying job, dramatically cut costs, build strong financial acumen, get all the money you can working for you, take on higher risk (and manage this risk appropriately), make use of the power of leverage, and be sure you are doing everything you can to minimize taxes.

If financial freedom in a relatively short period of time is your goal, it can be done. I should know. I did it. However, there should be no illusions to the fact that this goal will require more sacrifice, more hard-work, and more self-discipline than most people are used to.

If this sounds a little too much for you, then simply use the eight strategies discussed above to whatever level you feel comfortable with. If you don't want to live well below your means or take on more risk than you can stomach, then simply do what feels right. The choice is yours.

The Secret of Getting Ahead

Mark Twain once wrote, "The secret of getting ahead is getting started." This advice is so obvious, it almost seems too ludicrous to state. And yet so many of us never really follow this simple message. We are too scared, too indecisive, or too lazy to start.

"The secret of getting ahead is getting started."
- Mark Twain

Successful CEOs are different. They aren't scared, they are bold. They aren't indecisive, they come up with a plan and they follow it. And they aren't lazy, they take action. Most of all, they don't wait, they get started.

These CEOs know that they are required to increase their company's earnings every year, and they embrace this endeavour wholeheartedly. They pursue the goal of increasing their company's wealth with vigour and because of this they succeed. They succeed because failure is not an option, and they succeed because they get started. You need to do the same.

Just like the CEOs of successful companies, you need to embrace the goal of increasing your wealth. You need to believe, wholeheartedly, that this goal needs to get accomplished, you need to pursue this goal with vigour, and most importantly, you need to get started.

With all of the strategies now introduced, let's move onto the next chapter and start examining each strategy in greater detail.

Let's begin to think like a CEO, be bold, and start our journey towards financial freedom

KEY POINTS FROM CHAPTER ONE

- If you adopt the strategies used by successful CEOs, you will be able to grow your wealth much quicker than traditionally thought possible.

- Your financial freedom fund is your business and you are the CEO.

- Be diligent in the application of the strategies discussed and be relentless in the pursuit of financial freedom.

- Many people devote years training and working at their jobs, but devote no time to managing their money. This cannot be you.

- If you think and act like the herd, you will not achieve financial freedom.

- *Knowing is not enough; we must apply. Willing is not enough; we must do."* – Johann Wolfgang Von Goethe.

- *"The secret of getting ahead is getting started."* – Mark Twain.

CHAPTER TWO

Have a Business Plan

It was 2006, and after recently moving from Toronto to Vancouver for a new job in pharmaceutical sales, I was finally getting ready to meet my new sales manager, Allen.

Allen was a no-nonsense, straight talking, ex-hockey player from Calgary that had recently been put in charge of managing the sales teams in Western Canada and tasked with increasing the sales in our region.

As I waited for my new manager to arrive, I looked over my business plan. I had heard that Allen was especially big on having well thought-out business plans and I wanted to make sure our initial meeting went well.

My new manager walked into the restaurant where we were meeting and after a brief introduction, we soon started looking over the business plan I had created for my sales territory.

"Looks good, Tyrone," he said. He pushed the business plan aside and we started talking about our experiences in the company up until that point. Allen's accomplishments were impressive, to say the least. In each of the last five years, the sales teams he had managed had achieved either a first or second place ranking, in terms of total annual sales. These accomplishments had earned him a first-rate reputation within the company, and he was quickly climbing the corporate ladder.

"You know," he said, as he took a sip of his coffee, "I don't believe I'm smarter than anyone else in this company, but I'll tell you what it is I think I do better." He paused for a second to take another sip of coffee and then looked me directly in the eyes. "I take ownership of the business I'm in charge of and I take accountability. I expect all my employees to do the same."

Allen reached over and picked up my business plan. "In terms of ownership, this business plan is key. You can't succeed at anything without a well thought-out plan that is written down and top of mind. Look at this plan often and make sure you execute it."

He put the business plan back down and moved on to his second point. "The next thing is taking accountability. If you aren't successful, it's no one's fault but your own. If this is the case, you need to take accountability and do something about it. If your plan isn't working, then change it. Don't keep on doing the same things that didn't work in the past and expect a different result. And don't blame others." These were wise words that made perfect sense.

With my new manager's leadership, our sales team soon moved from last place in the national rankings all the way up to first. Moreover, I didn't just apply Allen's philosophy to my new sales job; I applied it to my quest for financial freedom as well. A few years later, my wife and I were financially free.

Business planning works. And it's not just businesses that need a plan. You need one too. Take ownership of your financial freedom fund, develop a well thought-out plan to achieve financial freedom, and then execute this plan. If your plans to achieve financial freedom aren't working, then take some accountability and do something about it.

Business Planning

All CEOs engage in business planning. Business planning involves coming up with an overall strategy and then formulating a detailed plan to achieve your goals. The clearer this plan is, the better your chances for success.

Successful CEOs realize the importance of business planning. They know that a well thought-out plan that is based on a proven strategy will keep a company focused on its goals, avoid procrastination, and dramatically increase the chances of success.

If you want to avoid delaying your financial freedom and dramatically increase your chances of success, you need to follow the lead of these successful CEOs. **You need a proven strategy and a well thought-out plan for generating wealth. Without these things, you will procrastinate saving for your future, you will lose focus, and you will not succeed.**

The Cost of Procrastination

One of the biggest advantages of having a business plan is that a detailed plan will help you to avoid the costly mistake of procrastination. Successful CEOs know that time is money. They do not procrastinate, and neither should you.

Every year you procrastinate will cost you dearly. The graph at the bottom of the following page highlights the cost of procrastination. This graph shows the growth in savings of two twenty-five year-olds whom we will call Bob and Barb.

Barb realizes that procrastination will be costly. She comes up with a plan and immediately starts contributing $10,000 a year to her financial freedom fund. She starts at age twenty-five and contributes $10,000 a year to her financial freedom fund until she is thirty-five years-old. She then stops contributing to her financial freedom fund altogether and simply lets her savings compound until she is ready to retire at sixty-five years of age (compounding is covered in chapter 8).

Bob, on the other hand, is a procrastinator. Unlike Barb, he never bothers to come up with a plan to save for his financial freedom. Because of this, he doesn't start saving for his retirement until ten years later when he is thirty-five years-old.

Bob starts saving for his retirement at precisely the same time that Barb stops saving for her retirement altogether. At thirty-five years-old, Bob diligently saves $10,000 a year for the next thirty years (twenty years more than Barb). Despite all this, because of his initial procrastination, he still winds up with less than Barb.

The Cost of Procrastination
(Assumes a CAGR of 7%)

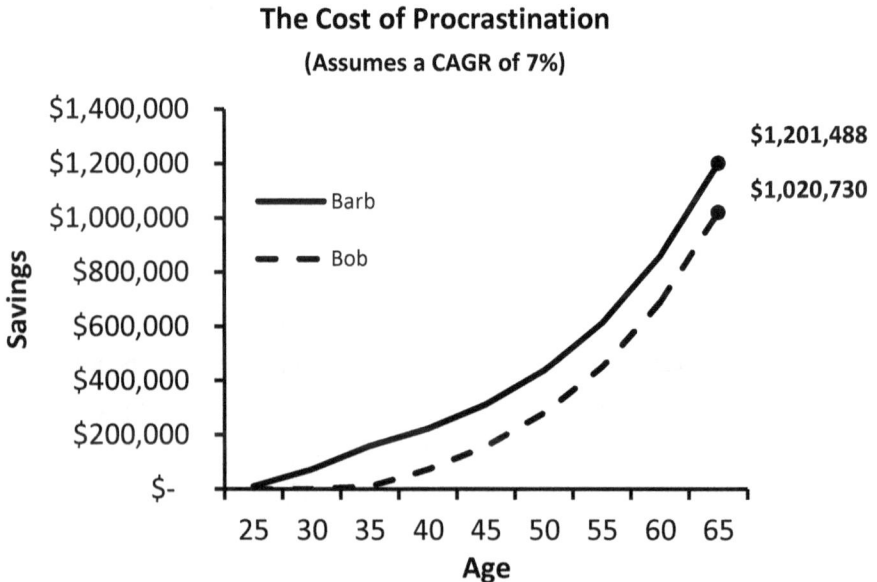

Chart legend: Barb (solid line), Bob (dashed line). End values: $1,201,488 and $1,020,730. X-axis: Age (25 to 65). Y-axis: Savings ($- to $1,400,000).

By the time Barb and Bob both reach sixty-five years-old, Bob has contributed $300,000 to his financial freedom fund and has a total of about $1 million dollars in savings. Barb, on the other hand, has contributed only $100,000 to her financial freedom fund, but with $1.2 million in savings, she still winds up with more than Bob.

Even though Barb stopped contributing to her financial freedom fund thirty years before Bob and contributed only one-third of what Bob did, she still winds up with roughly $180,000 more than Bob by the time they both reach sixty-five years of age.

In the bestselling book *Think & Grow Rich*, Napoleon Hill details his conclusions after spending years studying which personal characteristics can best lead to wealth. After studying several hundred people that had accumulated fortunes well over the million dollar mark, the author concluded that people who fail to accumulate money, *without exception*, have the habit of reaching decisions very slowly, if at all. This cannot be you.

Make coming up with your plan for financial freedom a priority. And just like my old sales manager advised, write this plan down and keep it top of mind. If that means hanging it up on your fridge or by your computer, so be it.

Human beings love to procrastinate. We say things like, "I'll do it later," and then "later" comes and goes and we still haven't done it. When it comes to saving for your financial freedom, you absolutely cannot procrastinate. Every year you wait will cost you more and more and mean your financial freedom will come later and later. The best time to start saving for your financial freedom fund was sometime in the past. The second best time is now.

Strategy

Before creating a business plan, successful CEOs work on developing an overall strategy that will position their company for success. You need to do the same for your financial freedom fund.

A corporation's overall strategy is often indicated in that company's mission statement. A mission statement is a brief statement comprised of one or two sentences that describe a company's goals, its main business, and its philosophies. An example of a properly written mission statement, taken from FedEx Corporation, is shown below.

> *"FedEx Corporation will produce superior financial returns for its shareowners by providing high-value-added logistics, transportation, and related business services through focused operating companies. Customer requirements will be met in the highest quality manner appropriate to each market segment served."*

It's clear from FedEx's mission statement that the corporation's main goal is to produce superior financial returns for its shareowners. Its main business is providing high-value-added logistics, transportation, and related business services through focused operating companies. And its main philosophy is that customer requirements will be met in the highest quality manner appropriate to each market segment served.

A mission statement is the first step in any sort of business planning. And just like large corporations such as FedEx, you need to have a mission statement, too. Your mission statement, however, will have nothing to do with transportation and logistics. Your mission statement will have to do with earning you your financial freedom. It should read the following:

"To achieve financial freedom by getting a reliable source of income and investing as much of this income as possible in long-term income producing investments such as stocks, bonds, and real estate."

Your main goal is to achieve financial freedom. Your main business is to have a reliable source of income, preferably a good-paying job. And your main philosophy is to invest as much of this income as possible in long-term income producing investments such as stocks, bonds, and real estate.

<u>Your Mission Statement Does Not Read Any of the Following:</u>

- "To give up reliable income in order to pursue risky alternatives that may or may not make money."

- "To try and get wealthy through get-rich-quick schemes."

- "To spend everything I have on material goods."

- "To leave all my money sitting in the bank and get none of it working for me."

No, your overall strategy is to have a reliable income coming in, to save as much of it as possible, and to invest these savings in proven long-term income producing investments such as stocks, bonds, and real estate. If you follow this strategy, you will achieve financial freedom.

Invest in Proven Income Producing Investments

Let's look at an example that illustrates how a strategy of finding a reliable, good-paying job and investing as much of your income as possible in proven income producing investments will lead to financial freedom.

Let's assume you have a good job that pays you $50,000 a year. Let's also assume that your living expenses are $40,000 a year and that any investments you make will earn a 7% annual rate of return.

Assuming you follow your strategy and invest as much of your income as possible, you would invest $10,000 by the end of the first year. If you do indeed invest this $10,000, you will make $700 a year in passive investment income (7% of $10,000) and $50,000 a year in employment income, for a grand total of $50,700 per year, from this point on.

In the following year, you would have an even greater sum of $10,700 to invest ($50,700 - $40,000). If you continue to invest as much as possible, you would invest $10,700 and have a total of $20,700 invested by the end of the second year. Your investments would now be earning you $1,450 a year (7% of 20,700) from this point on. If you add this $1,450 to the annual earnings you receive from work, you would now earn a total of $51,450 a year. You would have, in essence, given yourself a 3% raise, even though your boss might not have been as generous.

If you were to continue on like this each year, keeping your expenses at $40,000 and investing as much of your income as possible, you would be up to total earnings of roughly $54,000 a year, after five years. This amount would include $50,000 a year in employment income and $4,000 a year from investments.

Just like a successful corporation, you would be growing your earnings every year and making more and more money. More importantly, you would be starting to get your money working for you. Your money would be working for you, and every year more and more of your total earnings would be coming from your investments.

Now let's determine what your total earnings would be after a few years if you were to make $60,000 a year, live off of $40,000 a year, and invest $20,000 a year. While $20,000 a year sounds like a lot of money, if you and your significant other are committed to an early retirement and adopt a number of the strategies outlined in future chapters, I'll wager it could be possible.

With $20,000 of your earned income invested each year, you would be looking at total earnings of $68,000 a year, after five years. This $68,000 would be made up of $60,000 in employment income and $8,000 in investment income. Assuming you were still living off of $40,000 a year, you would now be generating 20% of the money you needed to live off of from your investment income alone. If you were to carry on like this for 16 years, you would get to the point where you would be earning $40,000 a year in investment income alone. You would now be able to pay for all your living expenses from your investment income alone.

I realize this example does not include taxes or inflation; nonetheless, this is an essential concept to grasp. **The fact that it is possible to have a substantial amount of income generated, year after year, from investments alone is something that many people fail to realize or appreciate.** Moreover, the fact that anyone can do it is something that not many people are aware of.

No one tells you this sort of information when you are growing up. It's not taught in schools and it is rarely taught by parents. Many people don't even realize it is possible.

Instead of saving and investing, most people work hard their whole lives, spend everything they earn, and save nothing. They never get their money working for them.

Some people believe they are not smart enough to invest, others believe investing is too risky. As future chapters will show, none of this is true. Investing can make anyone rich. Moreover, you don't have to be a financial genius or take on more risk than you are comfortable with. You will, however, need to make a plan.

The Business Plan

All CEOs have business plans. Successful CEOs know that increasing their company's earnings every year would not be possible without careful planning and flawless execution. You need to adopt the same mentality.

The importance of a well though-out business plan is difficult to overstate. A well thought-out plan is one that considers all options and then chooses the options that are most likely to lead to a successful outcome.

> *"Riches do not respond to wishes. They respond only to definite plans, backed by definite desires, through constant persistence."*
> - Napoleon Hill

A well thought-out plan also clearly lays out how each objective in the plan will be achieved. By writing down a plan that describes how you will achieve your objectives, you will guard against distraction, confusion, and procrastination, all of which can prevent you from achieving financial freedom. As author Napoleon Hill states, "Riches do not respond to wishes. They respond only to definite plans, backed by definite desires, through constant persistence."

The business plan shown on the next page is an example of a plan that is similar to the one my wife and I used to achieve our financial freedom. Many of the points in the plan will be discussed in greater detail in future chapters, so don't worry if you don't understand everything right now.

For now, just scan over this plan and try to get a feel for what your own business plan will look like. Once you have finished reading this book, come back to this plan and look it over in greater detail.

Financial Freedom Business Plan

1. Our goal is to be financially free in ten years. To be financially free, we will need the income from our investments to total $60,000 a year and we will need to be mortgage free. We will achieve these goals by doing the following:

   a. Building a financial freedom fund of at least $1.6 million that contains stocks, bonds, and real estate investment trusts (REITs). We would like our financial freedom fund to grow by 7% a year and to yield roughly 3.0% in dividends and income ($48,000 a year). We want our dividend growth to keep pace with inflation.

   b. We will also rent out the basement suite in our primary residence for $12,000 a year and raise the rent to keep pace with inflation.

2. Our strategy is to keep our jobs and to use our employment income to purchase income producing investments. These investments will eventually lead to our financial freedom (see chapters 2 & 3).

3. We will adopt a series of strict cost cutting measures and live well below our means. Our goal is to live off of one person's employment income. We will devote the other person's employment income and all the rental income from our basement suite to our financial freedom fund (see chapters 4 & 5).

4. We will invest $4,000 in employment income and $1,000 in rental income (basement suite) each month. We will pay ourselves first by having all of this money automatically deposited into our investment account. That way, we will not be tempted to use this money before we

can invest it. We will make purchases with these deposits on a monthly basis (see chapter 3).

5. We will contribute the maximum we can to all our tax-advantaged retirement savings accounts before investing outside of these accounts. We will also constantly look for ways to save on taxes (see chapter 10).

6. Our investments will be made in the stock market, the bond market, and the real estate market. We will diversify so that 50% of our holdings are in stocks, 25% of our holdings are in real estate, and 25% of our holdings are in bonds. We will always invest for the long-term, use proven investment strategies, and only buy investments that we hope we never have to sell (see chapters 6, 7 & 8).

    a. In the stock market, we will purchase low cost index funds or low cost exchange traded funds (ETFs) that focus on dividend paying stocks with a history of rising income and rising dividends (see chapter 7).

    b. In the bond market, we will purchase low cost ETFs that offer a mix of fixed income securities (see chapter 7).

    c. In the real estate market, we will purchase REITs or low cost ETFs focusing on REITs (see chapter 7), and we will purchase rental properties that generate positive cash flow on a monthly basis (see chapter 6).

7. We are targeting a CAGR of 7% on all our investments (see chapter 1). With this estimated return, it will take us fifteen years to reach our targeted savings of $1.6 million. Therefore, in order to meet our goal of

being financially free in ten years, we will need to use a strategy involving leverage.

8. To achieve our goal of financial freedom in ten years, we will need to borrow to invest. We will borrow to invest when we believe the long-term returns will be higher than the cost of borrowing. We will never borrow more than we can afford to lose or buy any investments that we may be forced to sell should they experience a temporary decrease in price. In this regard, we will position ourselves to handle a 50% drop in the value of all our investments without the need to sell. We will also invest for the long-term and position ourselves to comfortably handle all the interest payments that will be associated with this debt (see chapter 9).

Targets, Goals, and Actionable Items

CEOs always ensure their business plans have targets, goals, and actionable items. These are the three essential elements of any business plan.

Vague references as to how much money you will need to retire with and how much you will need to invest each month will not help you to succeed. Well thought out targets and goals, complete with actionable items that detail how money will be saved, how much money will be invested, what this money will be invested in, and what return you expect to generate, will.

Targets should always be the starting point in any business plan. It will be difficult to get to where you want to end up if you don't know where it is you are going. The targets in the business plan shown above are to have a financial freedom fund of $1.6 million and to generate $60,000 a year in income from investments. The goal is to be financially free in ten years. With these targets written down and top of mind, the owners of this plan know exactly where it is they are going. And if you know where it is you are going, you are far more likely to succeed in getting there.

Targets shouldn't be randomly pulled out of a hat. They should be written down after a careful reflection of exactly how much income it is you believe you will need to generate each year to be financially free.

It is obvious from the plan above that the owners of this plan have put some thought into their targets. They know how much income they need to generate to retire early and they know where this income will come from. They detail that they will achieve their target of $60,000 a year in investment income by generating $48,000 a year from their investments in the financial markets and by generating $12,000 a year in rent from their basement suite.

In coming up with their goal of $48,000 a year from the financial markets, the owners of this plan make the reasonable assumption that they can realize a dividend yield of 3.0% off an investment portfolio of stocks, bonds, and real estate, worth a total of $1.6 million dollars. A total dividend yield of 3.0% could be achieved if the stock portion of the portfolio yielded 2.2%, the bond portion yielded 2.8%, and the REIT portion yielded 4.8%.

With their targets established, the owners of this plan then move on to create a detailed list of actionable items (points 2 – 8) that will help them to achieve their goal of becoming financially free in ten years. They will focus on using their employment income to purchase income producing investments, drastically cut their costs, invest one individual's entire salary, and rent out part of their home so that they can earn even more money to invest. They detail how much money they will invest, when they will invest it, what they will invest it in, which accounts they will put their investments in (tax-advantaged retirement savings accounts first), and what return they expect to generate. There is no confusion or ambiguity. The plan is well thought-out and can be immediately put in place and acted upon.

In the last two points of the plan, the owners identify the fact that despite saving as much as they can, it will still take them fifteen years to reach their target of $60,000 a year in investment income. Given their goal is to be financially free in ten years; they develop some rules around borrowing to invest and decide that they will implement a strategy that involves the use of leverage.

Even though it is difficult to plan how much they will borrow and when they will borrow it (given their criteria for using leverage), the owners of this plan are aware of the fact that they can't reach their goal of retiring in ten years without implementing this type of strategy. They are prepared to take on a little more risk if it offers them the chance to leave the rat-race many years earlier.

Perhaps your targets will be higher or lower than the owners of this plan. Maybe your plan does not involve renting out part of your home. Possibly you plan to retire and supplement your investment income with part-time employment income. Maybe you are not able to save as much as the owners of this plan. Perhaps you are able to save more. Maybe you believe borrowing to invest is too risky. No matter what your decisions are, the important thing is that you come up with a well though-out plan and that you write this plan down. Then, keep this plan top of mind and act upon it.

Your journey towards financial freedom requires a map. Your business plan is that map. Make sure it shows you where you want to end up and make sure it shows you how you are going to get there. Then, start the journey. Don't just write a plan. Write a plan and go out there and execute it.

Let's conclude this chapter by looking at a famous business leader that exemplified business planning, setting goals, and avoiding procrastination. Let's look at the story of one of the richest people who ever lived, John D. Rockefeller.

The Richest Person Who Ever Lived

According to many, the richest private citizen who ever lived was John D. Rockefeller. Just how much was John D. worth? It has been estimated that at his peak wealth, John D. was worth the equivalent of $336 billion in terms of 2007 US dollars. To put this in perspective, Bill Gates was ranked by Forbes magazine as the world's richest person in 2016 with a net worth of roughly $75 billion.

John Davison Rockefeller, the son of a traveling salesman, was born on July 8, 1839, in Richford, New York. As a child, John D. set a goal for himself to become a millionaire. He would later recall that his life goal since early childhood was to make as much money as possible and then give away as much as he could. It was a goal he pursued with single-minded purpose and one that he would successfully achieve.

In 1863, at the age of 24, John D. entered the booming oil industry, and with the help of some partners, he bought his first oil refinery. In 1865, John D. bought out his partners and singlehandedly owned one of the largest refineries in the world. Then, five years later in 1870, John D. Rockefeller formed the Standard Oil Company of Ohio and became its president. By 1879, at the age of 40, John D. Rockefeller controlled 90% of the oil refining in the world.

By the end of his life in 1937, John D. Rockefeller had made the equivalent of what would today be considered hundreds of billions of dollars, and then he gave most of it away through his foundations. These foundations had a major effect on medicine, education, and scientific research.

How did John D. achieve this great success? At least part of his success is simply due to the fact that he set goals, came up with strategies to achieve these goals, and most importantly, took action.

John D. was constantly staying in his office for long hours, filling up chalkboards with unique game plans and different strategies to continue to grow his wealth. Then, once these plans were formed, he acted on them.

According to PBS.com, Rockefeller would come up with a plan and then, "he would act quickly and boldly to see it through to fruition."

John D. pursued his goals with vigour and he was determined to succeed. He is quoted as saying, "Singleness of purpose is one of the chief essentials for success in life, no matter what may be one's aim."

If you want to achieve financial freedom at a young age, follow this famous business magnate's lead. Set some goals, come up with a strategy and a plan to realize these goals, and then get out there and achieve them.

With your business plan created, let's move on and talk about where you are going to get the income to implement this plan. Let's move on and talk about your core competencies and getting your money working for you.

KEY POINTS FROM CHAPTER TWO

- Without a well thought-out plan that is based on a proven strategy, you will not achieve your goals.

- Do not procrastinate saving for retirement – every year you wait will costs you dearly.

- Your strategy is to have a reliable source of income and to invest as much of this income as possible in long-term income producing investments such as stocks, bonds, and real estate.

- "Riches do not respond to wishes. They respond only to definite plans, backed by definite desires, through constant persistence." - Napoleon Hill.

- Your business plan must contain targets, goals, and actionable items.

- Determine how much money you need for retirement, when you want to retire, and how much you need to save each month to achieve these goals.

CHAPTER THREE

Concentrate on Core Competencies

It was 2007, and I was parked outside a doctor's office, sitting in my car, trying to mentally prepare myself for my next sales call. It was already dark outside, and like most winter days in Vancouver, the rain was pouring down. Truth be told, I wanted nothing more than to end my gloomy day at work and start heading home. It had been just over a year since I had traded in my job in Toronto for a job as a pharmaceutical sales representative in Vancouver and I absolutely hated it.

Sales jobs are tough. You need to work hard for every little bit of success, and you often face a mountain of rejection along the way. Pharmaceutical sales jobs, in particular, require you to somehow work your way into the very busy lives of a whole whack of doctors who don't really want to see you. In fact, many times, these doctors hated seeing you. A fitting job description would read, "Candidates must be willing to show up every day so that they can be made to feel deeply unwanted and strongly unloved."

It used to be, before I started my sales job, that pharmaceutical salespeople could take doctors out for a round of golf or to a hockey game and discuss the company's medications with them during one of these fun outings. That little perk, however, had rightfully been shut down for fear that it was really just a way for a pharmaceutical company to bribe a doctor into using its medications.

In the years that followed this decision, relationships between doctors and pharmaceutical salespeople went from buddies on the golf course to, "I don't speak to salespeople." Left with little incentive for them to see me, it was a struggle to see any doctor at all. So, like most other pharmaceutical salespeople at the time, I would simply show up at doctors' offices with some free samples of the company's medications and try to get a quick word with these busy doctors in-between their appointments with their patients.

Needless to say, this wasn't always well received. On this particular day, I had already been verbally abused by one doctor and asked by another one to, "Stop talking and get out."

Nonetheless, as most salespeople know, the more people you see, the better your chances of increasing your sales. And the higher your sales, the higher your sales bonus. With this in mind, I stepped out of the car and into the next office.

"Oh no, not you again!" exclaimed the receptionist.

Despite all my complaining, this was still the best paying job I had ever had. I had concentrated on developing my skills over the years and it had paid off. I had worked as a researcher for a year at a biotech company for $45,000 a year, worked at the head office of a major pharmaceutical corporation for $65,000 a year (after getting an MBA), and was now working for roughly $90,000 a year (thanks to developing my sales skills and getting a large sales bonus) in pharmaceutical sales. Sure I didn't like my job very much, but was I about to leave it? Not a chance (not yet at least). I kept it and got more money working for me than ever before. I wouldn't be doing this job all my life, but for now, this job was my ticket to financial freedom.

It had only been two years since my wife and I had started our financial freedom fund, but it was now starting to get bigger than ever. I no longer felt that sinking feeling in my stomach that I had felt when I started off working in Toronto. Starting our financial freedom fund and focusing on making it grow had reinvigorated me. Every year my wife and I were getting more and more of our money working for us, and every year we were getting closer and closer to financial freedom.

Concentrate on Your Core Competencies

The CEOs of successful corporations know that the best way to make money is to buildup and to take advantage of a useful set of core competencies. Every year, large corporations use their core competencies to earn billions of dollars. Then, they take some of these earnings and reinvest them to earn even more money. You need to do the same.

You need to develop some useful, sought after skills and use these skills to get the best-paying job you can find. If you can develop these skills even further and get an even better paying job, then do it. Then, just like a successful CEO, take as much of this income as possible and use it to make even more money.

If you are young enough to be reading this book before you have chosen a career path, consider basing your career choice not only on what you enjoy doing, but also on what will offer a good chance of employment and provide a good annual income as well.

Have a Cash Cow

The CEOs of successful companies rely on their cash cows to provide them with a reliable source of income. Then, they take some of that income and invest it to make even more money.

For example, without the steady source of income initially provided by Kellogg's Corn Flakes (the cereal maker's first cash cow), Kellogg's would not have grown into the multibillion dollar company it is today. Kellogg's also would not have been able to create all its other cash cows such as Pringles, Eggos, Nutrigrain, and many others.

By this same logic, your job is your cash cow. It provides you with a steady source of income that you can use to create other cash cows. Keep trying to get the best paying job you can, and just like Kellogg's, use the income it provides to make even more money. Perhaps your job is not very exciting but, then again, neither is a bowl of corn flakes.

Even if your job isn't very exciting, if it takes advantage of some useful core competencies and provides you with a reliable source of high income, then you need to keep it. You need to keep it and use the steady income it provides to start buying income producing assets and start growing your wealth at an accelerated rate. This is your best plan for achieving financial freedom quickly.

Don't settle for a job that offers relatively low pay unless you are certain a job like this is the life you truly want. Be honest with yourself. Many people say money doesn't matter, but few really mean it. If you really can't stand your job, then try and get something else. Just try and get something else that offers you at least as much income as your previous job.

Furthermore, don't gamble your secure job on risky start-up businesses, most of which will fail in the first few years, or on risky jobs where salaries are based entirely on commission, unless you are absolutely sure a job change like this is what you truly want and that you will be able to succeed. **Get rich**

schemes will not lead to financial freedom. Good paying jobs coupled with aggressive saving and proper investing habits will.

If you are thinking of starting your own business, you might be better off picking one that many would consider boring. In their book *The Millionaire Next Door,* Thomas J. Stanley and William D. Danko indicate that the majority of entrepreneurs that wind up as millionaires own businesses that would be considered "dull-normal." Some of the businesses the authors list as being owned by the millionaires they studied include pest control services, sand blasting contractor, owners of mobile-home parks, paving contractors, and cafeteria owners.

Stanley and Danko then go on to write that many millionaire business owners know the odds of succeeding as entrepreneurs are very low and that very few of these millionaires would encourage their children to choose this path. Instead, according to Stanley and Danko, these millionaires encourage their children to become self-employed professionals such as physicians, attorneys, engineers, accountants, and dentists

The authors of *The Millionaire Next Door* also highlight the fact that is a common misconception that many millionaires suddenly strike it rich. **The truth is that many millionaires got their money by working hard for many years and simply saving and investing much more than the rest of us.**

After decades of studying how millionaires became wealthy, Stanley and Danko concluded that the real keys to becoming a millionaire are working hard, good savings habits, and investing your earnings.

Invest in Yourself

Led by their CEOs, all successful corporations spend time and money investing in themselves so that they can develop a profitable set of core competencies. Furthermore, if a company can earn more money by developing its core competencies even further, it does so. You need to do the same.

If your core competencies aren't earning you a lot of money, then maybe you need to spend some time and money developing some core competencies that will. This is a strategy that absolutely worked for me. I got an MBA and saw my annual income rise by nearly fifty percent. Then I got some sales experience and my annual income jumped up by nearly fifty percent again.

> *"An investment in knowledge pays the best interest."*
> - Benjamin Franklin

Benjamin Franklin once said, "An investment in knowledge pays the best interest." He was right. The table below is based on the 2014 earnings data taken from the U.S. Department of Labour's Bureau of Labour Statistics. It confirms that education plays a large role in determining your annual earnings.

Median Earnings for 2014 (over 25 years-old)*

Less than High School Diploma	High School Diploma	Some College	Bachelor's Degree	Professional Degree	Doctoral Degree
$25,376	$34,736	$38,532	$57,252	$85,228	$82,732

* Based on 2014 earnings data taken from the U.S. Department of Labour's Bureau of Labour Statistics.

Referring to this table, it can be seen that the median earnings in 2014 for individuals who were over twenty-five years-old and had a bachelor's degree were roughly $57,000. This compares to median earnings of only $25,376 for those who were over twenty-five years-old and never finished high school.

Furthermore, those individuals who were over twenty-five years-old and had a professional degree or doctoral degree, made even more money. In fact, those with a professional degree had median earnings of roughly $85,000 a year. This means these individuals earned roughly $60,000 more, each and every year, than those who never finished high school.

If you do have an advanced degree, or if you earn a salary equivalent to those that have an advanced degree, then chances are you've done a good job investing in yourself and have developed a good set of core competencies.

If this is the case, you will have an easier time achieving financial freedom compared to those that have not developed a good set of core competencies. If you do have a lower paying job, financial freedom is still possible, but it might take you a little longer.

Perhaps you don't earn a high salary but you are very happy with what you do and are content to live out the rest of your life this way. If this is the case, then congratulations, you have reached a level of happiness few people ever obtain and you are already living the life you truly want.

If you are not happy in your current situation, have a lower paying job, and are looking to get all the benefits associated with financial freedom, then investing in yourself may be the best thing you can do.

Keep in mind, however, that investing in yourself doesn't necessarily mean you should go back to school and try to get a PhD. This is especially true if this education will cost you an arm and a leg and the job prospects in your chosen field don't look very good.

Unless you feel it is your true calling, all the time, effort, and expense, involved in getting a degree in a field with poor job prospects might not be the best plan. **Instead, consider getting a degree or a diploma in**

something that not only interests you, but in something that will be worth it from a financial point of view.

Compare the costs of all the programs you are considering enrolling in and do some research to find out if the program that interests you will actually lead to a higher salary and a good chance of employment. If financial freedom is your goal, there is no point spending out on an education that will not lead to a higher paying job.

Earn Some Money on the Side

The CEOs of successful corporations also know that it is sometimes possible to earn some extra income outside of their day-to-day businesses. McDonalds' core business is its fast-food restaurants. However, this hasn't stopped McDonalds from selling its ground coffee in grocery stores all over North America.

McDonalds had something to offer that other people wanted; saw an opportunity to earn some extra money outside of its core business, and it took it. Perhaps you can do the same.

If your job pays lower than you would like and going back to school is not an option, perhaps you too can use some of your core competencies to generate some extra income on the side.

I've known plenty of people who have kept their day jobs and earned money on the side. I've know people that have taught another language a few nights a week, people that have created online businesses in their spare time, people that have taught at community colleges for one or two nights a week, and people that have worked in construction on the weekends. All of them kept their day jobs and did these other jobs on a part-time basis. Maybe you can do the same.

If you are handy and you are up for a challenge, you could even consider buying a fixer-upper to live in and do all the renovations yourself in your spare time. Imagine how much money you could save if you bought a dilapidated home, lived in it, and renovated it yourself. After a few years of renovating, you might even be able to sell your fixer-upper for a nice profit and then be able to do the whole thing all over again. I had a friend that did just that. He would buy a dilapidated house to live in, go home each day after work and fix it up, sell it for a profit, and then do the whole thing all over again. He made over $100,000 doing this in the few years that I knew him.

I'll bet if you put your mind to it, you could come up with more than a few ideas to earn a little extra money on the side.

Get Your Money Working for You

Once you have concentrated on building some core competencies that can provide a reliable income, your next task is to get as much of this income as possible working for you.

In order to achieve this, just like the CEO of a successful company, you will need to earmark some of your earnings for investments, devote some time into researching where to invest your money, and make sure you invest your earnings using strategies that have a proven history of growing wealth. Don't spend all you money, and don't stuff all of your money under your mattress. Get your money working for you.

If Kellogg's had just sat on all the money it got from its first cash cow, Kellogg's corn flakes, it would never have grown into the multibillion dollar company it is today. Instead of sitting on its money, Kellogg's invested its money and managed to create multiple streams of income. In addition to earning money from its cereals, Kellogg's now earns money from cookies, crackers, cereal bars, and frozen waffles (just to name a few). **You need to**

start using your money to create multiple streams of income, too.
And it all starts with earmarking some of your funds.

Earmark the Funds

Good CEOs know that if they don't put some of their company's earnings
aside and use these earnings to invest in their company's future, they could
find themselves in trouble sometime down the road.

A classic example of a company that failed to invest for its future is
Polaroid, makers of the now obsolete Polaroid instant film camera. During
the 1970's and the 1980's, Polaroid was generating huge earnings from the
sales of its instant film cameras.

Then came the 1990's. This new decade saw not only a rise in boy bands,
bleached hair, and Tickle Me Elmos; it also saw a rise in digital photography.
This rise in digital photography, combined with a decrease in the processing
times associated with analog photography, led to a huge fall in sales for
Polaroid. Having invested nothing to create any future cash cows, the
company was forced to file for bankruptcy in 2001.

A good CEO absolutely puts some earnings aside and invests some of the
company's money in its future. This rule is often in the company's business
plan and it is often strictly adhered to.

Whether it's the CEO of a pharmaceutical company putting millions of
dollars aside to discover the next medication that could be worth hundreds of
millions, or the CEO of a technology company putting millions of dollars
aside to come up with the next technological innovation that could be worth
billions, some of the money a company earns is absolutely earmarked for
future income producing investments. This simple act ensures continued
growth and survival. With regards to you and your finances, this act will

ensure that you eventually realize your financial freedom and will provide you with a never ending source of passive investment income.

You absolutely need to earmark some of the money you earn today and invest it so that you can continue to earn more money in the future. Moreover, you need to make this act of saving and investing automatic.

In his book *The Wealthy Barber*, David Chilton talks about the concept of forced savings and a rule he calls "pay yourself first." Chilton reinforces his belief in this rule in his follow-up book, *The Wealthy Barber Returns*. Paying yourself first refers to the idea of having a certain amount of your biweekly paycheck automatically put aside for investments. The money automatically gets debited from your account and invested before you have the chance to spend it. Chilton highlights the fact that unless you pay yourself first, you will, more than likely, just spend everything you earn.

Like it or not, we are a society of spenders. If you don't make a conscious effort to put money aside, it will get spent. Moreover, it will likely get spent on frivolous items or on money sucking maggots – purchases that continually use up all your earned income.

Chilton is not the only financial author to highlight a strategy of paying yourself first. In fact, some of the most popular books on personal finance ever written, including bestsellers such as *Rich Dad Poor Dad* and *The Richest Man in Babylon*, all highlight this important strategy.

How much money should you pay yourself first? This is entirely up to you. Keep in mind, however, that the more you are able to save, the quicker you will achieve financial freedom. Many people say that if you want to live a similar lifestyle in your retirement years, you should save roughly 10% of what you earn.

Here's a thought for you though. What if one person earns $50,000 a year and a second person earns $100,000 a year. If the first person can save $5,000 a year and live off of $45,000 a year, isn't it possible for the second person to save $55,000 a year and also live off of $45,000 a year? Of course it is. If the second person is willing to live significantly below their means, they will be able to save far more than the first person.

This is exactly what my wife and I did. We lived far below our means and earmarked my wife's entire salary for investments. Every time she got her paycheque, it went straight into an account dedicated to our financial freedom. The savings were automatic. We paid ourselves first and we used her entire paycheque to buy income producing investments. Seven years later, we were financially free.

We weren't the only ones to adopt this strategy. The famous investor and businessman Sir John Templeton, who was born into a poor Tennessee family in 1912, also initially followed a similar strategy of living a frugal life and investing 50% of the income that he and his wife generated. By the time Sir John died in 2008, he had amassed a fortune worth billions (the story of Sir John Templeton can be found at the end of chapter 11).

Earmark Your Time

It's not enough for a CEO to simply put money aside if no one knows what to do with it. Successful CEOs make it a priority to look for opportunities to invest their money in. They also make it a priority to understand all the investments they make. You need to do the same.

In order to properly manage your financial freedom fund, you need to become familiar with some of the most common investment vehicles out there. Real estate investments and other investments such as exchange traded funds (ETFs), mutual funds, real estate investment trusts (REITs), stocks, and bonds, will be the income producing investments that will lead to your financial freedom. You need to know a little bit about each of them. How can you succeed if you don't know or understand what it is you are investing in?

The good news is that understanding these investments is not as difficult as you might think. If you put in a small amount of time, doing things like occasionally reading the investment section of a reputable newspaper, reading an article or two in a magazine dedicated to investing, or reading a good book about investing, you will quickly begin to understand many of the investment tools and strategies out there. This book is an excellent start!

The most common investment vehicles, along with some proven wealth building strategies, will be covered later on in this book. With this knowledge, you will right away be able to start making some smart investments.

The simple truth, however, is that you cannot become wealthy without devoting some time and energy towards managing your finances. If we again refer to some of the research discussed in *The Millionaire Next Door,* we see that many of the individuals that eventually became wealthy prioritized their time so that managing their finances took precedence over all other activities. You need to adopt the same mentality.

"It has been my observation that most people get ahead during the time that others waste."
- Henry Ford

Henry Ford once said, "It has been my observation that most people get ahead during the time that others waste." Not only should you pay yourself first with regards to your earnings, you should also pay yourself first with regards to your time. Make it a priority to put some time aside and dedicate an hour or two a week towards building your financial knowledge and managing your finances. By scheduling in this time, you will also realize the advantage of keeping your financial goals top of mind. This benefit alone will dramatically increase your chances of success.

By the way, in case you are wondering, the wealthy people referred to in *The Millionaire Next Door* devoted roughly two hours a week to managing their finances. Two hours a week doesn't seem like a lot to ask, especially given the fact that many people work over fifty hours a week and work these types of hours their whole lives.

Do yourself a favour, block off some time each week and devote it to achieving financial freedom. These two hours might end up being the best paying hours you spend each week.

If you still aren't motivated to spend a little time each week building your investment knowledge, then consider this. Warren Buffett, one of the most successful investors of our time and the third richest man in the world according to a Forbes 2016 ranking, claims the best investment he ever made was not a stock or a bond, it was buying Benjamin Graham's book *The Intelligent Investor*. Warren Buffett used the knowledge he gained from this book, as well as other sources of investment knowledge, to create billions of dollars in wealth. Follow his lead and continue building your own investment knowledge as well.

Don't Just Save Your Money – Invest It!

After CEOs earmark money for investment, they do just that – they invest it. They don't let their money sit idly by; they get their money invested and working for them so that they can make even more money. You need to do the same.

"The biggest risk is not taking any risk - In a world that's changing really quickly, the only strategy that is guaranteed to fail is not taking risks."
- Mark Zuckerberg

Mark Zuckerberg, the CEO of Facebook, once said, "The biggest risk is not taking any risk – In a world that's changing really quickly, the only strategy that is guaranteed to fail is not taking risks." He is right. If you don't take any risks, you will have no chance of achieving financial freedom early on in life.

Return on Investment and Risk

When CEOs make investments, they always consider two key metrics. These two key metrics are return on investment (ROI) and risk.

ROI measures the profit an investment is expected to generate and is typically expressed as a percentage of the original investment. For example, if you invest $1,000 and this investment earns you $100 in profit, your ROI is 10%.

Risk, on the other hand, considers the possibility that an investment's return will be different from what is expected, including the possibility that the investment may lose money.

Risk is typically quantified using statistical terms such as standard deviation or variation. However, risk can also be stated in easier to understand terms that simply state what the chances of gaining or losing a certain amount of money are. For example, it could be stated that a certain investment has a 5% chance of losing more than 10% of its value and a 20% chance of earning more than 10% of its value in the next year.

Successful CEOs are good at maximizing their ROI while, at the same time, minimizing their risk. If a company believes that it can generate a good ROI by carrying out a certain project and believes that it faces minimal risk in doing so, then it undertakes the project. Even though there is always some risk in carrying out any type of project, as Mark Zuckerberg points out, there is also a risk in doing nothing.

If CEOs just sit on the money their companies make and don't take any risk at all, then profit growth stalls and share prices tumble. Just like a successful corporation, you can't afford to sit on your money. You need to take a little risk and get your money working for you.

Why Investing Beats a Saving Account

While it may be prudent to have some money in a savings account, having almost all of your money in a savings account, earning little to no interest, isn't prudent at all. It's a wasted opportunity.

> *"How many millionaires do you know who have become wealthy by investing in savings accounts?"*
> - Robert G. Allen

Sure, it's less risky keeping all your hard earned money in a savings account; the problem, however, is that this money is not earning you any meaningful ROI. To borrow a quote from famous financier Robert G. Allen, "How many millionaires do you know who have become wealthy by investing in savings accounts?"

Even worse, leaving all your money sitting in a savings account might actually be making you poorer.

Think about how much it cost you to buy things when you were a kid. Even more profound, think about how much it cost your parents to buy things when they were kids. I'll bet prices were much lower back then compared to what they are now. The reason for this is inflation.

Inflation is a measure of how much the cost of living goes up. Moreover, the central banks of most developed countries target a growth in inflation of 1-3% per year. **Therefore, even if inflation is at the low end of this spectrum and is 1% per year, unless the interest in your savings account is greater than 1%, the money you save is actually worth**

less and less every year. Rather than becoming wealthier, you are becoming poorer.

If you had invested $10,000 in the S&P 500 at the start of 1995 and then reinvested all the dividends you generated from this investment, you would have ended up with roughly $65,600 at the start of 2015. If you had invested this same amount in a typical savings account at the start of 1995 and let it compound annually until the start of 2015, you would have ended up with only $13,900 (based on historical average savings rates of Canadian Banks). That's a difference of about $51,700 in favor of the stock market. This difference gets even worse when you factor in inflation.

Investment professionals often label rates of return that do not factor in inflation as *nominal* rates of return. Faced with inflation, investment professionals find it more useful to calculate what they call the *real* rate of return. The real rate of return factors in the cost of inflation and is, therefore, a better indicator of how much a given investment has increased your actual wealth.

Let's assume, for example, that you invest $10,000. Let's also assume that a year later this investment is worth $10,500. If this $10,500 now buys you exactly the same as what $10,000 bought you a year ago, you have a nominal rate of return of 5%, but a real rate of return of 0%. In this case inflation is 5%, and it has effectively wiped out any benefit of a 5% nominal return and has resulted in a real return of 0%.

When inflation is factored into the analysis above, which involved putting $10,000 into either a savings account or the S&P 500 index from 1995-2015, we find that the results for the savings account are even worse than originally thought.

When you factor in the effects of inflation, it would have cost $15,346 at the start of 2015 to buy what $10,000 would have bought in 1995. Therefore, since you now only have $13,900 in your savings account, you cannot buy as much as you could have bought when you invested the money in the first place. By taking no risk at all and just leaving all your savings in the savings account, you have effectively become less wealthy. The table below highlights the results of this analysis.

Growth of $10,000 Investment from Jan 1, 1995 - Dec 31, 2014

	Savings Account (Interest Compounded)*	S&P 500 (Dividends Reinvested)
Initial Investment (Jan 1, 1995)	$10,000	$10,000
Nominal Value (Dec 31, 2014)	$13,900	$65,600
Nominal CAGR	1.7%	9.9%
Real CAGR (Adjusted for Inflation)	-0.5%	7.7%

* Based on historical average savings rates at Canadian banks

Yes, investing poses some risk, but as demonstrated above, there is also a risk in doing nothing.

Unfortunately, according to a survey by BlackRock Inc. conducted in the summer of 2015, a little more than half of all Canadians believe that investing is like gambling. Furthermore, almost half of all Canadians don't believe investing is for them. Sadly, this way of thinking will make it difficult for many Canadians to ever achieve financial freedom.

It will be extremely difficult to achieve any sort of financial freedom without taking some risk and investing some of your money. Stick with a strategy of getting a good-paying job, save as much of your income as you can, and then invest it.

The Average American Millionaire

How did the average American Millionaire accumulate his or her wealth? The answer to this question can be found in the research done by Thomas J. Stanley, and William D. Danko in their bestselling book *The Millionaire Next Door*. In this book, Stanley and Danko highlight their research findings after studying millionaires for over twenty years and interviewing more than five hundred of them.

These research findings can be summarized by the seven factors that Stanley and Danko found to be the common denominators among those who successfully build wealth. These seven factors are listed below.

Common Denominators Among Those Who Build Wealth

1. They live well below their means.

2. They allocate their time, energy, and money, efficiently in ways conductive to building wealth.

3. They believe that financial independence is more important than displaying high social status.

4. Their parents did not provide economic outpatient care.

5. Their adult children are economically self-sufficient.

6. They are proficient in targeting market opportunities.

7. They chose the right occupation.

Furthermore, Stanley and Danko also remarked that the millionaires they interviewed were both well educated (only one in five had less than a college education) and were fastidious investors (79 percent had at least one account with a brokerage company and almost all of these millionaires made their own investment decisions).

If you want to become wealthy at a young age, you should follow the wisdom of these millionaires. Build some sought after core competencies and get a good paying job. Then, live below your means, allocate time and energy towards building wealth, and invest your money wisely.

With our discussion about developing core competencies and getting your money working for you now complete, let's move on and focus on how you can get even more money working for you than you ever thought possible. Let's move on to discuss how you can aggressively cut costs, control expenses, and stop buying money sucking maggots.

KEY POINTS FROM CHAPTER THREE

- Develop your skills and get the best paying job you can find.

- Get-rich-quick schemes will not lead to financial freedom. Good paying jobs coupled with aggressive saving and proper investing habits will.

- Many millionaires got their money by working hard for many years and simply saving and investing much more than the rest of us.

- Invest in yourself. Develop your core competencies and get the best paying job you can find.

- Consider careers that you not only like, but ones that offer a high chance of employment and a good annual income as well.

- Consider using your core competencies to earn extra income on the side.

- Use your money to create multiple streams of income.

- Pay yourself first and make the act of saving and investing automatic.

- You cannot become wealthy without devoting some time and energy towards managing your finances and building your wealth.

- Keeping all your money in savings accounts will never lead to financial freedom and might actually result in a loss of wealth.

- To become wealthy you need to take some risk and invest your money.

CHAPTER FOUR

Cut Costs and Control Expenses

Nervous excitement filled the air. It was a cool autumn evening in 2007, and my wife and I were getting ready to submit an offer to buy our first home.

As anybody who has purchased a home knows, buying a home is no easy task. It is an emotionally draining one. And it is one that is filled with ups, downs, and plenty of anxiety. For my wife, all of this anxiety had finally boiled over.

"Oh my god!" she exclaimed, just as I was about to sign the offer. "Are we doing the right thing?"

We had been searching for a place to live for months. In the process, we had gone from looking at houses in downtown Vancouver, to looking at apartments in downtown Vancouver, to looking at houses in the suburbs of Greater Vancouver. We had also gone through three separate realtors and had seen somewhere between 10-20 properties. To be honest, I had lost count. Now, here we were, finally ready to submit an offer.

I understood my wife's anxiety. This was, without a doubt, the largest purchase we had ever made. That being said, I knew that buying this house was the right move. Unlike the homes we had started out looking at in Vancouver, this house was well below our budget. What's more, this house came with a rental suite that would enable us to save even more money.

In fact, when we factored in the potential rental income, the monthly mortgage payments were less than a third of what we had been approved for by the bank.

Now, instead of all our monthly income getting sucked into a large, unmanageable mortgage, we would be able to live off of only one person's wages and invest half of our total income.

Looking back, I am convinced that this was one of the best financial decisions we ever made. We were saving thousands of dollars each month and we were investing all of it.

Over the years, we never really noticed the smaller living space. What we did notice, however, was a dramatic increase in wealth.

Don't Try to Keep up With the Joneses

Keeping up with the Joneses refers to using your neighbours as a benchmark for the accumulation of material goods. Well I've got some news for you; the Joneses are not going to retire early. And if you want to achieve financial freedom but keep trying to keep up with them, then neither will you.

"Financial peace isn't the acquisition of stuff. It's learning to live on less than you make, so you can give money back and have money to invest. You can't win until you do this."

- Dave Ramsey

As financial guru and *New-York Times* best-selling author Dave Ramsey says, "Financial peace isn't the acquisition of stuff. It's learning to live on less than you make, so you can give money back and have money to invest. You can't win until you do this."

I once saw a presentation given by a retired executive from Harley-Davidson. He started his presentation by showing a large, muscular man, without his shirt on, at a motorcycle convention. This large, muscular man had the words "Harley Davidson" tattooed in big, bold letters over his entire body.

"At the most basic level, what is this man saying?" asked the retired Harley Davidson executive. Many people in the audience incorrectly guessed that, at the most basic level, this man was saying he loved Harley-Davidson.

"The correct answer," said the executive, is that this man is saying, "Look at me."

Most of us do the same thing when we use our hard-earned money to buy fancy cars and expensive houses. We are basically saying, "Look at me." We buy all these financial freedom sucking maggots in order to make ourselves feel as important as or more important than those around us.

Your plan must be to *not* keep up with the Joneses. If you want to achieve financial freedom in a relatively short amount of time, you must resist purchasing all those financial freedom sucking maggots that the Joneses have.

Sure you will sacrifice for a small window of your life, but you will, more than likely, end up being better for it. By leading a frugal life leading up to your financial freedom and, quite possibly, even after you achieve financial freedom, you will learn to appreciate what really matters in this life. And the things that really matter in life aren't materialistic.

My favorite part about being financially free is spending more time with friends and family. I spend more time with my two young children, more time with my parents, and more time with my wife.

Moreover, I guarantee you that living below your means is not as stressful as living above it. People who live above their means are always full of anxiety, stress, and worry. They struggle to make each bill payment and they constantly worry about whether or not they will have enough money to cover all their expenses. They see no way out of the rat-race and they feel as though they are moving farther away from the exits.

In contrast, people who live below their means, save some of their income, and invest these savings, replace all that worry and stress with optimism and satisfaction. They see a way out of the rat-race and instead of getting further away, they move closer to the exit every day.

Cut Costs and Control Expenses

Successful CEOs are always looking for ways to cut costs. In fact, every decision they make involves a careful consideration of costs. It doesn't matter if that cost is a major purchase, such as a factory, or if it's a smaller purchase such as the office supplies that go in that factory. It doesn't matter if it's the cost of employing their workers or if it's the cost of the internet used by those workers. No matter what the costs are, they are closely scrutinized so that more of the company's earnings can be protected and used to fuel its future growth. This needs to be your plan as well.

If you want to achieve financial freedom, you need to be constantly looking for ways to cut costs. You need to save as much as you can as often as you can, and you need to get this money invested and working for you.

In fact, when it comes to cutting costs and controlling expenses, most CEOs can be best described by just one word, "ruthless." They reduce headcounts wherever and whenever possible and they scrutinize even the most mundane expenses.

One of the most successful and well-known CEOs of the last century is Jack Welch. Jack Welch was the CEO of General Electric (GE) from 1981 to 2001 and was declared manager of the century in 1999 by *Fortune* magazine.

Jack Welch epitomized the relentless cost cutting behaviour embraced by most large, successful corporations. At the start of his tenure, Welch laid off thousands of employees and, in doing so, earned the nick-name Neutron Jack. Moreover, if a company or a division of GE was not first or second in its industry, Welch would either sell it off or shut it down.

I'm not sure if following Jack Welch's lead will make you manager of the century, but I am sure that **the more ruthless you are with your own cost cutting measures, the more successful you will be at growing your financial freedom fund.** Especially if you get all those savings invested and working for you.

CEOs, in general, have three types of large costs that they are always trying to control. These costs are labor costs, fixed costs, and variable costs. You need to control these types of costs too. You need to control these costs and invest all the money you save to make even more money.

The choice of how frugal you want to live is up to you. If you want to enjoy yourself more today and sacrifice less for tomorrow, then so be it. If you choose to eat out all the time, buy the biggest house you can afford, and take the most expensive vacations you can, then you won't achieve financial freedom anytime soon.

In contrast, if you buy a home for less than you can afford, take more humble vacations, limit the amount of times you eat out, and invest all these savings, you will greatly accelerate your time to financial freedom.

Control Labor Expenses

Labor expenses are some of the largest expenses many CEOs face. After all, it's usually someone's hard work that is responsible for a product or service that you receive. This being the case, CEOs are always trying to find ways to do more work with less people. You need to adopt this philosophy as well.

If you are paying a number of people to do things that you are perfectly capable of doing yourself, then you need to stop. Stop paying them and start paying your financial freedom fund instead.

Whether it was doing basic car repairs, filing my own taxes, managing my own investments, or redoing my roof, none of these things that I did myself ended up being as hard as I thought they would be.

Even better, doing them myself saved me tens of thousands of dollars. All of these savings got invested into our financial freedom fund and now, many years later; these savings have probably grown into hundreds of thousands of dollars.

Even if you don't feel comfortable doing your own home renovations or managing your own investments, I'll bet there are many other ways you can cut costs. What about making your own coffee in the morning? It doesn't get much simpler than that. I bet if you start looking for them, you will soon find numerous things that you can start doing yourself to save money.

Control Fixed Costs

A fixed cost is some specific type of cost that *needs* to get paid every month (or some other periodic interval). Good examples of fixed costs include mortgage payments, rent, or car payments. All companies face fixed costs. And just like labour costs, good CEOs do their best to keep fixed costs to a minimum. You need to do the same.

No CEO would ever buy a factory twice as big as the company needs, and no CEO would ever buy a factory that costs so much to run, it uses up all the company's earnings. You need to apply the same logic for all of your fixed costs. **Don't buy a home twice as big as you need, and don't buy or rent a home that uses up all your disposable income and leaves you with nothing left over to invest.**

Avoid the Trap of a Big Mortgage

There are few things in this world that can destroy your chances of financial freedom at a young age more than a big, unaffordable mortgage that uses up all your disposable income. You must avoid this trap at all costs. If you are in this trap, you need to get out. A large, unaffordable mortgage truly is one of the largest financial freedom sucking maggots out there.

A large mortgage will suck all the disposable income out of you. Moreover, it will do it every month for decades. If you get a mortgage that uses up every last dollar you earn, you will have nothing left over to purchase income producing investments. With nothing left over to purchase income producing investments, you will not be able to get your money working for you, and you will not be able to achieve financial freedom until much later in life, if at all.

Perhaps this is the reason that, according to *The Millionaire Next Door*, there were nearly three times as many households in 2010 with investments of $1 million or more living in homes valued at $300,000 or less than there were living in homes valued at $1 million or more. If that isn't enough to convince you to get a more affordable home, then consider this; Warren Buffet, one of the richest men in the world, still lives in the same home today that he purchased for $31,500 back in 1958. Adjusted for inflation, that amount in today's dollars is equal to roughly $260,000.

Let's look at the following example to illustrate how a large, unaffordable mortgage can destroy your chances for financial freedom. Let's assume, based on your monthly income, that the most expensive home you can afford costs $500,000. Let's also assume that if you buy this home, you will have nothing left over to invest in your financial freedom fund.

Now let's fast-forward twenty-five years to see how large your financial freedom fund could be if you buy a $400,000 home or a $300,000 home instead. Buying a home that is less expensive than what you can afford allows you to invest your leftover savings in your financial freedom fund and, as we will see below, could result in a very large amount of savings over the life of your mortgage.

For these calculations, let's assume a mortgage rate of 5% and an amortization period of twenty-five years. Let's also assume that you invest any leftover savings in an S&P 500 index fund that realizes a CAGR of 7%.

For simplicity, we will assume a zero down payment and will not factor in the affect that taxes might have on your savings. In this regard, let's assume you are channeling all your savings into every tax-advantaged retirement savings account available (see chapter 10).

For the $500,000 home, you would have mortgage payments of $2,900 a month and over the course of the twenty-five years, spend a grand total of roughly $870,000 on your mortgage. You would also be left with a rather disappointing financial freedom fund of $0.

For the $400,000 home, your mortgage payments would be roughly $2,300 a month and over the course of the twenty-five years, you would spend a grand total of $700,000 on your mortgage. However, given your lower monthly mortgage payments, you would now have an extra $600 a month available to invest in your financial freedom fund ($2,900 - $2,300). This extra $600 a month would grow to roughly $490,000 by the end of twenty-five years. Furthermore, this $490,000 would now earn you an extra $34,000 a year (assuming it continued to generate an annual return of 7%).

The growth of your financial freedom fund would be even more impressive if you were to purchase the $300,000 home. It's also worth noting that if you are able to rent out a portion of your home, the mortgage payments based on this lower amount might be possible, even if you were to buy a more expensive home. For example, once rental income is factored in, a mortgage payment of $2,000 a month is really more like a mortgage payment of $1,000 a month if you are collecting $1,000 in rent each month.

The $300,000 home would cost you roughly $1,750 a month in mortgage payments and cost a total of only $525,000 after twenty-five years. It would also allow you to contribute a total of $1,150 a month to your financial freedom fund, ($2,900 - $1,750) which, after twenty-five years, would be worth a staggering $938,000. With this much in savings, you would then be rewarded with roughly $65,000 each year from your investments alone (assuming your investments continued to generate an annual return of 7%).

Take a moment and think about this for a minute. You are mortgage free and now earn roughly $65,000 a year from your investments alone. The results of this analysis are presented in the graph below.

Growth in Savings After 25 Years

Assumes a $500,000 mortgage with a fixed rate of 5% uses up all disposible income and that left over monthly income from smaller mortgages is invested and earns a 7% CAGR

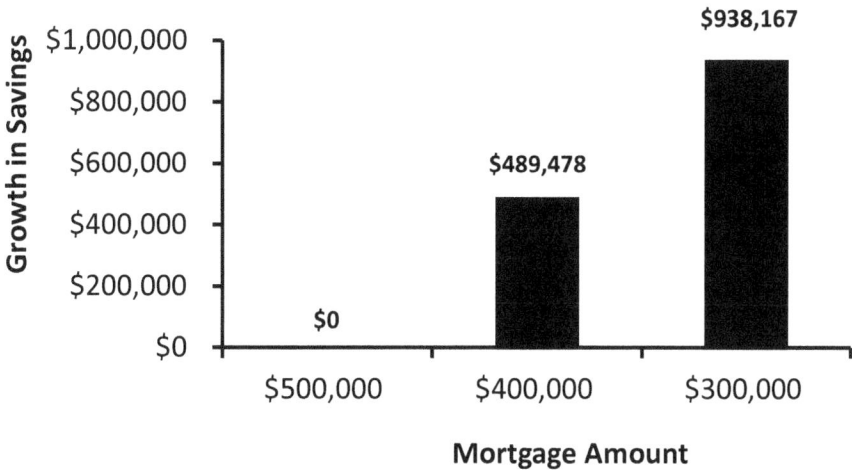

Some people might make the argument that because the value of a home would increase over time, it might be worthwhile to buy the more expensive home.

While it is true that homes are likely to increase in value over time, it is also true that a big expensive house won't pay you any income each month. Not unless you rent it out or sell it, move into a cheaper house, and invest your profits. If you want to invest in real estate then buy a house and rent it out.

Moreover, the stock market has historically offered a higher rate of return than the real estate market. Research in Canada has shown that in the twenty years leading up to 2013, stocks grew at an average rate of 8.3% a year while the national house price in Canada grew at only 4.5% per year. Furthermore, when you factor in all the costs involved with home ownership such as utilities, insurance, property taxes, and home repairs, this 4.5% return would become even lower.

Research in the U.S., according to Investopedia, has shown that between 1928 and 2012, the DJIA rose performed five times as well as the U.S. housing market. Warren Buffett seems to be aware of this fact and, when referring to the purchase of his own house, has been quoted as saying "I would have made far more money had I instead rented and used the purchase money to buy stocks."

Finally, if you take all your money and use it to buy the most expensive house you can afford, you end up putting all your eggs in one basket. Maybe your house will dramatically increase in value, but maybe it won't. A far better strategy would be to diversify your holdings and own at least some stocks, some bonds, and some real estate (see chapter 8).

Avoid Buying New Cars

Although not as costly as the trap of a big mortgage, an expensive new car is another large money sucking maggot that you would be better off avoiding. Billionaire and IKEA founder, Ingvar Kamprad, seems to agree with this philosophy. When asked about a 15 year-old Volvo he was driving, he responded, "She is nearly new, just 15 years old, or something like that."

Just like a large mortgage, buying a new car every few years will put a big dent in your disposable income and will reduce the amount of money you have left over to invest. And just like a large mortgage, this is something you must try to avoid.

I recently read an article that stated many people in Canada buy a new car every four years. Even worse, thirty percent of Canadian consumers, in 2015, had negative equity when they traded in their older cars for their new ones. This means the amount of money these consumers owed on their car loans was more than the value of the vehicles they were trading in. To buy their new cars, these consumers were forced to roll what was owed on their earlier cars onto the new loans for their newer vehicles. The result of this type of spending is a never-ending car loan that just gets bigger and bigger every time you buy a new car.

To be honest, I'm not sure why anyone who is looking to save money would buy a new car. As soon as you drive it off the lot, its value drops dramatically. You are far better off buying a less expensive second hand car that is only a few years old but still has a long, useful life ahead of it.

Better still, if your family owns two cars, see if you can get by with just one. Think of the money you could save each year in car payments, car insurance, gas, and maintenance, if you could eliminate that extra car.

As a child, I can remember my father buying a new car every five years. Unlike my father, I bought a 1999 Toyota Tercel in 2001 for about $10,000 and I have owned it ever since (15 years and counting). I believe that this decision alone has resulted in hundreds of thousands of dollars in extra savings over the years.

The average price of a new car in 2015 was just over $30,000. If you were to buy a used car for $10,000 and keep it for ten years, as opposed to buying a new car for $30,000 and keeping it for five years, the savings you could realize over a twenty-five year period would be huge.

If you bought a new car every five years, you would spend roughly $150,000 on new cars over a twenty-five year period (5 x $30,000). If you bought a used car for $10,000 every ten years, you would spend roughly $25,000 (2.5 x $10,000) over the same twenty-five year period. That is an immediate savings of $125,000. It gets even better.

What happens if, over a twenty-five year period, you were to invest all the savings you realized from your frugal car purchases into your financial freedom fund? If you were to invest an extra $400 a month into your financial freedom fund ($125,000 in savings divided by 300 months), you would wind up with something closer to $324,000 (assuming a CAGR of 7%).

Adding All the Fixed Costs Together

If you have the fortitude to live in a less expensive home, drive a second hand car, and invest all the savings you realize by making these decisions, then, assuming you realized all the savings mentioned above, your financial freedom fund would be over $1.25 million in twenty-five years. This $1.25 million would then generate an extra $87,500 a year (assuming it realized a CAGR of 7%).

These examples illustrate the important point that **many millionaires place a higher value on financial freedom than they do on social status**. The sooner you do the same, the quicker you will achieve financial freedom.

Control Variable Costs

Unlike fixed costs, such as monthly mortgage payments, variable costs change from month to month. Variable costs also, quite often, offer you a choice as to how much you will spend on a purchase. Most importantly, you usually don't need to make these types of purchases at all.

Examples of variable costs include renovation expenses, eating out, entertainment expenses...etc. Just like fixed costs, variable costs also need to be tightly controlled if you want to save as much of your earnings as possible and achieve financial freedom at a young age.

A better way to view variable costs might be to consider these types of costs as either *needs* or *wants*. A leaky roof is a variable expense that would probably be classified as a need, and you should, more than likely, pay to get it fixed (or better yet, fix it yourself, assuming you are safely able).

By comparison, cosmetic house renovations, like a new kitchen, are not needs, they are wants. And **if financial freedom is your primary goal, you need to try to minimize the amount of money you spend on your wants and try to maximize the amount of money you invest into your financial freedom fund.**

One of the richest and most successful business leaders that ever lived, Henry Ford, once said, "I sometimes wonder if we have fallen under the spell of salesmanship. The American of a generation ago was a shrewd buyer. But nowadays the American people seem to listen and be sold." Ford made this statement in 1926, and since then, hyper-consumerism has only gotten worse. Everybody seems to want the newest gadgets right away, and if they can't afford them, they borrow money and get them anyway.

Once again, the more you can curb your spending, the more you will have to invest. And the more you have to invest, the sooner you will achieve financial freedom.

Avoid Unnecessary Renovations

CEOs don't make renovations unless they believe these renovations will earn their companies more money. If financial freedom is your main goal, neither should you.

Sure, your bathroom may be a little outdated, but unless you are selling your home, I'm not sure updating it is going to help contribute to your financial freedom. And while it's true that everybody likes nice things, it's also true that the people with the nicest things are the ones that are going to have a much harder time achieving financial freedom.

Lower All Your Monthly Expenses

Besides saving on cosmetic home renovations, there are probably many other variable costs that you pay out each month that can be either lowered or eliminated completely.

Each month, I use to spend $60 on a landline phone, $40 on a newspaper, $40 on a gym membership, and a $100 on a cable TV subscription. This totaled close to $3,000 a year. A short while after coming to the realization of how much all these services cost, I decided to do something about it. I took action and managed to save thousands of dollars each year.

I cancelled the gym membership and started running outside, cancelled the newspaper subscription and started reading the newspaper online for free, and cancelled the subscription for the landline phone and bought a subscription to an internet phone that cost only $30 for the whole year. And although I wasn't able to cancel the cable TV, as it was part of the rental agreement with my tenant, I certainly would have cancelled it if it had been entirely up to me. It turns out I could watch almost all of the shows I liked online, either for free or at a much lower rate. These simple changes meant that almost $3,000 a year in savings could be realized with practically no change at all to my quality of life.

Spend Less on Vacations

There's no doubt about it, fancy vacations are fun. But, then again, so is never having to work again for the rest of your life. If you want to achieve financial freedom quickly, you need to start taking more modest vacations.

If you and your partner spend $5,000 a year on vacations, but this could be reduced to only $2,000 a year, that's another $3,000 a year in savings that could go into your financial freedom fund.

Maybe you always vacation in a foreign country or at a fancy beach resort. Now's your chance to take a few years exploring what your own local region has to offer. By exploring local cities, parks, and attractions, for the next few years, you will be able to contribute thousands more to your financial freedom fund.

If you really want to treat yourself, take a fancy vacation every three or four years instead. The savings you realize by doing this will help you to take a permanent vacation far quicker than most.

Then, after your mortgage is paid off and you are a millionaire, go back to taking a nice vacation each year, go live in Spain for a few years, or travel the world. You'll have earned it.

Minimize the Number of Times You Eat Out

No one is saying that you shouldn't enjoy yourself now and then, but if you have a good paying job and don't know where all the money is going, then looking at the amount of money you spend eating out would be a good place to start.

Assuming a couple could save $30 each time they eat dinner at home, reducing the number of times they eat dinner out from three times a week to once a week would save another $3,000 a year.

Even if you don't go out to dinner three times a week, you might still be able to save a lot of money, as previously mentioned, by simply having that morning coffee at home or by bringing your lunch to work each day.

Your mom probably packed you a lunch for close to a decade when you were going to school and I bet you never thought twice about it. If you and your significant other were to save two dollars each on coffee every day and eight dollars each on lunch every day, it would work out to roughly $7,300 a year in savings.

Adding All the Variable Costs Together

It is entirely up to you how lavish you want your lifestyle to be, depending of course on how much money you make in the first place, but remember, **the more frugal you can be early on in life, the wealthier you will end up later in life.**

This is because of the time value of money. Remember Bob and Barb from chapter 2? Bob waited ten years before investing for his retirement, and even though he contributed $200,000 more than Barb and contributed to his retirement for twenty years longer than she did, he still ended up with less money than she did when they both retired at age sixty-five.

All the variable savings listed above add up to over $16,000 a year, not including unnecessary renovations. If you and your partner ruthlessly cut as many variable expenses as possible, you might be able to save close to $1,000 a month or $12,000 a year. If this $12,000 a year was then invested and realized a CAGR of 7% a year, you would have an additional $800,000 in twenty-five years.

Adding All the Savings Together

Combining all the savings generated from cutting all your costs (fixed and variable) and investing them at a CAGR of 7%, results in roughly $2 million in twenty-five years. This sum of $2 million could then be used to provide you with roughly $140,000 a year, again assuming a CAGR of 7%.

Even though it might not be possible for you to realize all the savings discussed above, these calculations do illustrate just how much money one is able to save by dramatically cutting costs and controlling expenses. And even though not everyone will be able to realize all these savings by cutting their costs, I'd be willing to bet there are some families out there earning well over $100,000 a year in combined income that have no idea where the majority of their money goes. For these families, many of the cost cutting measure outlined above are probably a real possibility.

The bottom line is that the more you are able to cut costs, the quicker you will be able to achieve financial freedom. Again, the choice on how frugal you want to live is entirely up to you. If you are determined to achieve financial freedom in a short amount of time, you are going to have to sacrifice more compared to most. The good news is that if you are able to live a frugal life for a number of years while you are still relatively young and you invest all the savings you realize, you will be miles ahead of those who don't do these things.

My wife and I started living well below our means when I was twenty-nine years-old. Between seven and eight years later, we were financially free. We still live a fairly frugal lifestyle now, but given our mortgage is paid off and we don't need to relentlessly save as much as we used to, we now live a life that is pretty comparable to many other couples our age. We go out to eat at least once a week, we take vacations, and we sometimes splurge. The only difference between us and many other couples is that we are financially free and can live the lives we truly want without the need for a biweekly paycheck.

For seven or eight years we made a concerted effort to save as much as we could. In doing so, we were able to save and invest over $5,000 a month. The majority of this $5,000 a month was thanks to a dual income, avoiding the trap of a large mortgage, renting out part of our home, and buying less expensive second hand cars. However, we also saved more than a thousand dollars a month by watching many of the variable costs mentioned above. All of this saving and investing added up to hundreds of thousands of dollars over the first five years alone. It is now worth over a million dollars.

We earned even more money by building our financial acumen, leveraging ourselves, and paying close attention to our taxes. All of these strategies are discussed in detail in future chapters.

The graph below shows that if you started saving $5,000 a month at the age of twenty-five, you would make your first million at the tender age of thirty-six.

Growth of Investment Account

Assumes contributions of $5,000 a month and returns of 7% (compounded monthly)

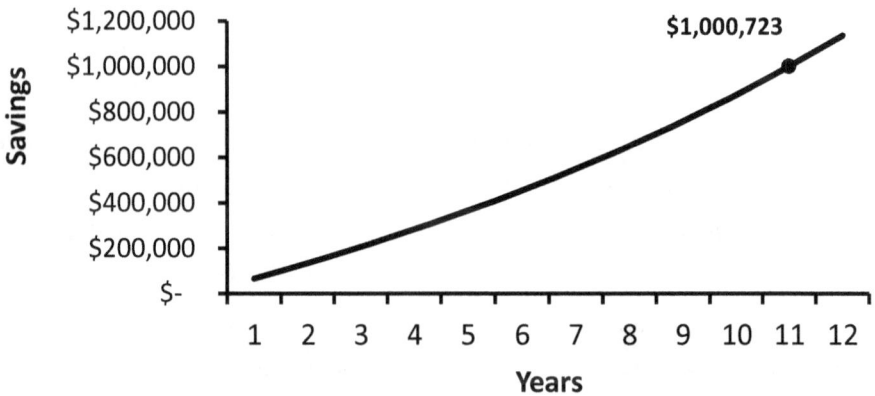

Picture that. You are a millionaire in eleven years. Sure your friends drove fancier cars and had more luxurious homes, but I'll bet, for the most part, they wouldn't have been all that much happier. Some of the happiest times in my life were spent in high-school and university, and I certainly didn't have an extravagant lifestyle back then.

"Regardless of what we achieve in the pursuit of stuff, it's never going to bring about an enduring state of happiness."

- Daniel Gilbert

Most of the research I have come across regarding happiness never mentions anything about achieving it by buying more stuff. In his book *Stumbling on Happiness,* Daniel Gilbert writes, "Regardless of what we achieve in the pursuit of stuff, it's never going to bring about an enduring state of happiness."

For most people, happiness comes from spending time with friends and family, helping others, and simply getting outside and being active. It has nothing to do with the car you drive. Moreover, isn't it worth it to live a happy, frugal life for eleven years if it could translate into a lifetime of financial freedom?

If eleven years isn't quick enough for you, it may be possible to achieve financial freedom even quicker. To do so, you will need to combine strong core competencies and relentless cost cutting measures with some leverage and make sure to take advantage of every tax avoidance strategy available.

Before we talk about leverage and taxes, however, we need to talk about financial acumen and the income producing investments that are going to make up your financial freedom fund. These topics will be covered in the next three chapters.

Let's end this chapter, however, by looking at one of the best cost cutting CEOs of recent history, Sam Walton. Sam Walton was the founder of

Walmart, and according to *Forbes* magazine, he was also the richest person in the U.S. from 1982-1988. Not only was Sam Walton rich, he was also notoriously frugal.

The Frugal Billionaire

In 1945, at the age of 26, Sam Walton began his career in retailing by purchasing a Ben Franklin variety store in Newport, Arkansas. By 1962, he and his brother, Bud, owned 16 stores in Arkansas, Missouri, and Kansas. On July 2, 1962, the brothers opened up their first Walmart store. And by 2010, Wal-Mart was the world's largest company. Sam Walton was the CEO of Wal-Mart until 1988 and remained active in the company until his death in 1992.

At the time of his death in 1992, Sam Walton was worth an estimated $65 billion. Despite this vast wealth, however, Walton was notoriously frugal. Walton almost always flew economy class and would often share budget hotel rooms when he went on business trips.

Moreover, according to the book *What I Learned From Sam Walton,* written by Michael Bergdahl, Walton lived in a humble house and his "corporate car" consisted of a beat up old pick-up truck. When once asked about his choice of vehicle, Walton famously replied, "What am I supposed to haul my dogs around in, a Rolls-Royce?"

Walton preached his frugal ways to his Wal-Mart employees as well. He is quoted as repeatedly telling employees that "Every time Walmart spends one dollar foolishly, it comes out of our customers pockets." This philosophy of minimizing costs was a big part of Walmart's success and it is a philosophy that is still ingrained in Walmart's culture today.

Sam Walton's goal was to try and help everybody live cheaper. If you want to get wealthy quickly, living cheaper is a goal that you should embrace as well.

KEY POINTS FROM CHAPTER FOUR

- If you want to achieve financial freedom, do not try to keep up with the Joneses.

- The more ruthless you are at cutting costs, the more successful you will be at growing your financial freedom fund.

- Stop paying people to do things that you are able to do yourself.

- Getting a smaller mortgage and investing the difference could result in hundreds of thousands of dollars in extra savings over the life of your mortgage.

- Buying less expensive, reliable second hand cars could result in hundreds of thousands of dollars in extra savings over your lifetime.

- Many millionaires place a higher value on financial freedom than they do on social status.

- To achieve financial freedom quickly, you need to control the amount of money you spend on *wants*.

- Unnecessary renovations, expensive vacations, and eating out all the time, will make it harder to achieve an early retirement.

- The more frugal you are early on in life, the wealthier you will end up later in life.

- The pursuit of stuff is unlikely to bring about an enduring state of happiness.

CHAPTER FIVE

Financial Acumen and Thinking Outside the Box

It was a rainy spring day in 2008, and the fate of our financial freedom hung in the balance.

My wife had just walked through the front door and she looked exhausted. She had just gotten home from work, after being stuck in traffic for well over an hour. She was leaving home just after seven-thirty every morning and was getting back home just after six-thirty every night. Like many people stuck in the daily grind, this was her daily routine.

On this particular day, however, my wife seemed like she had finally reached her breaking point. She wanted to be done with her long commutes, and judging by the look on her face, it seemed like it would be difficult to convince her otherwise.

"I want to buy a house in Vancouver," she said. I cringed in horror. The death of our financial freedom fund was staring me right in the face and it had to be stopped.

As anybody who has spent some time in Vancouver knows, Vancouver is not only one of the most beautiful cities in the world; it's also one of the most expensive. What can literally buy you a palace in some parts of the world, can buy you a dirty, old shack of a house in Vancouver.

In fact, the morning paper recently printed an article about castles in France that cost less than condominiums in Vancouver. That's right; you can buy a castle in France for the same price as a condominium in Vancouver.

I immediately started calculating how a move to Vancouver would affect our financial freedom fund. A new house in Vancouver would cost an extra $2,000 a month in mortgage costs, and if this new house didn't have a rental suite, we would lose an additional $1,000 a month in rental income.

We stood to be down $3,000 a month or $36,000 a year. Losing $36,000 a year in contributions to our financial freedom fund would absolutely kill the dream of achieving financial freedom anytime soon. The important point here is that I was aware of this fact and that I was determined to do something about it.

In fact, as opposed to moving to Vancouver, we would have been better off if my wife just quit her job and stayed home. If she stayed home, we would save $750 a month on each child's daycare costs (for a total of $1,500 a month), $2,000 a month in extra mortgage payments, and $1,000 a month in lost rental income. This meant we could save about $4,500 a month or $54,000 a year by not moving to Vancouver. This $54,000 a year was more than the after tax take-home pay my wife earned at her job.

We discussed my wife taking a year off work to stay home with the kids, switching jobs, or working part-time. In the end, however, we kept our house in the suburbs of Greater Vancouver, my wife put up with the awful commutes for a little longer, and we continued investing her salary for a few more years until we both achieved financial freedom. This ended up being the best financial decision of all.

Develop Your Financial Acumen

Having a business plan, having a reliable income producing job, and cutting your costs, are all things that are essential to achieve financial freedom. So too, however, is strengthening your financial acumen.

Financial acumen is the ability to make good financial decisions, the kind of decisions that will enable you to achieve financial freedom much quicker than most. The fact that many CEOs come from a financial background underscores the importance of possessing good financial acumen. And given you are now the CEO of your financial freedom fund, you need to make sure you possess the ability to make smart financial decisions, too.

Even though you have a well thought-out strategy and a well thought-out business plan, you will still be faced with a number of important financial decisions in your life that aren't covered by your strategy or your business plan. And even though these decisions may not be covered in your business plan, they will still play an important role in determining how quickly you will be able to achieve financial freedom. For this reason, you must develop your financial acumen.

Let's start developing some financial acumen right now and examine two of the more common financial decisions that many people will face at some point during their lives. The first financial decision will involve buying a home and choosing a mortgage. The second financial decision will involve deciding whether or not you should pay down debt or invest.

Buying a Home and Choosing a Mortgage

It's worthwhile to note that for many people, their primary residence will be the biggest investment they ever make. Moreover, their mortgage will likely be the largest debt they ever incur. It is also worthwhile to note that, assuming you live in the U.S. or in Canada, your primary residence will, quite likely, be one of the few large investments you ever make that will not be subjected to capital gains tax when you sell it.

This being the case, it makes good sense to try to buy a primary residence that will show above average appreciation over time and to try to save as much as possible on your mortgage.

Buying a Home

Choosing a primary residence that will show above average appreciation over time is easier said than done. However, it is definitely worth the effort to try and accomplish this goal. There are plenty of people in Vancouver that have saved nothing their whole lives but have still ended up as millionaires, thanks to the price appreciation of their homes.

Of course, these people won't realize the benefit of this price appreciation unless they downsize or they find somewhere less expensive to live. Nonetheless, this is still a nice option to have.

When buying your primary residence, assuming you have a choice, look for cities where the demand for housing is expected to rise and the supply of housing is not expected to keep up with this rising demand.

Factors such as increasing employment opportunities, increasing disposable incomes, a growing economy, and a growing population, will all fuel a rise in the demand for housing. Falling interest rates, which make owning a home more affordable, will also help to increase demand.

In contrast, rising interest rates, increasing unemployment, decreasing wages, a failing economy, and a decreasing population, will all lead to weakening demand for housing.

Within a given city, look for neighborhoods that can be expected to generate strong demand thanks to things like good schools, low crime rates, easy access to public transportation, and easy access to nice parks and good restaurants.

Finally, as most savvy real estate investors already know, it is usually better to have a not so nice house in a really nice area than to have a really nice house in a not so nice area.

In terms of supply, the biggest factor affecting the future supply of housing is simply the amount of space a city or a neighborhood has left to build on. If there is no more space left to build on, or certain zoning restrictions prevent an increase in the supply of a certain type of housing, it will be difficult for builders to increase the supply.

This topic is covered in greater detail in the next chapter on real estate investing (chapter 6). For now, just realize that the future supply and demand for the type of housing you purchase will play a large role in determining your home's future price appreciation. Bearing this in mind, try to buy accordingly.

Choosing a Mortgage

The best way to save money on your mortgage is to get the shortest, most affordable mortgage you can and to pay this mortgage off as quickly as you can. While things such as biweekly payments and prepayment options are all great, if you don't want to be bogged down with large mortgage payments for the rest of your life, get a small mortgage and pay it off fast.

The time it takes to pay off your mortgage will be determined by your mortgage's amortization period. And the longer the amortization period, the more you will end up losing in interest payments.

To illustrate how longer amortization periods end up costing homebuyers more in interest payments, let's look at the monthly mortgage payments and the total interest paid over the life of a typical fixed rate mortgage, using three different amortization periods - ten years, twenty years, and forty years.

For this analysis, we will assume a mortgage of $400,000 and a fixed rate mortgage of 4%. The results of this analysis are shown in the table below.

Total Cost of $400,000 Mortgage (4% fixed) with Different Amortization Periods

Amortization Period	Monthly Payments	Total Principal Paid	Total Interest Paid	Total Cost
10 years	$4,050	$400,000	$85,200	$485,200
20 years	$2,420	$400,000	$180,000	$580,000
40 years	$1,660	$400,000	$400,000	$800,000

The table above shows that an amortization period of ten years results in some hefty mortgage payments of $4,050 a month, especially when these mortgage payments are compared to the monthly mortgage payments that result from choosing an amortization period of twenty years or forty years. Don't be fooled, however, by these higher monthly payments. In the long-run, the shorter the amortization period, the more money you save.

Referring to the table above, it can be seen that the total interest paid on the mortgage with the ten year amortization period is $85,200. The total interest paid on the mortgage with the twenty year amortization period, however, amounts to a much larger $180,000. Even worse, the total interest paid on the mortgage with the forty year amortization period is a staggering $400,000.

With the forty year amortization period, you originally borrow $400,000 but end up paying $800,000 in total costs. With the ten year amortization period, you end up borrowing $400,000 and paying total costs of only $485,000 for the same home.

While there are sometimes valid reasons for getting a mortgage with a long amortization period, more often than not, longer amortization periods are simply a way for homebuyers to go out and buy the most expensive homes they can get their hands on.

As a result of this type of behaviour, many homebuyers end up with large, unaffordable mortgages that drain all of their disposable income. These types of homebuyers end up paying so much on their mortgages that sadly, they never have any money left over to get working for them.

Let's look at an example to illustrate this point. Let's examine how higher amortization periods can result in homebuyers buying homes they might not otherwise be able to afford and evaluate how this decision could end up costing these homebuyers a lot more money over the long-term.

Let's assume that you are able to afford monthly mortgage payments of $2,500 a month. Given these monthly mortgage payments, you would be able to buy a $400,000 home with a twenty year amortization period or a $600,000 home with a forty year amortization period.

Let's see what the total cost of these two options works out to be. We will again assume a fixed rate mortgage of 4%. The results of this analysis are illustrated in the table below.

Total Cost of Different 4% Fixed Rate Mortgage Amounts with Different Amortization Periods but Identical Monthly Payments

Mortgage Amount	Amortization Period	Monthly Payments	Total Principal Paid	Total Interest Paid	Total Cost
$400,000	20 years	$2,420	$400,000	$180,000	$580,000
$600,000	40 years	$2,500	$600,000	$600,000	$1,200,000

The table above shows that if you purchase the less expensive $400,000 home, using an amortization period of twenty years, you are looking at mortgage payments of roughly $2,420 a month. These monthly mortgage payments end up costing you roughly $180,000 in interest and result in total costs of $580,000, over the life of the mortgage.

By comparison, the table above also shows that if you buy the $600,000 home, using the forty year amortization period, your monthly mortgage payments will be almost identical to the monthly mortgage payments involved with the $400,000 home with the twenty year amortization period. However, even though your monthly mortgage expenses will almost be identical, your total costs, with the $600,000 home, will be dramatically higher.

In fact, the $600,000 home, using the forty year amortization period, will cost a whopping $600,000 in interest payments alone. This is about $420,000 higher than the interest payments paid on the $400,000 home. When you add these interest payments to the principal, it means your total cost for the $600,000 home is a stunning $1.2 million.

By purchasing the less expensive $400,000 home, using the lower amortization period, you can save yourself $420,000 in extra interest expenses and $200,000 in extra principal. This means you wouldn't just realize total savings of $200,000 (the difference in the purchase price), you would realize total savings of $620,000.

Purchasing the less expensive home, using the twenty year amortization period, would also mean that you wouldn't be paying a mortgage for forty years. Imagine the financial benefit of not having to pay a monthly mortgage for an extra twenty years. Furthermore, imagine how much larger your financial freedom fund would be if this extra $620,000 was used to buy investments that actually earned you money.

As mortgages rates go up, the advantages of buying a more affordable home and paying off your mortgage as quick as possible become even more apparent. A $600,000 mortgage with a fixed mortgage rate of 6% and an amortization period of forty years would end up costing the homebuyer closer to $1.5 million in total payments and almost $1 million in interest payments alone.

Should You Pay Down Debt or Invest?

The choice of whether or not to pay down debt or invest is one of the more common dilemmas many investors face during the course of their lives. When faced with this dilemma, a savvy investor with good financial acumen always examines all the information available before coming to any conclusions. Sometimes it makes sense to pay down debt, and other times it may make sense to invest.

For example, if you have a large debt on your credit card and this credit card charges you 20% interest, then you should pay down your debt. Do not even think about investing. This makes sense because even if the stock market offers a CAGR of 10%, you would make less money in the stock market than you would lose in interest payments on your debt.

Unfortunately, by the end of 2015, the average Canadian had close to $22,000 in debt sitting on their credit cards. This debt should absolutely be paid off before any money is used to purchase investments.

However, if your only debt is your mortgage, your mortgage rate is 4%, and you believe you can earn a 7% ROI by investing in the stock market, then it may make sense to invest in the stock market and not pay down your mortgage. This would make even more sense if your investments were to receive some sort of tax advantage (see chapter 10).

In fact, **whenever you believe you can earn a higher return on your investments than the cost of the interest you pay on your debt, you should consider investing your money.** If you invest, the returns from the investments would likely be able to cover the interest on the debt and more.

Sometimes these decisions are not as straightforward as just discussed. Quite often, considerations such as taxes and risk also need to be factored into the analysis. For example, if the 7% return you expect to earn on your investments faces taxes of 30%, then the return from your investments after taxes is more like an uncertain 4.9%. An uncertain return of 4.9% and a mortgage of 5% would mean you are probably better off just paying down your mortgage (assuming the mortgage interest is not tax deductible).

Canadian Residents Only

Some Canadian residents might do well to consider the option of paying down their mortgage debt and investing their money all at the same time. This is because of the opportunity to convert their non-tax-deductible mortgage interest into tax-deductible mortgage interest. This topic is discussed in greater detail in the next section in the chapter. But, for now, let's look at some math to see if a strategy that involves paying down a mortgage and then borrowing this money back against a home to invest it, could make sense for a Canadian resident.

At the time of writing this, unlike residents of Canada, residents of the United States are already entitled to claim their mortgage interest, up to a certain amount, as a tax deduction.

If a Canadian resident were to pay down a 5% mortgage, borrow the funds back at 4% with a home equity line of credit (HELOC), and then invest this money in a diversified stock portfolio, this investor would, more than likely, be entitled to claim this 4% interest expense as a tax deduction. Assuming this investor was in a 30% tax bracket, this tax deduction would result in the interest on the money borrowed to invest being closer to 2.8%. If this investor was then able to realize a 7% return on his or her investments, and these investment returns got taxed at half of his or her marginal tax rate (15%), this investor's profits would be closer to 3.2% (6.0%-2.8%). With an expected return of 3.2%, this would be a strategy well worth considering.

If you are a Canadian resident and you are thinking of implementing this strategy, be sure you research and follow all of Revenue Canada's rules before you begin. Generally speaking, the borrowed money must be used to purchase investments that generate income. Also, you are not allowed to claim a tax deduction on your interest if you borrow money to invest in some sort of tax-advantaged retirement savings account such as an RRSP or a TFSA.

Notice how some of the best financial options are not always the most obvious. The key is to make sure you spend some time working through all of your options.

I've heard numerous people comment on how it makes no sense to invest in tax-deferred retirement savings accounts (RRSPs in Canada, or IRAs in the U.S.) because you just end up owing taxes later on. I've also heard others say that you should never borrow money to invest under any circumstances. Rather than just accept or dismiss these claims, I've looked into them myself. I've exercised my financial acumen and I've come to my own conclusions.

Incidentally, I have come to the conclusion that it does make sense to invest in tax-deferred retirement savings accounts (see chapter 10) and, depending on the circumstances, it does make sense to borrow money to invest (see chapter 9).

Think Outside the Box

Successful CEOs thrive on innovation and thinking outside the box. Think of companies such as Apple. Over the last decade, Apple has brought some truly innovative products to market. Innovations such as the iPod, the iPhone, and the iPad, have revolutionized the way people listen to music, use phones, and connect with the internet. Apple's reward for this way of thinking has been record sales. In 2015, Apple became a $700 billion company, the biggest company the world has ever seen.

"Innovation distinguishes between a leader and a follower."
- Steve Jobs

Steve Jobs, one of the founders of Apple, once said, "Innovation distinguishes between a leader and a follower." And one of the most famous minds the world has ever known, Albert Einstein, once said, "We cannot solve our problems with the same thinking we used when we created them." When it comes to saving and investing for your financial freedom, you need to listen to these two titans of innovation and start thinking outside the box.

"We cannot solve our problems with the same thinking we used when we created them."
- Albert Einstein

If you are a follower, and you do the same old things everyone else does, you will end up achieving financial freedom at the same time everyone else does - much later in life. If you think outside the box, cut your costs, and come up with better ways to save and invest your money, you will retire well ahead of everyone else.

Below is a list of options that many people don't think about when trying to save and invest for their financial freedom. Nonetheless, these are options that many would do well to consider. Read them over and see if you could benefit from them. Then, try to think outside of the box and come up with a list of your own.

Thinking Outside the Box for Financial Freedom

- Live in another city or another country.
- Live with family, rent out part of your home, or downsize.
- Make your mortgage interest tax deductible (residents of Canada). Consider minimizing your mortgage payments and maximizing your investments (residents of the U.S.).
- Give some of your inheritance to your loved ones while you are still alive.

Live in a Different City or a Different Country

Here's a thought for you. If you are living in an extremely expensive city (like Vancouver), then maybe you would be financially better off if you moved.

CEOs choose to set up their businesses in locations that will allow them to realize the most income. You should try to do the same. Ideally, you should try and find a job in a location where your employment income will be high and your cost of living will be low.

If there is another city where you could get a higher paying job and spend less of your income on your cost of living, you might want to consider moving to this city. Just imagine how much quicker you could achieve financial freedom if you earned much more from your job and your cost of living was much lower.

When my wife and I moved to Spain, believe it or not, we actually saved money. Our financial freedom fund paid out the same amount in Spain as it did in Canada, but the cost of living in Spain was much less expensive than the cost of living in Canada. In fact, the savings on my son's preschool costs alone paid for the cost of renting our home by the beach.

If you have an opportunity to work in another city or another country where it is cheaper to live, salaries are higher, or taxes are lower, this is definitely something worth considering.

In addition to all the monetary savings you might realize, the non-financial rewards of moving to another country, including learning another language and experiencing another culture, could be rewarding enough by themselves to merit a move.

If you already have some savings or have access to some sort of pension, but you are unable to retire where you currently live, then perhaps the option of retiring abroad is the solution you've been looking for. Perhaps, even though you are unable to retire where you currently live, the cost of living in another country is so low, you could retire quite comfortably over there.

I've heard of plenty of people retiring oversees for this very reason. In fact, I even met some of them while I was in Spain. Sometimes you don't even need to hold a foreign passport to retire oversees. Many countries will give you residence status if you buy a home in their country or if you can demonstrate to them that you have a certain amount of guaranteed income available to you. There are countries like this in South America, Asia, Central America, and Europe.

You might find that not only are some of these countries less expensive to live in, but their weather, their focus on stress-free living, and their focus on family, are a welcome change from what you could be used to in your home country.

Live With Family, Rent Part of Your Home, or Downsize

What about the option of sharing a home with family or friends? Sharing a home with family or friends could allow you to cut your cost of living by a huge amount.

Maybe you could continue to live in the same home as your parents for a little longer. Maybe you could share a home with your siblings for a couple of years. Even though this may seem strange to those of us who grew up in North America, there are plenty of other places in the world that have close family members living together under the same roof. Not only do they get the benefit of having their family close by, they also get the benefit of saving a bundle on their living expenses.

My mom has spent the last few years living with my family in the lower level of my home and it has benefited us all tremendously. After selling her house, my mom was able to invest the proceeds of this sale and generate a large monthly income that she otherwise would not have had access to. Moreover, my mom helps us look after our two young children, and we help my mom out with some of the things she needs help with. The truth is we all benefit from this arrangement.

If you don't want to live with family members or friends, then what about renting out your basement or downsizing? I'll bet many of us don't need half the space we have in our homes.

Furthermore, a smaller living space might even motivate you to get outside more. My wife and I rented a smaller place when we moved to Spain and we found it encouraged us to spend more time outside in parks and on beaches. It was a welcome change.

No matter how you do it, imagine how much better off you would be if you cut your mortgage payments in half. Then imagine how much more money you could generate if you started getting those savings working for you.

Make Your Mortgage Interest Tax-Deductible (Canadian Residents Only)

Whether you live in a big expensive house or in a reasonably sized condominium, a good way for residents of Canada to save money is to make their mortgage interest tax-deductible.

If you are a resident of Canada, the mortgage interest on your primary residence is not tax-deductible. However, even though the mortgage interest is not tax-deductible in the traditional sense, it is possible to make this mortgage interest tax-deductible through various indirect methods.

If you are a resident of the U.S. then, at the time of writing this, you are eligible to claim the interest on your mortgage payments as a tax deduction (up to a certain amount). Strategies for U.S. residents pertaining to mortgage payments and investing are discussed in the next section.

The difference between having a mortgage with tax-deductible interest and having a mortgage with non-tax deductible interest could conceivably add up to hundreds of thousands of dollars over the life of your mortgage. If there was ever a situation that could benefit from the use of some financial acumen, it is this.

Let's consider a couple of ways that Canadian residents are able to turn non-tax deductible mortgage interest into tax-deductible mortgage interest and, thereby, realize substantial savings.

This simplest way to make the mortgage interest on your primary residence tax-deductible (Canadian residents only) would be to sell some of the non-registered investments you already have, use the proceeds to pay down your mortgage, and then borrow back the same amount of money against your home and use it to repurchase some income producing investments. By doing this, you would swap non tax-deductible mortgage interest for tax-deductible interest on the money you borrowed to invest.

For example, if you had $100,000 in non-registered investments and a $100,000 mortgage on your primary residence, you could sell the investments and use the proceeds to pay down the mortgage. You could then borrow this money back against your home, usually in the form of a home equity line of credit (HELOC), and simply repurchase the investments. After doing all of this, you would still have $100,000 in debt and $100,000 in investments, however, given the debt is now being used to purchase income producing investments, the interest on this debt would now be tax-deductible. By following this strategy, you would have just changed the interest payments on $100,000 in debt from non-tax-deductible interest into tax-deductible interest.

Be aware of the fact that whenever you sell any investments, whether to implement this strategy or not, you may end up owing capital gains tax (see chapter 10). As well, make sure you check all of Revenue Canada's rules and talk to a tax accountant before you implement this strategy. You want to be absolutely sure the interest on your debt will, indeed, be tax-deductible.

Once again, the general rule is that as long as the debt is being used to purchase investments that earn income and is not being used to purchase investments in any sort of tax-advantaged retirement savings account, such as an RRSP or TFSA, the interest on this debt should be tax-deductible.

Even if you don't have the benefit of having $100,000 in non-registered income producing investments lying around, you may still be able to implement this strategy. Assume, for example, that you have a $100,000 mortgage and no investments, but that you diligently pay down your mortgage each month or are about to make a lump sum payment to pay down your mortgage principal. Faced with this scenario, you would simply pay your mortgage as planned, immediately borrow back any principal you have paid down (again using a HELOC), and then use the borrowed funds to purchase non-registered income producing investments. Under this scenario, you would be able to slowly build up an investment portfolio over time, using your home as collateral for a loan with tax-deductible interest.

This is an extremely powerful strategy, especially given the cost of procrastination (see chapter 2) that would be involved in delaying the purchase of income producing investments until after your mortgage was completely paid off. Imagine the advantage of building your investment portfolio up over the life of your mortgage, as opposed to not buying any investments until twenty or thirty years later.

This is a strategy that my wife and I made full use of. We would often use her entire salary to prepay our mortgage and then immediately borrow this sum right back, using a HELOC, and invest it.

Now just to be clear, borrowing to invest is not without some risk. And anytime you borrow to invest, you must be sure this strategy actually makes sense (see chapter 9).

You must also manage these risks appropriately (see chapters 7, 8, & 9) and make sure the math behind this type of strategy makes sense. There's no point borrowing money to invest if it will cost more to borrow this money than the return you expect to generate.

Nonetheless, borrowing money to invest and making your mortgage interest tax-deductible is a powerful wealth building option.

If you think about it, anytime you have a sum of money you plan to invest and an outstanding mortgage, you are usually presented with two options. The first option is to simply purchase the investments. The second option is to prepay the mortgage, borrow back against your home, and *then* purchase the investments. If you are not interested in purchasing any investments, you would simply pay down the mortgage. If you are interested in purchasing investments, however, these are your two options.

These two options are illustrated in the chart on the next page. This chart assumes that you have a $100,000 mortgage and $100,000 in available funds that you would like to invest. Even if you don't have $100,000 available to invest, the logic would be the same for any sum of money up to and including the mortgage debt.

Option one is to invest the $100,000 directly in the stock market. This option is illustrated on the left side of the chart. By following this option, you end up with $100,000 in investments and a $100,000 mortgage with interest payments that are non-tax-deductible.

Option two is to pay down the mortgage with the $100,000, borrow the $100,000 back, and *then* invest it. This option is illustrated on the right side of the chart. Option two also results in $100,000 in investments and $100,000 in debt, however, unlike option one, this $100,000 in debt now has interest payments that are tax-deductible (see figure below).

CONVERTING NON TAX-DEDUCTIBLE MORTGAGE INTEREST INTO TAX-DEDUCTIBLE INTEREST (RESIDENTS OF CANADA ONLY)

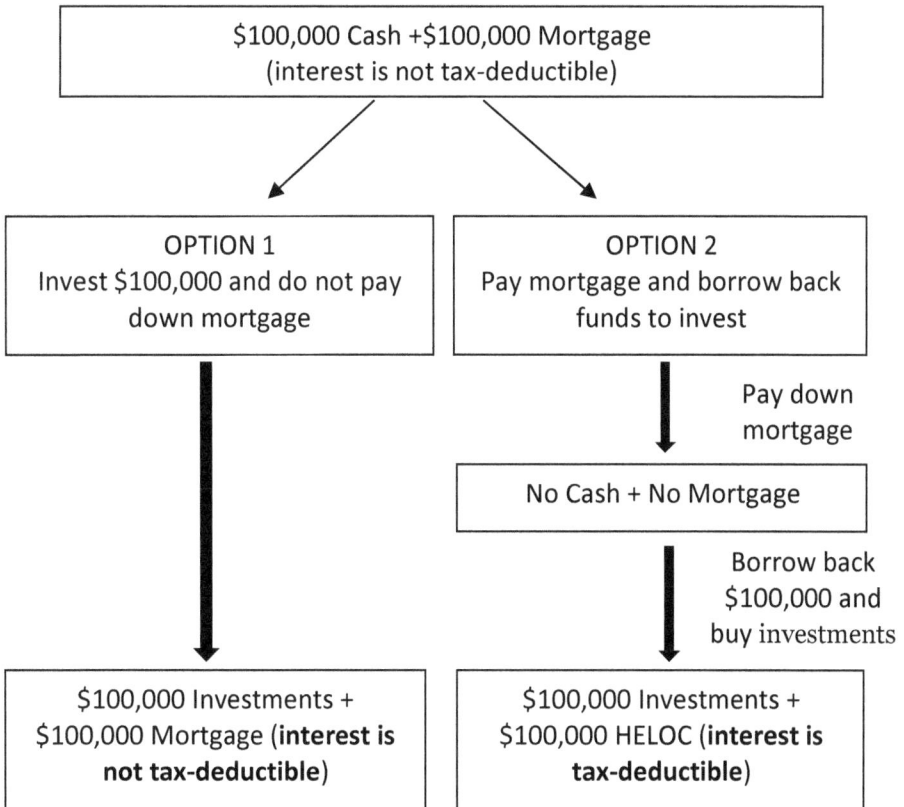

```
         ┌──────────────────────────────────────────┐
         │  $100,000 Cash +$100,000 Mortgage         │
         │     (interest is not tax-deductible)       │
         └──────────────────────────────────────────┘
              ↙                              ↘
┌───────────────────────┐      ┌───────────────────────────┐
│       OPTION 1         │      │         OPTION 2          │
│ Invest $100,000 and    │      │ Pay mortgage and borrow   │
│  do not pay            │      │ back                      │
│  down mortgage         │      │      funds to invest      │
└───────────────────────┘      └───────────────────────────┘
                                          │  Pay down
                                          ↓  mortgage
                                ┌───────────────────────────┐
                                │  No Cash + No Mortgage     │
                                └───────────────────────────┘
                                          │  Borrow back
                                          │  $100,000 and
                                          ↓  buy investments
┌───────────────────────┐      ┌───────────────────────────┐
│ $100,000 Investments + │      │ $100,000 Investments +    │
│ $100,000 Mortgage      │      │ $100,000 HELOC (interest  │
│ (interest is           │      │ is                        │
│ not tax-deductible)    │      │ tax-deductible)           │
└───────────────────────┘      └───────────────────────────┘
```

Minimize Your Mortgage Payments and Maximize Your Investments (U.S. Residents)

If you are a resident of the U.S., unlike residents of Canada, you don't need a strategy to make your mortgage interest tax-deductible. For the 2016 tax year, you can claim a tax deduction on all of your mortgage interest, up to $1 million in principal, on the home in which you live.

This means that if you have a mortgage of $500,000, for example, all of the interest on your mortgage is tax-deductible. If, however, you have a mortgage of 1.2 million, only the mortgage interest on the first million dollars of principal is tax deductible.

It is also important to note that in order to qualify for the mortgage interest tax deduction in the U.S., you are required to forgo the standard deduction and itemize your tax deductions. Therefore, you should check to see if itemizing your tax deductions and claiming your mortgage interest actually saves you more money than not itemizing and simply claiming the standard deduction.

"I would not pre-pay. I would invest instead and let the investments cover it."

- Dave Ramsey

In the U.S., if mortgage rates are relatively low and made lower by the tax deductibility of mortgage interest, then you may have access to a significant amount of borrowed money at a very low rate. Under these circumstances, it might be worthwhile to minimize any payments you make towards prepaying your mortgage and to maximize the contributions you make to your financial freedom fund. This type of idea has also been expressed by financial guru Dave Ramsey in his quote, "I would not pre-pay. I would invest instead and let the investments cover it."

Once again, you would need to ensure that the math behind this strategy makes sense. There is no point investing more in the stock market if your expected returns (after taxes) are less than your expected mortgage interest (after taxes).

If your expected mortgage interest is more than your expected returns, pay down your mortgage as fast as you can. If your expected returns are higher in the stock market, consider investing more in the stock market and worrying less about paying off your mortgage quickly.

Also, keep in mind that there is obviously more risk involved in maximizing your investments in the stock market compared to paying off your mortgage. You must be sure that you are comfortable with this risk and that you manage this risk appropriately (see chapters 7 & 8). Nonetheless, if the math adds up, then this is a risk that may be worth taking.

Moreover, the math is more likely to add up by making investment in the stock market that benefit from certain tax advantages, such as maximizing your contributions to your 401(k), especially if you receive some sort of matching benefit from your employer.

Minimizing your mortgage payments and maximizing your investments in 401(k)s, IRAs, or Roth 401(k)s, would allow you to realize the significant tax advantages associated with these plans (see chapter 10). In fact, even if the money were to be invested outside of these types of plans, it may still be eligible for certain tax advantages, assuming the investments generated dividends and/or capital gains (see chapter 10).

Give Some Wealth to Your Loved Ones While You Are Still Alive

Here's a radical thought, why don't you help out your loved ones while you are still alive instead of waiting until you are dead.

By financially helping out your loved ones earlier on in their lives, as opposed to later, not only will you get the satisfaction of seeing the difference your contributions make, your contributions could also have a much larger impact.

In addition, depending on how much wealth you have available to give away or bequeath, and depending where you live, giving this wealth away before you die could result in substantial estate tax savings. Walmart founder, Sam Walton, seemed to be acutely aware of this fact and wrote in his book, *Made in America,* that "The best way to avoid paying estate taxes is to give your assets away before they appreciate."

I'm not sure how easy it would be to have this conversation with your parents, but just because it might be difficult, doesn't mean it's not a discussion worth having. This is particularly true if you plan to properly invest any money you get gifted to you and your parent's are sitting on a large pile of uninvested money that they might not ever need.

It is a discussion that is especially worth having if your parents are planning on leaving you a large sum of money and this money is sitting in a bank account earning 0.1% interest while you are paying off a large fixed rate mortgage of 5%, or this money is sitting in a bank account earning 0.1% interest while you are unable to contribute any money to a tax-advantaged retirement savings account.

Let's consider an example involving three fathers who all have different ideas about giving money to their children. The first father (father A) decides that he will deposit $10,000 in a bank account and will bequeath these savings to his son (child A) when he dies.

The second father (father B) decides that he will invest $10,000 in an index fund that mirrors the S&P 500 and will bequeath this investment to his son (child B) when he dies.

The third father (father C) believes his son is financially responsible and decides that he will gift $10,000 to his son (child C) right away so that his son can invest the money in his tax-free retirement savings account. Child C humbly accepts this gift and uses the money to purchase an index fund that mirrors the S&P 500. Child C makes the investment inside his tax-free retirement savings account.

Twenty years later, child A and child B receive their inheritance. Let's compare these inheritances to the savings realized by child C over the last twenty years, in order to see which child has benefited the most.

Assuming father A received a CAGR of 1% on the $10,000 deposited in the savings account, this $10,000 would be worth roughly $12,200 twenty years later. We will assume that father A paid all the income taxes associated with the investment before he died. Under these circumstances, and barring any estate taxes, child A will inherit $12,200.

Given that father B invested the $10,000 in an index fund that mirrors the S&P 500; we will assume that this $10,000 realized a CAGR of 7% over the twenty years it was invested. This would mean that the $10,000 would be worth roughly $38,700. However, upon the death of father B, this $38,700 would be subject to capital gains taxes before it could be passed on to child B. If we assume capital gains tax of 15% (and it could be higher), then the actual amount available to be passed on to child B is, in fact, $32,900, (assuming there are no estate taxes). It is also worthwhile to note that father B would have been paying income taxes on all the dividend income this $10,000 had generated up until the year he died.

Now let's consider child C. Because father C gave the $10,000 to child C to contribute to a tax-free retirement savings account, neither father C or child C would have paid any income taxes on any dividends or capital gains that this investment generated over the last twenty years. Unlike the other children, there is also no chance of any estate taxes being levied on this gift. Again, assuming the investment achieved a CAGR of 7% over the last twenty years, it would now be worth $38,700.

This means child C would wind up with approximately $26,500 more than child A and approximately $5,800 more than child B.

Given these results, it's not hard to see how a strategy of helping your adult children contribute to their tax-free retirement savings accounts now, versus a strategy of bequeathing your savings to your children much later on, could lead to tens of thousands of extra dollars in their hands.

On the other hand, if you are a parent who is considering making a large monetary gift to your adult children, it will be important for you to ensure that your children recognize the importance of good saving and investing habits before they get this money. **Gifts of money should be used to help children achieve financial freedom, not to support economic dependence or frivolous purchases.**

If you do feel your children are responsible enough to receive a monetary gift and invest it properly, one of the best things you could do for them, assuming they are financially unable to do it themselves, would be to help them contribute to a tax-free savings account. The tax savings, compound growth, and lack of estate tax, all mean that this gift would, very likely, have a much larger impact if given early on in their lives, compared to bequeathing the money to them at a later date.

In Canada, at the time of writing this, adult parents are allowed to gift as much money as they want to their *adult* children with no gift tax applied and with no risk of having this money attributed back to them for income tax purposes. Gifting money or property such as stocks, bonds, or real estate, to a child who is a *minor* (child under the age of 18) would, however, trigger the attribution rules. In this case, income generated from the gift would be attributed back to the gift giver for income tax purposes. However, capital gains or capital losses would remain in the hands of the minor.

In the U.S., there are certain limits on the amount of money that can be gifted tax free. The 2016 gift exclusion amount was $14,000 and the federal estate tax exemption was $5.45 million per person. However, again at the time of writing this, the payment of tuition or medical expenses for someone other than yourself is exempt from gift tax in the U.S.

Before you can give any money away, however, you will need to make it. Let's move on and turn our attention to the different investments that are going to grant you your financial freedom. These investments are investments in real estate, investments in the stock market, and investments in the bond market. We will start by considering investments in real estate.

Before moving onto the next chapter, let's end this chapter by looking at the story of one of the wealthiest and most innovative American businessmen that ever lived. Let's look at the story of Henry Ford.

<u>The Relentless Innovator</u>

Henry Ford was born in 1863 on a farm in Greenfield Township, Michigan. Not having a great interest in farming, Ford would eventually leave his family's farm in Greenfield Township to start work as an apprentice machinist in Detroit.

In 1891, Ford became an engineer with the Edison Illuminating Company, and in 1893, he began conducting his own personal experiments with gasoline engines and automobiles. Ten years later, in 1903, Ford opened the Ford Motor Company. And in 1908, Ford introduced the world to his revolutionary Model T automobile.

By 1918, half of all cars in America were Model T's and Henry Ford was on his way to becoming one of the richest men in America and one of the richest private citizens of all time.

What were some of the secrets to Ford's success? First and foremost, he thought big and relentlessly pursued his goals. Ford was determined to be successful and to not let anything stand in his way. He is quoted as saying, "There is no man living who can do more than he thinks he can," and "Obstacles are those frightful things you see when you take your eyes off a goal."

Without his innovation and financial acumen, however, Ford would not have been nearly as wealthy. Over his lifetime, Ford was awarded an amazing 161 patents. Not only that, he was also constantly on the hunt for greater efficiency and lower costs.

In 1913, Ford developed the first automotive assembly line, allowing him to eventually achieve his lofty single-minded goal of building 1,000 cars a day. By 1920, Ford was producing over 1 million cars a year. This efficiency allowed Ford to produce cars at much lower costs compared to the other car manufacturers of that time.

With prices low, demand for automobiles skyrocketed. For the first time in history, a cheap abundant automobile was available to the masses, and the sale of the Model T made Ford rich. At his peak wealth, Ford was worth a staggering $199 billion dollars (inflation adjusted 2013 US dollars).

Ford's innovations didn't just stop at the assembly line. He also used his financial acumen to lower his overall labour costs, as well. Ford ingeniously realized this objective by paying his workers more money, not less.

By 1913, the pressure and monotony of Ford's assembly line proved so difficult to take, he needed to hire more than 52,000 men to keep a workforce of only 14,000. In 1914, against the advice of his managers and other business leaders, Ford raised his employee's wages from $2.34 a day to $5 a day, (more than double the average wage of the day). What followed was an increase in employee retention, an increase in production, and an increase in sales. Ford had correctly predicted that the money lost due to increased wages, was more than offset by the savings realized by increased production and lower employee turnover.

Take a page out of Henry Ford's playbook - exercise your financial acumen and look for innovative ways to build your wealth, too.

KEY POINTS FROM CHAPTER FIVE

- Financial acumen is the ability to make good financial decisions. It is essential in order to achieve financial freedom.

- The best way to save money on your mortgage is to get the most affordable mortgage you can and to pay this mortgage off quickly.

- Whenever you believe you can earn a higher return on your investments than the cost of the interest you pay on your debt, you should consider investing your money.

- If you are a follower, and you do the same old things everyone else does, you will achieve financial freedom much later in life.

- Consider living in another city or another country that has a lower cost of living, so that you can accelerate your time to financial freedom.

- Consider living with family, renting out part of your home, or downsizing, in order to save and invest more money.

- If Canadian, consider making your mortgage interest tax-deductible.

- Understand all the risks involved before you borrow to invest.

- If interest rates are very low, consider maximizing your investments and minimizing any prepayments to your mortgage.

- Give some of your wealth to your loved ones while you are still alive. Have them use this gift to maximize their contributions to their tax-advantaged retirement savings accounts.

- Monetary gifts should be used to help the recipient achieve financial freedom, not to support economic dependence or to encourage frivolous purchases.

CHAPTER SIX

Real Estate

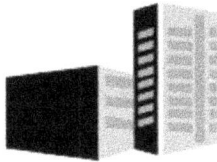

It was 2008, and my wife and I were getting ready to buy our second house in as many years.

"Honey, we're buying a house in Winnipeg." I can still remember my wife's shock after I said those words.

Winnipeg was a three hour flight from Vancouver, and temperatures there reached a balmy negative forty degrees during the winter. It had actually made headlines in Canada, one day, for being colder than the planet Mars.

The cold temperatures didn't really matter to me. After all, I wasn't planning on living there. What did matter, however, was that property in Winnipeg, at that time, was a great investment.

We could buy a house in Winnipeg, rent it out easily, and, even after paying all the monthly expenses (mortgage, insurance, property taxes...etc.), still make thousands of dollars in extra income each year.

Moreover, we were buying in a good neighborhood where demand for housing was strong, vacancy rates were low, and rental income was high. Put all of these factors together and you've got yourself a solid real estate investment.

Thankfully, my wife and I hadn't used up all our available credit when we bought our primary residence. We had bought our own home for much lower than we could afford. This meant we were now able to buy this investment property and have our money earn us even more money.

This property in Winnipeg, the rental suite in our home, and our investments in the stock market, soon become the core components of our financial freedom fund. In the years ahead, all of these investments appreciated more and more and provided more and more income every year.

It had been three years since we had started our financial freedom fund, and financial freedom in the next few years no longer felt like some sort of faraway dream. Instead, it was starting to feel like a real possibility, and it felt good.

Real Estate

Real estate has long been a favourite way for CEOs and their companies to generate wealth. This fact is illustrated in Robert T. Kiyosaki's book *Rich Dad Poor Dad*, which describes a meeting in 1974 between Ray Kroc, the founder and first CEO of McDonalds, and some MBA students whom he had just finished giving a presentation to.

During this meeting, as described in *Rich Dad Poor Dad*, Kroc famously asked some of these students what type of business he was in. To the surprise of the students, his answer was not that he was in the hamburger business; it was that he was in the real estate business.

Kroc understood the value of real estate. McDonalds started out by leasing all its land and buildings and then subleasing these lands and buildings to franchisees at markups of 20%-40%. The franchisees were responsible for not only running the restaurants, but also responsible for paying the rent, insurance, and taxes, associated with the real estate. This ensured a steady profit for McDonalds for as long as the restaurants stayed in business. Later on, McDonalds took out mortgages to own many of the buildings and much of the land it was leasing.

According to *Rich Dad Poor Dad*, McDonalds now owns real estate on some of the most valuable intersections and street corners in all of America and, furthermore, is one of the largest holders of real estate in the world.

Just like it has done for CEOs and corporations, real estate investing can make you wealthy too. It can do so because it forces you to save, invest, and take advantage of the power of leverage. As outlined in the beginning of this book, these are some of the key principles involved in generating wealth.

Forced Saving and Leverage

Real estate forces you to use two proven wealth building strategies. It forces you to save and invest your money and it forces you to use leverage. As already discussed, the CEOs of all successful companies use these two strategies to generate wealth.

By requiring you to pay the monthly mortgage payments, real estate investments force you to save and invest your money. Not only that, real estate investments force you to pay yourself first. If those monthly mortgage payments weren't lurking over your shoulder each month, instead of investing in real estate, you would be more inclined to spend your money frivolously.

Real estate investments also force you to leverage yourself. They force you to borrow money and invest it. As future chapters will show, leverage can be a powerful tool in your quest to achieve financial freedom (chapter 9).

Let's leave the detailed discussions surrounding leverage until chapter 9, but, in the meantime, let's look at a quick example that illustrates how leverage can lead to larger investment returns.

Let's assume an investor purchases an investment property for $100,000, pays $20,000 for the down payment, and then borrows the other $80,000 in the form of a mortgage. If after a year, the investment property goes up by 5%, then, assuming the rent covered all the expenses (mortgage payments, insurance, taxes...etc.), this investment would have generated a profit of $5,000 (5% of $100,000).

On the other hand, if this same investor had simply invested his or her $20,000 in the stock market and had earned an equivalent return of 5%, again after one year, he or she would have only generated a profit of $1,000 (5% of $20,000).

Borrowing to invest resulted in a return that was five times larger than not borrowing to invest. This is true even though both investments increased by 5%. In fact, by borrowing to invest in the investment property, this investor didn't only earn a 5% return; he or she actually earned a return of 25% ($5,000 return on $20,000 invested).

It is important to realize, however, that **leverage doesn't only offer the possibility to generate higher returns; it also comes with the risk of suffering larger losses.**

If, for example, the real estate investment mentioned above had dropped in price by 5%, then the investor would not have lost $1,000 (5% of $20,000), he or she would have actually lost $5,000 (5% of $100,000). This would translate into a loss of not only 5%, but a loss of 25% ($5,000 loss on $20,000 invested).

It is because of the larger variation in returns, including the possibility for much larger losses, that leverage is considered riskier than no leverage at all.

The risk of losses associated with real estate investments can, however, be mitigated by carefully researching any real estate investment before you buy, knowing and attempting to mitigate all the risks involved with becoming a landlord, and by positioning yourself to hold the investment for the long-term.

In the short-term, prices may go up or down, but in the long-term; history has shown that real estate prices are far more likely to go up.

Do Your Research

Before you make any real estate investment, it is important to do some thorough research.

Successful CEOs don't invest in anything without doing extensive research first. They research all the costs involved, they research the return they expect to generate, and they research the risks they expect to face. If you want to be successful in real estate, you need to do the same.

With real estate, just like any other investment, it makes sense to try and buy properties that are undervalued. Properties are more likely to be undervalued if the growth in their demand is expected to exceed the growth in their supply. They are also more likely to be undervalued if they are selling for far less than comparable properties.

Spend some time trying to determine if the property you are thinking of buying is undervalued before you attempt to buy it. Also, be sure you research many properties before you actually buy any of them. Research different locations and different types of properties and try to find properties that offer the biggest expected return for the least amount of risk.

Know as Much as You Can About Any Real Estate Investment

- Know the rental income you can expect to generate.
- Know the costs involved in holding the real estate investment.
- Estimate how long the property might stay vacant.
- Calculate your monthly cash flow.
- Try and estimate the future supply and the future demand for the type of property you are interested in.

Get familiar with researching important details such as how much rent you can expect to generate, how long your property might stay vacant, and what you expect the future supply and demand situation for your property to be. Also, spend some time figuring out what your monthly costs will be and what type of cash flow your property will generate.

Furthermore, make sure you know all the risks involved in becoming a landlord and that you how to mitigate these risks. All of these topics are discussed below.

Don't Buy Overvalued Properties

CEOs make investments when it is most profitable to do so and refrain from making investments when they believe it will not be profitable. You need to apply this same logic to all of your investments.

If you believe it will cost more to own a certain investment than the return that investment will generate, don't buy it.

This seems obvious, but the problem is that many of us often get caught up in irrational behaviour. We only purchase investments when they have gone up to an unreasonable price, then we assume that the prices of these same investments will, somehow, continue to go up forever.

If you are considering buying a certain real estate investment because prices have been going up by large amounts each year, but the rent comes nowhere close to paying for the property's expenses, you might be in for an unpleasant surprise.

Just ask anybody that invested shortly before the housing market crash of 2008. Usually, if the monthly costs involved in renting a home are way cheaper than the monthly cost involved in owning a similar home, this is a warning sign that home prices could suffer a retreat.

Generally speaking, it is difficult to time the purchase of any investment so that you buy low and sell high. It is worthwhile to remember, however, that periods of extreme greed will causes investments to be overpriced, and that periods of extreme fear will cause investments to be underpriced.

> *"Be fearful when others are greedy and greedy when others are fearful."*
> - Warren Buffett

One of the most famous investors of our time, Warren Buffett, once said, "Be fearful when others are greedy and greedy when others are fearful." This philosophy is true for both real estate investments and investments in the stock market. You would do well to remember it.

Where to Buy

Overall, as discussed in the previous chapter, the best areas to invest in real estate are areas where you expect there will be a strong demand for the type of housing you wish to purchase and areas where the supply for the type of housing you wish to purchase will be unable to keep up with the demand.

Demand

From a demand perspective, things like low and decreasing unemployment, rising incomes, a growing economy, and positive net migration, will all fuel price increases. Even if net migration is low, if a lot of foreign buyers are purchasing property anyway, this could still have the same effect as positive net migration. This is true even if those foreign buyers are not moving into these properties.

At least part of the reason why cities like Vancouver and London (London, England) have seen their property values rise so much in recent years, is because of a steady increase in foreign buyers, some of whom don't even live in these cities.

Again, as previously mentioned in the last chapter, neighborhoods with good schools, low crime rates, and easy access to parks and restaurants, would all be good signs that you are buying in a location that will continue to generate interest from potential home buyers and one that will result in high demand.

Two other major factors that can affect housing demand are interest rates and the availability of mortgages. Part of the reason home prices increased so much in the years leading up to the 2008 real estate crash in the U.S., was because of low interest rates and the large amount of banks willing to provide subprime mortgages. Falling interest rates can boost housing demand by making monthly mortgage payments more affordable. The availability of mortgages, subprime or not, also results in more buyers. Rising interest rates and a lack of mortgage availability would have the opposite effect (lower demand).

Supply

From a supply perspective, the best areas to buy in are often those areas in which there isn't any room left to build. Another reason Vancouver has become so expensive is that it is pretty difficult to increase its housing supply, especially in terms of single detached homes.

It doesn't help that the city is surrounded by mountains and water. Unless you are willing to demolish something in order to build up and make condominiums, it is very difficult to increase the supply of housing in Vancouver. Hong-Kong is faced with a similar dilemma. There is simply no space left to build on.

What to Buy

For my real estate investments, I've always preferred detached houses over condominiums or townhouses. As condos age, units becomes less attractive and tend to underperform the newer buildings that inevitably pop up. As well, in terms of a long-term investment, it's hard to argue with the value of a single detached house, especially in major urban centres.

In major urban centres it's easier to increase the supply of condominiums, by building upwards, than it is to increase the supply of single detached housing. Therefore, the supply of condominiums increases and the supply of detached housing remains fixed. With supplies fixed and rising demand, detached houses usually see higher price appreciations in the long-run.

Rents and Vacancy Rates

In my experience, the best real estate investments are the ones where the rent you receive covers all the expenses the investment incurs and leaves some money left over for a rainy day.

As mentioned at the beginning of the chapter, McDonalds initially subleased their real estate holdings at markups of 20% - 40%, even after they had their franchisees pay for the major expenses associated with their real estate investments.

To find properties such as these, you need to become familiar with researching rents and vacancy rates. If you are considering buying real estate in Canada, the Canadian Mortgage and Housing Corporation (CMHC) offers excellent reports detailing the average rents and vacancy rates for a variety of properties in a variety of Canadian cities.

Even if you can't find some sort of housing report for the city you are interested in, rents can easily be found by searching various advertisements from landlords looking to rent out their properties.

Vacancy rates are a little more challenging. Nonetheless, they are an important piece of the puzzle. Vacancy rates are important because they let you know what percent of the rental units in any given area are sitting empty.

This means vacancy rates offer a good indication of how difficult it will be and how long it may take to rent out your rental unit. If vacancy rates are high, let's say 10%, it might take a few months to rent out a unit to a good tenant. If vacancy rates are low, let's say 1% or 2%, it might be possible to rent the unit out to a good tenant right away.

If you are unable to find a report listing the vacancy rate for the area and the type of property you are interested in, you may be able to get a feel for how long it will take to rent out the property by monitoring how long similar properties in the area are advertised for before their ads get removed. If all the ads seem to disappear fairly quickly, then chances are good that vacancy rates are low and that you won't have many problems renting out a similar property in the area to a good tenant.

Real Estate and the Seven Percent Cash Flow Rule

If you know the amount of rent you can expect to receive and you know all the costs your real estate investment will incur, you can determine what sort of cash flow your real estate investment will provide.

This means that you can determine if your investment will give you some extra cash at the end of each month or if it will take some of your hard-earned cash away.

It is absolutely possible to become wealthy because your real estate holdings increase in value. This is one of the main goals of owning real estate in the first place. However, this won't help you if you've got a leaky roof that needs fixing right away. For this type of situation, you will want to have some solid rental income that can cover all your monthly expenses and leave you with a little bit of cash left over each month.

CEOs know that cash flow is essential. You need to think this way too. If there is no cash to keep a business running, it will fail. By the same token, if there is no cash available to pay for some of the expenses your real estate investments might incur, then they may fail as well.

To guard against this potential risk, I search for properties where I can receive enough rental income to pay for all my expected expenses each year and, on top of that, generate at least an extra seven percent of my down payment in the form of free cash flow.

The table on the following page shows how to calculate a property's monthly cash flow and how to calculate the property's cash flow return on investment (CFROI).

MONTHLY CASH FLOW

MONTHLY INCOME

Estimated Rental Income	**$1,500**

MONTHLY EXPENSES

Mortgage	$775
Insurance	$75
Property Taxes	$250
Repairs and Maintenance	$100
Total Expenses	**$1,200**

MONTHLY CASH FLOW	**$300**

Down Payment	$50,000
Annual Cash Flow	$3,600
CFROI	**7.2%**

The monthly cash flow statement shown above is very similar to the one that my wife and I used when we bought our rental property in Winnipeg. The house cost roughly $200,000, we put $50,000 down as a down payment, and we were faced with mortgage payments of approximately $775 a month.

To calculate the property's cash flow, we estimated our monthly rental income at $1,500 a month and then subtracted all of our expected monthly expenses (such as mortgage payments, insurance, property taxes, and repairs and maintenance). We estimated these monthly expenses to be $1,200 a month. This resulted in an expected cash flow of $300 a month or $3,600 a year.

To calculate the property's CFROI, we divided our annual cash flow of $3,600 a year by our down payment of $50,000 to get a CFROI of 7.2% ($3,600 / $50,000).

Keep in mind, your CFROI is outside of any returns that you would expect to generate from the appreciation of your property (referred to as capital gains). Your property may go up in value or it may go down in value, however, rise or fall, it will provide you with $300 a month in extra cash and grow your total earnings by $3,600 a year.

A 7% CFROI has always been the minimum I have been willing to accept on any real estate investments. The reason for this is not only because I want some extra cash for unexpected expenses, it's also because of the time and energy involved in real estate investing compared to the time and energy involved with investing in the stock market.

As you will see in future chapters, I believe it is possible to invest money in the stock market and get a similar return for far less work than that involved with real estate.

Know the Risks of Becoming a Landlord

Successful CEOs identify all the risks their businesses face and put plans in place to manage these risks appropriately. You need to do the same. You need to identify all the risks involved in owning real estate and you need to develop plans to mitigate these risks. Some of the major risks involved in becoming a landlord are listed below.

Risks Faced by Landlords

- Risk of bad tenants.
- Risk that the property stays vacant.
- Risk of unexpected repairs.
- Risk the property decreases in value.

The Risk of Bad Tenants

The risk of having bad tenants that damage your property and/or don't pay rent can be mitigated by meeting all prospective tenants in person and by conducting proper background checks.

Have all prospective tenants fill out rental application forms that require them to list previous landlords, places of employment, and other references. Then follow up and call these references. Also consider conducting a credit check. Furthermore, keep in mind that a low vacancy rate will increase the odds of finding a good tenant in a relatively short amount of time.

The Risk the Property Stays Vacant

As previously discussed, the risk that the property stays vacant for a long period of time, can be mitigated by buying properties in areas with low vacancy rates.

The Risk of Unexpected Repairs

The risk of unexpected repairs can be managed by ensuring you have a good amount of positive cash flow each month. If you don't have any extra cash at the end of each month, make sure you have a way to pay for these types of extra costs when they invariably pop up.

Proper insurance that is able to cover events such as fire or flooding is also essential. Moreover, have a property inspector do a proper inspection before you buy any type of property. You want to make sure you know about any necessary future repairs before you make the purchase.

Try to avoid properties that are very old or rundown. Furthermore, no matter what property you buy, always try and estimate the yearly maintenance costs and include these costs in the calculations used to determine your monthly cash flow. The older the property is, the higher you can expect the maintenance costs to be.

The Risk the Property Decreases in Value

Finally, the risk of having a property that decreases in value can be somewhat mitigated by considering all the supply and demand factors associated with the type of property you plan to purchase. As previously discussed, try to buy properties you expect will eventually be in high demand and in short supply.

You can also guard against price declines by ensuring you are in a position to hold your property for the long-term.

Invest For the Long-Term

Successful CEOs invest for the long-term. You need only look back to the 2008 financial crisis to see what happens when companies let a lack of risk management and short-term greed creep into their business decisions.

In the years leading up to the financial crisis, many banks incentivized their employees to sell as many mortgages as possible and had little regard for the quality of the mortgages they gave out or the risks these mortgages posed. And while these banks were rewarded with short-term profits, they failed to adequately plan for the long-term. As a result, many of these banks were forced into bankruptcy when the subprime mortgage crisis hit.

> *"Successful investing takes time, discipline, and patience. No matter how great the talent or effort, some things just take time: You can't produce a baby in one month by getting nine women pregnant."*
> - Warren Buffett

You absolutely want to make sure that you not only invest in a fairly valued property, but that you also invest for the long-term. To borrow another quote from Warren Buffett, "Successful Investing takes time, discipline, and patience. No matter how great the talent or effort, some things just take time: You can't produce a baby in one month by getting nine women pregnant."

If you think you will need to sell an investment property in the next few years, then maybe this isn't the right investment for you. If prices should suddenly drop and you are forced to sell in a down market, you could stand to lose a lot of money. For example, if you put down $50,000 to buy a $200,000 home and three years from now prices are down 10%, you could stand to lose up to 40% of your original investment ($20,000).

If you can hold on to your investment for the long-term, however, you are in a much better position to earn a decent return. History has shown that those who invest for the long-term are able to weather any short-term drops in the market and are eventually able to sell at a profit.

If you can find a suitable rental property and hold it for the long-term, it's hard to believe you won't end up making money. The forced savings and leverage that a mortgage provides means that even if you bought a house for $250,000 and it didn't increase in value at all, you would still end up with a $250,000 home after your tenants paid the mortgage for you.

Moreover, the rental income an investment property provides can usually be increased each year as the cost of living rises. This means your rental income is able to keep up with the cost of inflation.

The Famous Restaurateur - or Is It the Famous Real Estate Mogul?

In 1961, Ray Kroc purchased the McDonalds restaurant company and transformed it from a local restaurant chain to the world's largest chain of hamburger fast food restaurants. What was the secret to Kroc's success? In Kroc's own words - "The most important requirements for major success are: first, being in the right place at the right time, and second, doing something about it."

For Kroc, the right place at the right time was his initial meeting with the McDonalds brothers in 1954 at their original McDonalds restaurant in San Bernardino, California. Once there, Kroc saw how the brothers had created a restaurant that operated with the efficiency of a Henry Ford assembly line, cranking out orders that traditionally took 20 minutes in less than 60 seconds. Kroc immediately realized the franchising potential. And he immediately did something about it. He entered into an agreement to be the brother's franchising agent, and then in 1961, he eventually bought the brothers out to retain full control of the company.

Despite the restaurant's initial popularity, however, and the fact that Kroc was opening numerous McDonalds in the company's early years, he still found that he was barely making enough money to cover his expenses. Then Kroc met Harry Sonneborn.

Sonneborn had the idea that McDonalds should be investing in real estate and that McDonalds should become the landlord to its franchisees. McDonalds started buying properties and then leasing them out to its franchisees at large markups. At one point, Sonneborn actually made this statement - "We are not technically in the food business. We are in the real estate business."

McDonalds is now one of the biggest real estate companies in the world. It owns roughly $28 billion in real estate (before depreciation) and continues to lease out the land and /or the buildings in many of its locations.

Finding valuable real estate and being able to lease this real estate out for a profit is one of the core strategies McDonalds and Ray Kroc used to achieve great success. The same strategy can work for you, too.

My personal belief, however, is that nothing can beat investments in the stock market. Even better, the stock market won't call you late one night and ask you to come and fix a broken hot water tank or deal with a flooded basement.

Let's move on and continue learning about the investments that are going to earn you your financial freedom. Let's move on and focus our discussion on one of the most powerful wealth building opportunities around - the stock market.

KEY POINTS FROM CHAPTER SIX

- Real estate investing can help generate wealth because it forces you to save and invest and because it forces you to take advantage of the power of leverage.

- Leverage offers the possibility for larger returns, but also comes with the risk to suffer larger losses.

- Know as much as you can about any real estate investment. Know the rent you can expect to receive, how long the property might stay vacant, what the costs will be to hold the property, what cash flow you can expect, and estimate the property's future demand and supply.

- Real estate prices will be affected by the future supply and demand for the type of real estate in question.

- Try to purchase real estate investments that offer positive cash flow.

- Meet all prospective tenants in person, conduct background checks, and consider conducting a credit check.

- Try to buy properties in areas that have low vacancy rates.

- Position yourself to be able to hold the property for the long-term.

CHAPTER SEVEN

The Stock Market

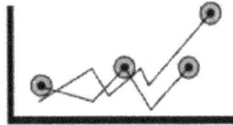

I can still remember my first purchase in the stock market. I was eighteen years-old, and thanks to a summer job, I finally had some money to invest.

Even though I only had $1,000 available to invest, I was convinced that I would be a millionaire in no time. I walked into the bank and waited for an appointment with someone licensed to sell mutual funds. Not too long after that, the mutual fund salesperson invited me into her office and handed me a glossy covered booklet that detailed all the different mutual funds the bank had to offer.

"That's amazing," I thought, as I looked over the list of mutual funds and found one that had grown by 50% the year before. I put all my money in that one mutual fund and then went home thinking how smart I was.

A few months later, that same mutual fund fell in price by 10-20%, and I sold it in a somewhat panicked rage, all the while complaining that the stock market had stolen my money.

Therein lies the problem that many individuals face with the stock market. They become greedy, they become fearful, and they become irrational. Moreover, they don't invest using a proven strategy.

Putting all your money in an investment just because it went up by 50% the previous year, is not an investment strategy that has worked out well for many investors. Investing in an index fund or investing in companies with a proven history of rising earnings and rising dividends, and staying invested for the long-term, however, is.

It is greedy to buy a stock just because it dramatically went up in price the year before and to then expect its price to continue to go up at an impossible rate. It is fearful to sell a stock just because it experiences a short-term drop in price when over the long-term, it may be positioned to do well. And it is irrational to put all your eggs in one basket, buy a few risky stocks, and then expect to be wealthy in no time.

What is rational is using a proven investment strategy and buying a broad spectrum of stocks that are diversified across many different industries. It is also rational to invest in many different asset classes (stocks, bonds, and real estate), and to be patient and expect these investments to go up at a reasonable rate over the long-term.

If, when I was eighteen years-old, I had just stuck my $1,000 in an index fund that mirrored the S&P 500 and then left this investment alone, that $1,000 would have been worth roughly $7,300 at the start of 2015 (assuming I had reinvested all the dividends and not accounting for the management fees).

Instead, I acted irrationally by not diversifying or having any sort of investment strategy, greedy by buying an investment just because it had gone up so much the year before, and both greedy and irrational by expecting to get the same impossibly high returns the investment had delivered in the past. Finally, and worst of all, I acted fearful by withdrawing all my money from the market.

I had learned a lot since those early days in my investing career. It was now spring 2008, and my wife and I had been diligently saving and investing for the last three years without committing any of those previously mentioned mistakes.

Thanks to our proven strategies and our investing discipline, our financial freedom fund was now worth hundreds of thousands of dollars and was getting bigger all the time. All the meticulous saving and careful investing was paying off. I was now convinced that we would be able to achieve financial freedom in our mid-thirties.

Of course, at that time, I didn't know what was lurking just around the corner, but we'll leave that for the next chapter.

The stock market is able to make you wealthy. All you need to do is use a proven strategy and not let fear, greed, or irrational behaviour, get in your way.

What is the Stock Market?

The stock market is a collection of stocks that are listed on stock exchanges. A stock, in turn, represents the equity of an individual company. Stocks are partitioned into shares and sold on the stock exchanges. Stock exchanges are, therefore, places where one is able to buy and sell (trade) stocks.

There are numerous stock exchanges all over the world. In the U.S., most people know of the New York Stock Exchange (NYSE) or the National Association of Securities Dealers Automated Quotations (NASDAQ). In Canada, most people are familiar with the Toronto Stock Exchange (S&P/TSX), as well as the NYSE and the NASDAQ.

If you buy the shares of one of the companies that list their stocks on a stock exchange, you become a part owner of that company. Therefore, **if you want to own part of the biggest, most successful companies in the**

world, all you need to do is buy some of their shares. Once you own some of a corporation's shares, you will be entitled to a portion of that corporation's future profits.

Most corporations will do one of two things with their profits; they will reinvest these profits back into the company (in order to make more money) or they will distribute these profits out to their shareholders as dividends.

Imagine this for a moment. You could be a part owner of McDonalds, Walmart, The Coca-Cola Company, or many other large, successful corporations that make more and more money every year.

Not only that, because you are a part owner, these corporations will pay you a share of their profits. You don't need to work at any of these corporations, and you don't have to make any of the business decisions needed to run them, you just need to own some of their shares. If you own some of their shares, you will get paid some of their profits.

Just like real estate, the stock market has produced many millionaires (and even billionaires) in recent times. What's important to realize, however, is that it's not just investing legends such as Warren Buffett, Carl Icahn, and George Soros, that have become wealthy, it's also many everyday people who don't know the first thing about managing multibillion dollar investment companies.

A 2015 study by Spectrum Group found that there were 10.1 million households in the U.S. with $1 million or more in investable assets in 2014 (excluding the value of their primary residence). Moreover, a 2015 survey by Fidelity Investments found that approximately 80% of people who have a net worth of over $1 million, built up their wealth without a trust fund or inheritance. Fidelity Investments has also demonstrated that **one of the most common strategies that self-made millionaires employ is investing in equity (stocks).** With all this in mind, it's time that you started using the stock market to grow your wealth, too.

This will probably be the most complicated section of the book, especially if you don't have any previous investing experience, so grab a coffee, settle in somewhere quiet, and get comfortable. It's time to find out about the different types of investments that are going to make up your financial freedom fund and lead to your financial freedom.

Financial Securities

The term, "financial securities" is used by investment professionals and academics to describe all the different types of investments available to investors on the financial markets (stock market, bond market, options market...etc.).

It is beyond the scope of this book to go into a detailed discussion about all the different types of financial securities out there, but we will summarize the most common types of financial securities available and examine their risk and return characteristics.

The financial securities we will discuss in this book are: common shares, preferred shares, bonds (fixed income securities), real estate investment trusts (REITs), mutual funds, and exchange traded funds (ETFs).

You should view this discussion as an introduction only and, as previously discussed, continue to build your investment knowledge through further reading.

Common Shares

Common shares are some of the most popular types of investments traded on the financial markets. As mentioned above, shares are equity in a given company and represent partial ownership of that company. As such, shares entitle the shareholder to receive a portion of a company's profits in the form of a dividend.

Dividends, however, may or may not be issued. The issuing of dividends will depend on whether or not a company chooses to reinvest all of its profits or chooses to distribute some of these profits to its shareholders.

With regards to the expected returns offered by common shares, as already mentioned in chapter one, the long-term average return of the stock market has been approximately 8% per year for the ten year period between 2005 - 2015 and closer to 11.4% a year for the thirty year period between 1985 - 2015 (CAGR of the S&P 500 assuming dividends reinvested).

This return information does not, however, suggest that you will earn an 8% return on your investments in the stock market each and every year. Some years the stock market goes up, and some years it goes down.

The fact that you might not get the return you expect each and every year is why the stock market contains risk. Let's examine these fluctuating returns a little more closely and try to better understand the risk one faces when investing in common shares.

To do this, let's examine how many times the stock market has generated positive returns and how many times the stock market has generated negative returns, in any calendar year, over the thirty year period between Jan 1985 – Jan 2015. Let's also examine how many times the stock market has gained more than 10% or lost more than 10% of its value, again in any calendar year. Finally, let's also examine how many times the stock market has gained or lost more than 20% of its value in any calendar year, again over the thirty year period between Jan 1985 – Jan 2015.

Over this thirty year period, the stock market has generated positive annual returns twenty-five times and has generated negative annual returns only five times. It has gained more than 10% of its value nineteen times and has lost more than 10% of its value only three times. It has gained more than 20% of its value ten times and has lost more than 20% of its value only two times. Again, this assumes reinvestment of dividends and does not take into account any costs to purchase or hold these investments.

Looking at the returns discussed above, it is obvious that the stock market does go down some years, but over the long-term, it goes up more often than it goes down.

There is a risk, in any calendar year, that we may not generate our expected 7% return. However, if we are diversified and invest for the long-term, the risk that we will not achieve a CAGR that is close to 7% becomes greatly diminished.

Preferred Shares

Just like common shares, preferred shares also represent partial ownership of a company. There are, however, a few differences between common shares and preferred shares.

For starters, preferred shareholders have a higher claim on a corporation's earnings and assets than common shareholders do.

Moreover, a preferred share's dividend *needs* to get paid out before any dividends get paid out on the common shares. And, unlike common shares, a preferred share's dividend *must* get paid out on a regular basis. This ensures that preferred shareholders receive guaranteed dividend income for as long as they own their shares and the company remains solvent.

Their guaranteed dividend income, combined with their higher claim on assets and earnings, means that preferred shares are, typically, considered less risky than common shares. Moreover, historically speaking, the value of preferred shares does not fluctuate as much as the value of common shares. This means these types of shares should have less risk.

However, because a preferred share's price is based predominantly on the income it pays out, it usually does not experience the same increase in value that a company's common shares would, if that company is able to continually increase its earnings. Therefore, the expected returns for preferred shares are, quite often, not as high as the expected returns for common shares.

Furthermore, as discussed below with bonds, preferred share prices are often affected by a change in interest rates. Generally speaking, a rise in interest rates should cause a fall in the value of a preferred share, and a fall in interest rates should cause an increase in the value of a preferred share. However, this might not always be the case. Some preferred share issues have special clauses to address interest rate risk and many adjust their payouts according to these clauses.

Preferred shares are sometimes referred to as a hybrid of common shares and bonds (discussed below). Because preferred shares represent partial ownership of a corporation in terms of equity and have no maturity date, preferred shares are like common shares. However, because preferred shares pay a predetermined amount of income at regular intervals, they are also like bonds.

Bonds (Fixed Income)

Bonds belong to a larger class of investments called *fixed income* investments. Other types of fixed income investments include financial securities such as treasury bills (T-bills), guaranteed investment certificates (GICs), mortgage backed securities (MBS), and many others. These financial securities are called fixed income securities because they pay out a certain amount of fixed income at regular intervals.

Unlike common shares, fixed income investments do not represent ownership of any kind. They are not equity instruments, they are debt instruments. Bonds and other debt instruments get issued by governments, corporations, or other entities, that need to borrow money.

For the privilege of borrowing an investor's money, bond issuers guarantee the holders of their bonds a certain amount of regular income in the form of interest payments. These interest payments usually get distributed to investors at regular fixed intervals.

Bond issuers also guarantee to return the original money invested in their bonds (the principal) at the bond's maturity date. Common shares don't guarantee fixed payments, don't have any type of maturity date, and don't guarantee to return the original amount of money invested in them.

On top of all of this, bond holders also have a higher claim on a corporation's assets compared to common or preferred shareholders. Therefore, in the event a company gets liquidated, bond holders get paid out first.

It is because of these characteristics that bonds and other types of fixed income investments are, in general, considered less risky than common or preferred shares.

This lower risk, however, often comes with a lower expected return. Simply put, if a bond issuer can guarantee to offer an investor a series of periodic fixed interest payments and guarantee to return the principal invested, investors are usually willing to accept a lower rate of return compared to the return they would expect from common shares.

It is important to realize, however, that fixed income investments come in many different forms, offer many different rates of return, and come with many different levels of risk.

On the whole, the shorter the investment period, and the more creditworthy the issuer, the lower the risk is. And the lower the risk, the lower the expected return.

For example, a fixed income security such as a T-bill issued by the U.S. government, maturing in thirty days, would be far less risky and offer a far lower return than a bond issued by a small start-up company that matures in ten years. After all, the risk of the U.S. government going bankrupt in thirty days is pretty remote. U.S. T-bills are considered to be some of the safest investments around. In fact, many people would say they are the closest thing to a risk-free investment that you can get.

One of the best ways to determine a bond's risk is to evaluate the creditworthiness of its issuer. This can be accomplished by referring to ratings issued by credit rating agencies such as Moody's or Standard & Poor's. These credit rating agencies use certain scales to rate a bond's risk. Quite often, a bond is rated as either *investment grade* or *non-investment grade*.

Investment grade bonds are considered to pose minimal risk to investors, in terms of meeting payment obligations, while non-investment grade bonds (junk bonds) are considered to pose higher risk. It is because of this higher risk that non-investment grade bonds need to offer higher returns than investment grade bonds before most investors will consider buying them.

In addition to the credit worthiness of the issuer and the length of the investment period, interest rates pose a special risk to bonds. Just like preferred shares, bond prices are inversely correlated with interest rates. This means that when interest rates go up, bond prices usually go down, and when interest rates go down, bond prices usually go up.

The risk of losses due to increases in interest rates can by mitigated, to some extent, by holding shorter term bonds and by using more complex fixed income strategies such as bond laddering. Bond laddering involves buying a variety of bonds with a variety of different maturity dates. Complex strategies such as this, however, are often best left to professional bond managers.

Rather than buying individual bonds, I've often found it much easier to buy an ETF or a mutual fund (see below) that specializes in holding a variety of different bonds. This approach has the additional benefit of having a professional bond manager at the helm. These professionally managed bond funds often allow individual investors to get more diversification for fewer costs and, quite often, offer valuable strategies such as bond laddering.

Now that we understand what bonds are and how they work, let's see how their risk and their expected return measures up to common shares. To provide a comparison, let's refer to some of the data compiled by the Federal Reserve Bank of St. Louis, which has measured the returns of stocks, T-bills, and 10-year Treasury bonds (T-bonds) since 1928.

Referring to this data from 1928-2015, stocks have averaged a compound annual return of 9.5%, T-bonds have averaged a compound annual return of 5.0%, and T-bills have averaged a compound annual return of 3.5%.

Furthermore, stocks have shown positive returns in sixty-four of the eighty-eight years evaluated (73%), T-bonds have shown positive returns in seventy-two of the eighty-eight years evaluated (82%), and T-bills have shown positive returns in all eighty-eight calendar years evaluated (100%).

Based on this data, common shares offered the highest return, bonds offered the second highest return, and T-bills offered the lowest return. However, given that they only generated positive returns in 73% of the years evaluated, common shares also had the highest risk.

On the other hand, despite their lower returns, bonds offered somewhat lower risk (positive returns for 82% of the years evaluated). T-bills had the lowest return but offered no risk at all.

It can, therefore, be reasoned that the greater safety associated with bonds comes at the price of a lower expected return. Furthermore, as illustrated with T-bills, the safer the investment is, the lower the expected return.

Real Estate Investment Trusts (REITs)

Remember the previous chapter on real estate? Well what if I told you there was a way to own a share of some of the biggest office buildings, shopping centres, and apartment buildings out there and, on top of that, have none of the burdens of being a landlord. Would you be interested? If the answer is yes, then maybe real estate investment trusts (REITs) are for you.

REITs offer the individual investor an opportunity to buy into a real estate trust that is managed by a professional real estate company. The real estate company pools all the individual investors' money, uses this money to buy a large portfolio of commercial real estate, and then manages these investments for the individual investors.

REITs also, very often, offer investors monthly payouts that are derived from the rental income received from their tenants.

There are many different types of REITs available. Some REITs only buy and manage office buildings, some only buy and manage residential properties, and others only buy and manage industrial properties. In addition to these types of REITs, there are also REITs that buy and manage more specialized properties such as retirement homes. Finally, there are REITs that own and manage properties in all of the above mentioned categories, all in the same trust.

What's more, REITs usually trade on stock exchanges. This means that REITs can easily be purchased by most individual investors.

How do REITs compare to common shares and to bonds in terms of risk and return? Based on the calendar returns for all the REITs in the FTSE NAREIT US Real Estate Index from 1972 – 2014, REITs have generated a compound annual return of roughly 9.9% (assuming reinvestment of dividends). Furthermore, this index has generated positive returns in thirty-three of the forty-three years evaluated, roughly 77% of the time.

Besides offering an easy way to own real estate and the ability to save yourself the headaches involved in managing real estate investments yourself, REITs can also be a nice way to better diversify a portfolio of stocks and bonds (see chapter 8).

Mutual Funds

Mutual funds are investments made up of a collection of stocks, bonds, and other financial securities. These financial securities are bought, packaged together, and then managed by a professional portfolio manager. The money used to buy these investments comes from the pooled money of many individual investors. This pooling allows each individual investor to hold a large variety of securities for a cost that might otherwise be prohibitive.

There are many different types of mutual funds available. Some mutual funds will only invest in stocks, some will only invest in bonds, and others will specialize in investing in a variety of asset classes, all in the same fund (usually called a balanced fund).

What's more, some mutual funds specialize in different sectors of the economy. For example, some mutual funds only invest in health-care companies, while others only invest in oil and gas companies.

Other mutual funds might choose to specialize in different geographies, investing only in China or only in Europe, for example.

Furthermore, different mutual funds can employ different investment strategies (discussed later in the chapter). Some mutual fund managers employ an active strategy and make many trades (in an attempt to generate higher profits), while other mutual fund managers employ a passive strategy and simply buy and hold all the securities in an index.

As previously mentioned, mutual funds often offer the advantages of diversification and professional portfolio management at a cost that might otherwise be prohibitive to some individual investors. For these services, mutual fund companies charge their investors some sort of fee. This fee usually takes the form of a management expense ratio (MER). However, many mutual funds companies often charge a variety of other fees as well. These fees might be associated with the buying and selling of their funds, switching from one of their funds to another, or trading their funds in a short time period (just to name a few).

These fees can vary widely. They often depend on the company issuing the funds, how long you hold the funds for, and the strategy the mutual fund manager employs. If, for example, the manager is continually trading many different financial securities, the MER will, quite likely, be much higher than the MER of a fund where the manager is just buying and holding.

Fees can quickly add up, and high fees are something that can really eat away at your investment returns. Because of this, fees are something you will want to carefully consider whenever you make any investments in mutual funds.

Moreover, if a mutual fund charges high fees and consistently fails to deliver a higher return than a mutual fund that charges lower fees, you are clearly better off investing in the mutual fund with the lower fees. The effect of fees on investment performance will be discussed in greater detail later in the chapter.

Mutual funds are not sold on stock exchanges. Instead, they are bought and sold directly through the companies that manage these funds. That being said, you can usually purchase mutual funds from the mutual fund companies offering the funds, through financial planners, through brokers, or through online brokers by using self-directed investment accounts.

The risk and the return characteristics of mutual funds vary widely and will depend on the type of holdings in each mutual fund. If a mutual fund only holds T-bills, for example, you would expect it to earn a lower return and to possess less risk than a mutual fund that exclusively holds common shares.

Often times, you are able to access information concerning the risk and expected return of a given mutual fund directly from the mutual fund company itself. It is also possible to obtain risk and return evaluations from private companies such as Morningstar.

Exchange Traded Funds (ETFs)

Exchange traded funds (ETFs) combine some of the features of mutual funds and some of the features of stocks, all in one tidy package. ETFs are similar to mutual funds in that they hold a collection of different financial securities and are managed by professional portfolio managers. However, ETFs are also similar to stocks in that they are traded directly on stock exchanges.

Just like mutual funds, you can buy ETFs that specialize in fixed income, specialize in stocks, or specialize in holding a variety of different financial securities. And just like mutual funds, ETF's can specialize in a variety of different sectors or a variety of different countries. You can also find ETFs that are actively managed, meaning they perform a lot of trading, or ETFs that are passively managed, meaning they often simply buy and hold all the companies in an index.

As well, just like mutual funds, ETFs also charge fees. Unlike mutual funds, however, ETFs do not have investment minimums, and they can be bought and sold right away without worrying about possibly triggering some sort of short-term trading fee.

ETFs are bought and traded directly on stock exchanges. This means you will owe your broker commission charges whenever you buy or sell ETFs.

Again, you would be wise to pay close attention to the fees charged by different ETFs. If a certain ETF seems to be charging much higher fees compared to other ETFs, then you should expect its return to be high enough to merit these larger fees.

Also, just like mutual funds, the risk and return characteristics of different ETF's vary widely and will depend on their core holdings. You are again often able to get risk and return information directly from the company that manages the ETF or through private companies such as Morningstar.

How to Buy and Sell Financial Securities

To buy and sell stocks and other financial securities yourself, all at a reasonable cost, you will want to set up a self-directed online investment account with an online brokerage.

Once this is accomplished, you will be able to trade an array of financial securities yourself, all at the touch of a button. Moreover, online brokers often provide all the information you would ever need to research any of the financial securities you are interested in trading. More often than not, these online brokers give you access to a company's financial statements, to analyst reports, and to up-to-the-minute news.

All of these benefits come at a cost that just keeps on getting lower. It used to be, when I started trading stocks online, that it cost anywhere between $25 and $50 a trade. Now, most online brokers charge something like $6.99 a trade.

It is because of the easy access to research and the low cost of trading that I consider a self-directed investment account with an online broker to be one of the best ways to buy and sell stocks and other financial securities yourself.

This is assuming you are actually interested in managing your investments yourself. If you are not interested in making these purchases and managing your portfolio yourself, then one option would be to find a good financial advisor.

A good gauge as to whether or not you should get a financial advisor or manage your investments yourself would be whether or not the thought of learning about investing interests you.

If the thought of glancing over the investing section of a newspaper or an investment magazine interests you, then you are halfway there to managing your portfolio yourself. You also need to be sure you are able to do *all* of the following:

Keys to Managing Your Own Portfolio

- Come up with an investment plan and follow some sort of proven strategy.

- Have the discipline to buy a diversified portfolio of quality investments.
- Don't sell all your investments when they temporarily go down in price.

If you have an interest in investing and are able to do these three things, then you may be able to invest in the stocks and other financial securities that will eventually earn you your financial freedom all by yourself. If you don't believe you can do all of these things, you should consider using a financial advisor or getting some other form of help.

If you do choose to go with a financial adviser, be sure to shop around and meet a few of them before you commit to working with any of them. As well, be sure to ask for references from other clients and to compare fees.

As previously mentioned, even if you do choose to go with a financial adviser, you will want to have at least a little bit of knowledge around investing. And you will especially want to understand the effects of high fees on your portfolio's performance (discussed later in the chapter). Always remember, **no one should have a bigger interest in your money than you.**

If you can't find a financial advisor that you like for a fee that you like, and you are not confident enough to do everything on your own, then you could also consider trying a robo-advisor.

Robo-advisors, also called online advisors, offer an alternative that is halfway between a do-it-yourself investor and a real life financial advisor. Robo-advisors will help you setup a diversified investment portfolio (usually using low cost ETFs), and will then monitor and rebalance (see next chapter) your portfolio for you at a cost that is usually half as much as what a real-life financial advisor would charge.

Rather than meeting with a real life advisor, robo-advisors usually work by having you fill out an online questionnaire. Therefore, if you would rather talk to someone in person, this option might not be for you.

Investment Strategies

Successful CEOs always follow a proven strategy when they make investments. You need to do the same. Before you start buying any financial securities, you need to invest a little time and energy deciding on an appropriate investment strategy.

There are many investment strategies out there, and regardless of the one you choose, the important thing is to actually have one. **Have an investment strategy with a proven history of success and stick with it.**

Whatever you do, don't make up your strategy as you go along. And don't just continually trade in and out of stocks in an attempt to make quick profits. The most successful strategies require time, discipline, and patience.

Let's look at two proven strategies that my wife and I have used in the past. Both of these strategies are easy to adopt and are ideal for most individual investors. **These two strategies are: (1) index investing, and (2) dividend investing.**

Before we delve into these two strategies, however, it will be important for you to decide if you will be an active investor or a passive investor.

Active Investing Versus Passive Investing

Active investors believe that with time, effort, and research, they are able to find undervalued financial securities that will eventually outperform the market. This being the case, active investors adopt some sort of stock picking strategy.

Passive investors, in contrast, believe that financial securities are always priced fairly. Passive investors believe in the *efficient market hypothesis*. This hypothesis states that financial markets are so efficient at processing information, the moment any new information comes out that could affect the price of any given financial security, this information gets immediately processed and instantaneously reflected in the price of the financial security it affects. According to this hypothesis, financial securities are, therefore, always priced fairly.

Subscribing to the efficient market hypothesis, passive investors believe that trying to find financial securities that will outperform the market is a waste of time and money. Given this philosophy, passive investors often adopt a strategy of index investing (see below). Passive investors don't try and pick individual stocks; they just buy a small amount of all the stocks on the stock market index.

So which type of investor does better – active or passive? To answer this question, let's look at: (1) a stock picking contest between blindfolded monkeys and active investors, and (2) some scorecards that get released twice a year by S&P Dow Jones Indices that compare active investing returns to passive investing returns.

Blindfolded Monkeys Versus Active Fund Managers

Active investment management versus passive investment management has been debated for decades. It was such a hot topic of contention that after economist Burton Malkiel argued in his book *A Random Walk Down Wall Street* that a bunch of blindfolded monkeys throwing darts at a newspaper's financial pages could select a stock portfolio that did just as well as one carefully crafted by experts practicing an active investment approach, the *Wall Street Journal* decided to put his claim to the test.

In 1988, some *Wall Street Journal* staffers, acting as the monkeys, threw darts at a stock table and then compared the results of their randomly chosen portfolio against the results of the experts' portfolios.

In 1998, after one-hundred contests, the experts won sixty-one times, and the "monkeys" won thirty-nine times. However, the experts only beat the DJIA fifty-one times, which meant that passively investing in the DJIA index would have almost performed just as well as the experts. Moreover, the analysis didn't take into consideration the transaction costs involved in active investing. As previously mentioned, the transaction costs involved with active investing can have a large effect on a portfolio's performance.

SPIVA Scorecards

More recent research into active versus passive investment strategies can be found by analyzing the S&P Indices Versus Active Funds research scorecards (SPIVA) that get released every six months by S&P Dow Jones Indices.

The mid-2015 SPIVA U.S. scorecard showed that over the five and ten year investment horizons, roughly 80% of large-cap managers failed to deliver incremental returns over the benchmark.

A SPIVA Canada scorecard released in mid-2015 showed similar results. Over the previous five years, only 23% of actively managed funds in the Canadian Equity Funds Category outperformed the S&P/TSX Composite Index.

"Most investors, both institutional and individual, will find the best way to own common stocks is through an index fund that charges minimal fees."
- Warren Buffett

This research definitely seems to support a passive investment strategy. And as judged by the following comment - "Most investors, both institutional and individual, will find the best way to own common stocks is through an index fund that charges minimal fees," even legendary investor Warren Buffett seems to agree that a passive investment strategy makes the most sense for most investors.

If you think you want to adopt a passive investing strategy, then you will want to adopt a strategy that involves index investing and focus on making sure you pay the lowest fees possible. Let's take a closer look at this type of strategy right now.

Index Investing

In his book *Millionaire Teacher,* Andrew Hallam details how he became a millionaire on a teacher's salary by saving his money and investing it in low cost index funds.

This strategy is a passive strategy. Moreover, it is a strategy that would be fairly easy to implement with a self-directed online investment account. For the portion of your portfolio invested in domestic equities, it would simply involve holding the same securities in your portfolio as a stock market index such as the DJIA, the S&P/TSX Composite, or the S&P 500. This can easily be accomplished by using either mutual funds or ETFs specifically designed for this purpose.

When adopting an indexing strategy, the most important thing to consider would be the fees charged by each fund. There is almost no reason why you wouldn't just go with the index fund that charges the lowest fees. **Fees eat away at your returns each year, and over the course of many years, they can severely limit your overall returns.**

On that note, if you have a financial advisor that always encourages you to buy mutual funds that charge a lot in fees, you should definitely ask your advisor to explain to you why he or she has made these choices. You should also have him or her compare your investment returns to those of the appropriate index. If your returns are consistently below the index, this is a good sign that you might be better off adopting an index investing strategy.

The impact that large fees can have on long-term returns was highlighted by John C. Bogle, the founder of Vanguard, in a *Frontline* episode titled "401(k)s: The New Retirement Plan, For Better or Worse" that aired in 2006.

In the episode, Bogle stated that management fees and trading costs can take up to 2.5% of an investor's annual returns and can cost an investor up to 80% of his or her long-term gains.

Bogle goes on to give an example to prove his point. If one were to invest $1,000 and let it compound for 65 years at 8%, then one would end up with total savings of about $149,000. If, however, one were to invest $1,000 and let it compound for 65 years at 5.5% (thanks to 2.5% in fees and trading costs), then one would end up with total savings of only $32,500.

John C. Bogle invented the world's first index mutual fund back in 1975 and has been a staunch supporter of investing in low cost index funds ever since. The company he founded, Vanguard, is an investment management company that specializes in low cost ETFs. Vanguard offers investors the opportunity to purchase funds in both Canada and the United States and charges management fees as low as 0.05%.

If you implement an indexing strategy, you still want to ensure that you are diversified not just across stocks (which you are when you buy an index fund that mirrors a stock index), but that you are also diversified across many different asset classes.

This means you would also want to hold investments in bonds and real estate as well. Moreover, you would also want to try and diversify some of your stock holdings across different geographies. Again, all of this could easily be accomplished through index funds. Some of the big ETF companies out there include Vanguard, BlackRock's iShares, and Invesco's PowerShares. All of these companies offer low cost index funds.

If you are a Canadian investor, be careful to not just buy an index fund based on the S&P/TSX. The problem with this strategy is that the S&P/TSX is inherently poorly diversified, both by individual sectors and by individual stocks.

In fact, at the time of writing this, 70% of the S&P/TSX is represented by only three sectors; energy, financials, and materials. Moreover, four of the top ten companies on the S&P/TSX are banks and four more are large energy companies. A far better index to passively invest in, as far as diversification is concerned, would be the S&P 500.

Investing in the S&P 500 would result in more diversification across different industries and more diversification across different companies. It would also, however, expose non-American residents to the risks of currency fluctuations. Therefore, if you are not living in the U.S., make sure that any mutual fund or ETF you buy to mirror this index uses currency hedging strategies (see chapter 8).

How to start a passive investment strategy:

1. Open a self-directed online investment account with an online broker.

2. If you are a U.S. investor, buy an ETF mirroring the S&P 500 (Vanguard S&P 500 ETF, for example). If you are a Canadian Investor, buy an ETF mirroring the S&P 500 that is hedged against currency risk, (ishares Core S&P 500 Index ETF (CAD – Hedged), for example).

Dividend Investing

The second strategy we will discuss focuses on investing in companies with a history of consistent and growing dividend payments. This strategy is an active strategy and involves buying larger blue chip companies (established companies that are valued over $1 billion) that pay investors increasing dividends and have reliable, increasing earnings. Think of companies like Johnson and Johnson or Toronto Dominion Bank.

Even though this strategy may be considered an active one, it does not involve a lot of buying and selling. It involves buying great companies and holding them for the long-term.

The advantage of this strategy is that companies with a long history of increasing earnings and increasing dividends are usually financially stable and often tend to outperform the market over the long-term.

As well, owners of dividend paying companies get to enjoy the income their stocks generate. If you want to retire or take a break from work, then, assuming you own enough shares in these types of companies, you may be able to live off the income provided from the dividends alone.

Even better, in many cases dividend income gets taxed at rates less than half of what normal employment income gets taxed at (see chapter 10). This lower tax rate means that you don't have to earn as much of this type of income as you would have had to earn from employment income in order to realize the same after-tax income.

If you are not ready to retire, you can reinvest the dividends and use them to buy even more shares. This way, you can earn even more dividends in the future. Moreover, because the best companies often increase their dividends every year, a dividend investing strategy ensures that the income from your investments, in all likelihood, will keep up with the rising cost of goods. More specifically, it means that the income from your investments will keep up with the cost of inflation.

Personally, I really like a dividend investing strategy. **Buying shares in companies that continually increase their earnings and continually increase their dividends, ensures you are investing in good companies and not speculating in bad ones.**

If a company is able to increase its revenue, increase its earnings, and increase its dividend, year after year, then it is a company I consider investing in. Often, I don't use any complicated formulas or fancy algorithms when I invest. I just review the financial statements of the companies I'm interested in (using my self-directed online investment account) and see if the company meets the above mentioned criteria. If the company consistently increases its revenue, earnings, and dividends, each year, then I consider investing in it.

If you aren't interested in researching individual companies, you could consider buying a mutual fund or an ETF that invests in companies using this strategy. One of the best ways to do this would be to buy an ETF that tracks the S&P Dividend Aristocrats Index.

The S&P Dividend Aristocrat Index is made up of companies in the S&P 500 index that have a twenty-five year continuous history of raising dividends. What's more, by the end of 2014, the S&P Dividend Aristocrats Index boasted a five-year total average annual return of 17.5% and a ten-year total average annual return of 10.5%. These returns compare to five-year and ten-year average annual returns of 14.4% and 7.6%, respectively, for the S&P 500 index. At the time of writing this, ProShares sells an ETF that mirrors the S&P Dividend Aristocrats Index under the ticker symbol NOBL.

Here is an example a company that, at the time of writing this, meets the requirements of increasing revenue, increasing earnings, and increasing dividends. The company is Johnson and Johnson (JNJ). At the time of writing this, JNJ has a market capitalization of about $280 billion USD and is listed on the NYSE under the symbol "JNJ".

The following table summarizes some of the information from the company's last four available income statements. This information was easily found using my online discount broker. It could have also easily been found at Yahoo finance or a variety of other websites.

Selected Financial Information for Johnson and Johnson (JNJ:NYSE)

	2011	2012	2013	2014
Total Revenue (in millions of $USD)	65,030	67,224	71,312	74,331
Basic Normalised Earnings Per Share (EPS)	$4.70	$4.85	$6.37	$6.43
Dividends Per Share (DPS) Common Stock, Primary Issue	$2.25	$2.40	$2.59	$2.76

Referring to the table above, you can see that in each of the last four years, JNJ has been able to increase its revenue, increase its earnings per share, and increase the dividends it gives out for each share owned. In fact, at the time of writing this, JNJ has increased its dividend for fifty-three consecutive years.

JNJ brought in over $74 billion in revenue in 2014 and paid its investors $2.76 for each share that they owned. Given its size and its history of growing revenue, increasing earnings, and increasing dividends, a dividend investor would consider JNJ a good investment.

Another example of a company that meets the requirements of increasing revenue, increasing earnings, and increasing dividends, at the time of writing this, is Toronto-Dominion Bank (TD).

TD is a Canadian bank that has operations in the U.S. and in Canada. It is listed on the S&P/TSX and the NYSE under the symbol "TD". At the time of writing this, TD has a market capitalization of almost $100 billion and is one of the largest banks in Canada.

The following table summarizes some of the information from the company's last four available income statements, again easily found using my online discount broker.

Selected Financial Information for Toronto-Dominion Bank (TD:TSX)

	2012	2013	2014	2015
Net Interest Income After Loan Loss Provision (millions $CAD)	15,026	16,074	17,584	18,724
Basic Normalised Earnings Per Share (EPS)	$3.40	$3.51	$4.16	$4.53
Dividends Per Share (DPS) Common Stock, Primary Issue	$1.45	$1.62	$1.84	$2.00

Instead of "revenue," the table above lists a similar metric for banks, "net interest income after loan loss provisions." As banks generate a great deal of their income by lending out money, this metric details the interest income that banks generate on the money they lend out and adjusts this income for any losses banks expect to incur from any of their loans not getting paid back.

The table above shows that TD was able to increase its net interest income in each of the last four years, and that TD brought in roughly $18.7 billion in net interest income (after loan loss provisions) for 2015.

The table above also shows that, just like JNJ, TD was able to increase its earnings per share and its dividends per share every year for the last four years. In fact, at the time of writing this, TD has raised its dividend more than sixty times since 1970. Therefore, just like JNJ, it would be a company that dividend investors would consider investing in.

As you can see from the examples shown above, dividend investing is easy to understand. If you see a company consistently increasing its earnings and consistently increasing its dividends, then owning it just makes sense.

Compare a dividend investing strategy to a different strategy that may require you to buy the shares of a company that is not generating any earnings or not paying out any dividends, and you may find that strategy is a little harder to make sense of. An investment in a company with little to no earnings is better described as speculating, not investing. Moreover, if investing legends such as Benjamin Graham and Warren Buffett like to invest in companies with a solid dividend, then so do I.

Of course, past performance does not guarantee future performance. Moreover, no one can predict with absolute certainty that a company will continue to increase its earnings, continue to increase its dividend, and continue to do well.

Nonetheless, a company with a history of rising revenue, rising earnings, and rising dividends, is definitely more reassuring than a company without these things.

For an extra layer of security, some dividend investors also evaluate the safety of the dividend payout. In order to do this, some investors calculate a company's payout ratio.

A payout ratio is the proportion of a company's earnings that gets paid out as dividends. It is typically expressed as a percentage. Dividend investors like companies with payout ratios well below 100%. A payout ratio that is over 100% would mean that a company was paying out more in dividends than it actually earned in income. This would imply that the dividend could be at risk, especially if the company's earnings were to unexpectedly fall.

At the time of writing this, JNJ had a payout ratio of about 55% and TD had a payout ratio of about 47%.

How to buy shares of any company or ETF on a stock exchange:

1. Open a self-directed online investment account with an online broker.

2. Buy as many shares of the company or the ETF as you would like. If you want to buy $1,000 worth of shares and the shares are selling at $50 a share, buy 20 shares.

Key Success Factors for Investing

Successful CEOs have a list of key success factors that they follow in order to ensure their businesses thrive. You need to adopt the same strategy when you invest in the financial markets.

Key success factors are based on a careful analysis of what has worked in the past and what is expected to work in the future. For example, if a company was in the food services industry, its key success factors might include high quality food, excellent customer service, and an inviting atmosphere.

Just like a good CEO, you also need to reflect on the things that you need to do in order to succeed. More specifically, you need to come up with a list of key success factors for investing in the stock market. Fortunately, a great deal of research has already been done to answer this.

Let's create a list of key success factors for investing in the stock market that is based on this proven research. By following these key success factors, you will dramatically increase your chances of success.

Key Success Factors for Investing in the Stock Market

- Be an investor and not a speculator.
- Keep transaction costs low.
- Buy and hold.
- Only buy investments that you understand.
- Diversify.

Be an Investor and Not a Speculator

The more you start investing, reading about investing, and talking to your friends about investing, the more you will hear stories about some great stock that has produced incredible returns and will, *undoubtedly*, continue to do so.

You will hear all about recommendations to buy these types of stocks. You will hear these recommendations in the media and you will hear these recommendations from your friends. The problem, more often than not, is that these recommendations won't be to purchase financially stable blue chip stocks with a history of increasing earnings and increasing dividends, they will be recommendations to purchase risky speculative stocks that might end up losing you money.

You must be careful to tune this type of noise out. Make sure you always remain an investor and not a speculator. Don't speculate that just because a stock has gone up in the past, it will continue to do so (especially if the earnings growth isn't there). This is the type of risky behaviour that cost investors dearly during the dot-com bubble.

During the dot-com bubble, between 2000 and 2002, speculation was rampant and investors were loading up on shares in companies with absolutely no earnings. The end result of all this speculation was the NASDAQ Composite index losing 78% of its value.

More often than not, speculating results in: (1) excessive trading costs, as you keep chasing profits from the latest socks you hear about, and (2) financial losses, as you end up buying right at the top of a price increase and selling the moment the price drops.

> *"The individual investor should act consistently as an investor and not a speculator."*
> - Benjamin Graham

Warren Buffett's mentor, Benjamin Graham, once said, "The individual investor should act consistently as an investor and not a speculator." If you want to follow in the footsteps of some of the greatest investors of our time, you would be wise to follow this advice.

Keep Transaction Costs Low

Another key to success, when it comes to investing in the stock market, is to keep your transaction costs low. This means you need to avoid, as much as possible, all the fees charged by mutual fund and ETF companies. You also need to avoid excessive trading costs.

If a mutual fund company is charging you a few percentage points in fees each year, you would be wise to ask yourself if your investment returns actually merit these high fees. If a mutual fund does as well as the market, and you are paying this fund 3.5% in fees, you might have just lost half of your total return.

Except for the cost to buy and sell them, holding individual stocks in your portfolio won't involve any fees, (unless you are working with a financial advisor who's fees are based on your holdings), however, a large amount of trading will. This is especially true if one acts more like a day trader and less like an investor.

If you engage in speculative behaviour that involves many purchases and many sales, then not only are you jeopardizing your future returns, you might also be costing yourself a great deal of money in fees. Engaging in this type of speculative behaviour usually doesn't result in any significant long-term profit. More often than not, it just results in a great deal of transaction costs.

Buy and Hold

If you have bought the shares of a variety of good companies that have a history of increasing their earnings and increasing their dividends, or if you have simply opted to buy some index funds, the next thing you need to concentrate on doing is not sabotaging your returns. This means you need to buy and hold.

The best way to sabotage your returns is to sell all your holdings when the stock market experiences a temporary downturn. Do not do this.

If there is some fundamental change in one of the companies you are holding and you believe this company will not be able to continue to increase its earnings and its dividends, consider selling it. However, if nothing has changed with the company's business and its price is lower because of a general market downturn, hold on to it.

In the short-term, stock markets can go up or down, but over the long-term; history has repeatedly shown that they eventually always go up. At the time of writing this, the last great stock market crash was the great recession of 2007-2009. During this bear market, the DJIA lost about 54% of its value from October, 2007 – March, 2009. Investors who sold at the bottom of this crash lost over half their money. Investors who held onto their holdings went on to make it all back and more.

Chances are, if you sell all your holdings when the market falls and try to buy your holdings back before the market rebounds, all you will do is miss out on the rebound and suffer the loss.

If the companies you own are the same good companies they were when you bought them, then hold onto them, continue to collect your dividends, and consider buying more.

Having made it through a few market downturns, rather than sell my core holdings, I've often thought I should have bought a little more. Most of the time, I did.

Only Buy Investments That You Understand

It goes without saying that you shouldn't buy financial securities that you don't understand. When things become too complicated, you are probably speculating and not investing.

Don't be fooled by anyone claiming that a particular investment or a particular type of financial security is guaranteed to make a lot of money. An old finance professor of mine used to love to say, **"There is no such thing as a free lunch,"** and when it comes to investing in the stock market, this is absolutely true.

"No free lunch" is a common expression in the investing world that refers to the fact that you can't get high returns from an investment without taking on high risk. It also refers to the fact that an investment is usually priced appropriately.

If you hear someone say a particular investment is guaranteed to make you a lot of money, chances are, you should look the other way. At the very least, you should look at that particular investment with a great deal of scrutiny.

I have often seen advertisements claiming that investors are able to earn a great deal of money by trading complex financial securities such as options or derivatives. Options and derivatives are the types of financial securities that were, in part, to blame for the 2008 financial crisis. Moreover, these types of financial securities can be very difficult to understand, even for professional investors. I have taken university courses on trading these types of financial securities and I still can't imagine using them.

Options and derivatives don't offer investors some sort of special way to beat the market. Instead, they are priced such that the return you can expect to generate is appropriate for the risk being taken on. They do not offer a "free lunch."

My feeling is that given there is no advantage to using options or derivatives, and given they are rather complicated to understand, you stand a better chance of losing money with these types of investments as opposed to gaining any.

"Never invest in any idea you can't illustrate with a crayon."
- Peter Lynch

One of the most successful investors of our time, Peter Lynch, once said, "Never invest in any idea you can't illustrate with a crayon." By following this philosophy, Peter Lynch was able to grow the Fidelity Magellan Fund from $20 million in 1977 to $14 Billion in 1990 and average an annual return of 29%. Instead of investing in things you don't understand, keep it simple and invest in companies with rising earnings and rising dividends. Or keep it even simpler and just invest in index funds.

Diversify

Even though the next chapter of the book is devoted entirely to managing risk, let's get a jump on the topic right now and introduce one of the most important risk mitigating strategies around - diversification.

Proper diversification is a must. CEOs know that diversification across product lines, industries, and countries, is key to managing risk and generating stable returns. You need to adopt this strategy too.

Johnson and Johnson has thousands of products, spanning multiple industries. And these products get sold in many different countries. This diversification has played a large role in the company's ability to deliver stable, increasing dividends to its shareholders for over fifty years. Other successful corporations such as Colgate-Palmolive, Proctor and Gamble, and 3M, are no different. They all have large diversified businesses that have rewarded shareholders with increasing dividends for decades.

Diversification is all about not putting all your eggs in one basket. In order to reduce your risk, you need to buy a variety of good companies in a variety of industries. Not only that, you also need to hold investments in a variety of different asset classes (see chapter 8). Asset classes such as stocks, bonds, and real estate, should all be included in your financial freedom fund. By owning all these different asset classes, you will ensure that if one asset class does poorly, your whole portfolio won't do poorly. Diversification isn't hard. It can easily be accomplished through simple purchases of ETFs or mutual funds, as well as through individual stock purchases.

The exact percentages of each asset class you hold will be up to you to determine yourself. However, the general rule is that the shorter your investment horizon and the more dependent you are on your investments, the more you will want to invest in less risky assets (such as bonds).

The other factor to consider is whether or not the level of risk you have in your portfolio will let you sleep at night. Imagine how you would feel if all your investments were in stocks and those investments fell by 40-50%, as they did during the financial crisis of 2007-2009. If you don't think you could stomach that type of risk without the possibility of selling all your holdings at the worst possible time, then you may want to hold a higher percentage of your portfolio in something a little less risky, such as bonds.

Given its importance to your investing success, the next chapter of this book will be devoted entirely to exploring the topic of risk. Before we move on, however, let's explore the story of Ronald Reed, a Vermont gas station attendant and janitor who followed many of the key success factors for investing mentioned here and amassed an $8 million fortune.

<u>The $8 Million Dollar Janitor</u>

In June 2014, Ronald Reed, a 92 year-old Vermont gas station attendant and janitor, died. Despite Reed's lifetime of relatively modest wages, his estate was anything but modest. In fact, his total estate was valued at close to $8million. Most of this fortune was amassed by investing in stocks.

How did Reed amass such a large fortune on such a modest salary? He did it by living a relatively frugal life and by following many of the key success factors for investing mentioned in the previous section.

First and foremost, Reed was frugal. It was reported by CNBC that neither his friends nor his step-children had any idea that he was wealthy. As well, Bridget Bokum, one of the associates from Wells Fargo that assisted in the settling of Reed's estate, is quoted in the *Wall Street Journal* as saying, "If he could save a penny, he would." It has also been reported that Reed drove a second hand Toyota Yaris and would often park it far from where he was going just to avoid paying a parking meter. This type of frugal living made it possible for Reed to save and invest a great deal of his wages over his lifetime.

Secondly, Reed was an investor and not a speculator. He only invested in what he could understand and he never bought any type of technology stocks.

Instead, Reed favoured large blue chip stocks that paid regular dividends. Reed's attorney, Laurie Rowell, was quoted on CNBC as saying, "He only invested in what he knew and what paid dividends."

Thirdly, Reed was not an active trader. He would buy his stocks and then hold onto them for the long-run. In fact, Reed held onto most of his stocks for many decades. On top of this, he continually reinvested the dividends he received. In doing so, he was able to take advantage of the power of compounding and generate even larger gains (compounding and dividend reinvestment are described in greater detail in the next chapter).

Finally, Reed was well diversified. At the time of his death, Reed owned 95 stocks across many different industries including, railways, banks, telecoms, health care, consumer products, and utilities. This diversification allowed Reed to prosper even though some of his individual stocks, such as Lehman Brothers, failed.

It's also worth noting that Reed would make it a point to read the Wall Street Journal daily. As previously mentioned, reading up on investments and increasing investment knowledge are key characteristics of many millionaires.

Ronald Reed wasn't a famous businessperson or a rich CEO. He was just a regular guy who thought like a CEO and got rich. You can too.

KEY POINTS FROM CHAPTER SEVEN

- You can own a part of some of the biggest, most successful companies in the world by simply purchasing some of their shares.

- One of the most common strategies used by self-made millionaires is investing in stocks.

- Popular financial securities for individual investors are: common shares, preferred shares, bonds, REITs, mutual funds, and ETFs.

- Keys to managing your portfolio yourself: having a plan, using a proven strategy, buying a diversified portfolio, and not giving in to emotions.

- No one should have a bigger interest on your money than you.

- Invest using a proven strategy and stick with it.

- *"Most investors, both institutional and individual, will find that the best way to own common stocks is through an index fund that charges minimal fees."* – Warren Buffet.

- Fees eat away at your returns each year, and over the course of many years, they can severely limit your overall returns.

- Buying shares in companies that increase their earnings and their dividends will ensure you invest in good companies and not speculate.

- Be an investor and not a speculator.

- Keep transaction costs low.

- Buy and hold.

- Only buy investments you understand.

- Diversify.

CHAPTER EIGHT

Manage Risk

It was now February 2009, and my wife and I had now been saving and investing as much as possible for the last four years. Six months earlier, after the stock market had fallen by 20%, we had used a HELOC to borrow some money against our home and had invested it all in dividend paying stocks. The thought at the time was that the 20% drop had presented an ideal opportunity to buy some good stocks at depressed prices. Unfortunately, this move didn't quite work out as planned.

Right after we borrowed and invested the money, the worst financial crisis since the Great Depression sent shock waves through the financial markets. The stock market fell by another 30%, and we immediately lost close to one third of the new money we had invested. The Great Recession had arrived, and it had given our financial freedom fund a beating.

Thankfully, we didn't sell our stock holdings just because they fell in value. After all, they were still the same great companies they had been a few months before their plunge in prices.

In fact, despite the financial crisis, many of the companies we had bought kept on raising their earnings and kept on paying out increasing dividends. We reinvested these dividends and bought more shares of the same great companies at even lower prices.

Even though not selling our investments was the right move, we had made one critical error. And the Great Recession had made us acutely aware of it. We had not properly managed our portfolio's risk.

We had a number of different stocks in our portfolio, but nothing else. We had no bonds of any kind and had not diversified into any other asset classes. All we had was stocks. And not being properly diversified over a number of different asset classes really hurts when the stock portion of your portfolio drops by 40-50%.

If you plan to retire in five to ten years, a stock market crash like the one in 2008 could put a severe dent in your plans. To avoid this potentially disastrous scenario, you need to make sure you properly manage risk.

Risk

CEOs make it a priority to manage risk. You need to do the same. If companies don't properly manage risk, they could find themselves in deep trouble.

As I write this, many companies in the oil industry are grappling with a severe downturn in the price of oil. In fact, the price of oil has dropped from a high of over $100 a barrel in 2014, to a low of below $30 a barrel in 2016.

Companies in the oil industry can now be broadly divided into two groups: (1) companies that managed risk appropriately, and (2) companies that didn't manage risk appropriately.

The companies that managed risk appropriately are set to ride out the decreased price of oil and profit by purchasing distressed companies at depressed prices. The companies that didn't manage risk appropriately are in danger of collapsing.

One of the large, successful companies that did manage risk appropriately is Canada's largest oil company, Suncor.

Over the twenty year period between 1995 and 2015, Suncor has seen its share price increase by over 1,500%. Moreover, over the ten year period between 2005 and 2015, Suncor has increased its dividend payouts by more than 800%. Despite this impressive performance, it is not the increase in its share price or the increase in its dividend payouts that has resulted in its CEO recently being named CEO of the year (for 2015) by *Report on Business* magazine. It is because of the way that Suncor manages risk.

Unlike some other oil companies, Suncor has an integrated business model. Besides oil exploration and production, Suncor also runs world-class refineries and has a large network of retail stations. This means that Suncor is better diversified than many of its rivals.

Unlike many of its competitors, Suncor generates earnings from three different businesses, not just one. This diversity has enabled Suncor to weather the risk of low oil prices much better than many of its competitors.

Moreover, when the oil crisis hit, Suncor possessed a large war-chest of billions of dollars in saved funds. This war-chest, thanks to a quasi-religious zeal for controlling costs, (one of the important strategies covered in chapter 4), means that while other oil companies are in danger of going bankrupt, Suncor is viewing the downturn in oil prices as an opportunity to use its war-chest of funds to buy weaker rivals.

With regards to your financial freedom fund, you need to be sure you manage risk like Suncor, not like its rivals. You need to ensure your financial freedom fund is never at risk of collapsing, you need to diversify, and you need to position yourself to take advantages of temporary market declines.

Let's look at the major risks facing your financial freedom fund and consider how to manage these risks. There are three main types of risks that can affect your financial freedom fund, and you need to make sure you manage all of these risks appropriately.

Main Risks to Your Financial Freedom Fund

1. Systematic risk.
2. Unsystematic risk.
3. Currency risk.

Systematic Risk

Systematic risk, also called market risk, is the risk of large economic events, like the 2008 global financial crisis, causing broad declines in the entire market. It cannot be eliminated by diversifying your stock holdings and can only be mitigated by diversifying into a variety of asset classes. Systematic risk is unpredictable and impossible to completely avoid.

The major problem systematic risk causes, like the problem the 2008 financial crisis caused for many, is that if investors need to dig into their principal when prices are down, they end up selling their holdings for lower than they bought them for and end up losing money.

This is why **selling all your holdings after a large market decline rarely makes any sense.** Not only do you lose the income stream associated with your investments, you also lose a portion of your capital as well. If you own good companies and they are still the same good companies they were before the market downturn, hold on to them and consider buying more. The stock market will recover. It always does.

The best way to manage systematic risk is to invest in different asset classes and to stay invested for the long-term. By investing in different asset classes such as stocks, bonds, and real estate, as opposed to just stocks alone, you are better able to buffer your portfolio against large drops in any one of these asset classes.

The reason for this reduced risk is due to the fact that different asset classes, quite often, react differently to different market shocks. While one asset class might go down after of a certain market event, another asset class might actually go up.

It is also a good idea to hold a small portion of your portfolio in cash. This cash can be used for emergencies, such as a temporary loss in employment, or it can be deployed to purchase undervalued investments should the market collapse.

Unsystematic Risk

Unsystematic risk, also known as diversifiable risk, is caused by the uncertainty individual companies face while conducting their day-to-day business. Unsystematic risk is not the risk of a market wide event driving down the prices of all the stocks in the market, it is the risk that an individual company falters and the price of this individual company's shares falls.

Unlike systematic risk, **unsystematic risk can be greatly reduced by diversifying your holdings.** Diversify your holdings so that each asset class contains investments in many different companies, in many different industries, in many different countries. Don't invest in one good company, invest in many good companies.

Currency Risk

Diversifying your holdings often involves investing in different countries. When you invest in different countries, however, you usually expose yourself to another kind of risk - currency risk.

Currency risk is the risk for losses that develops when investments are held in a foreign currency. This risk is due to the fact that foreign exchange rates can fluctuate over time.

To mitigate currency risk, many mutual funds and ETFs adopt a strategy of hedging their foreign investments against a falling exchange rate. Check for this this type of hedging strategy whenever you purchase ETFs or mutual funds that invest in foreign markets.

With a better understanding of the three main types of risk that all investors encounter and how one is able to mitigate these risks, let's now take a look at how you can create a portfolio that delivers the highest return for the least amount of risk. To accomplish this, you need to understand a little bit about *Modern Portfolio Theory* (MPT).

Modern Portfolio Theory

As mentioned above, diversification is a must. And **the best way to diversify is to create a portfolio of investments that offers the highest return for the least amount of risk.**

In order to accomplish this, you need to learn about and apply some of the rules of MPT. Let's introduce the concept of MPT right now and explore how you can use it to earn the highest return for the least amount of risk.

The Highest Return for the Lowest Risk

We have all heard the old adage that you shouldn't put all your eggs in one basket. Nowhere is this more important than with your financial freedom fund.

However, what is the best way to store your eggs? In other words, what should you do to get the highest return for the least amount of risk?

To answer this question, we need to take a look at MPT. MPT is the Nobel Prize winning work of American economist Harry Markowitz. MPT was developed in 1952 and is still widely used in the financial industry today.

The main finding of MPT is that yes, holding a variety of investments offers lower risk, however, **holding a variety of investments whose returns differ over time (whose returns are not correlated), offers the *best* return for the *lowest* amount of risk.**

Therefore, all other things being equal, owning two investments that produce similar returns each year is not as good as owning two investments that produce returns that can differ from each other each year.

This is why investing in a variety of asset classes makes sense. Generally speaking, the returns of most of the stocks in the stock market are more closely correlated with each other than they are with the returns of other asset classes.

Therefore, when systematic risk strikes (and one day it will), the prices of all the stocks in a certain portfolio might go down while, at the same time, the prices of all the bonds in the same portfolio might go up.

Sure, owning ten stocks is better than owning one stock, but if the whole stock market crashes, it would have probably been better to own some stocks, some bonds, and some real estate.

By owning a variety of investments in a variety of asset classes, you will be able to achieve a far better *risk-adjusted* return. A better risk-adjusted return means that the risk you take on to produce a similar return is lower.

Even if investing a portion of your portfolio outside of stocks causes your expected return to be a little lower, the trade-off is still worth it. Why? It is worth it because you get a much better return for the risk you take on. It is worth it because that slightly lower return comes with *substantially* lower risk.

Even better than putting your eggs in many baskets, put some eggs in one basket, some bread in another basket, and some cheese in another. That way, even if disaster strikes and you drop all of your baskets, you will still have something to eat.

How to Invest Using MPT

What are the different asset classes you should hold in your portfolio to be properly diversified? **Most investors will do just fine holding stocks, bonds, real estate, and a little bit of cash for emergencies.**

The percentages of each asset class you hold will be up to you, however, a simple allocation of 40% stocks, 30% bonds, and 30% real estate, would probably be ideal for most investors.

If you have a long time horizon and have the benefits of a good paying job, consider holding a higher percentage of your portfolio in stocks and real estate. If you have a shorter time horizon or will need to dig into some of your principal, consider holding more of your portfolio in less risky investments such as bonds.

The stock section of your portfolio should be invested in either index funds or invested using some other proven strategy, like dividend investing. Remember to always have a strategy and to always invest for the long-term. Do not speculate.

The bond portion of your portfolio can be made up of any type of fixed income investments you like, but just like stocks, remember that high yields are often associated with more risky investments.

The highest yielding bonds (junk bonds) tend to produce investment returns that are more closely correlated with stocks than with bonds. According to MPT, this positive correlation would imply that a portfolio of junk bonds and stocks would offer a lower risk-adjusted return compared to a portfolio comprised of investment grade bonds and stocks. On the other side of the spectrum, government T-bills would probably not be risky enough. T-bills would be better suited for holding the cash portion of your portfolio.

A mix of investment grade corporate bonds and higher yielding government debt would likely be the best alternative for the bond portion of your portfolio. This mix of bonds can be found in various ETFs offered by the previously mentioned ETF companies (Vanguard, BlackRock's iShares, and Invesco's PowerShares).

The real estate section of your portfolio can be invested in either REITs, investment properties, or both. As discussed in chapter six, try and buy investment properties that can generate rental income high enough to cover the costs of owning the property in the first place and provide you with a little extra each month. If this is not possible, consider just sticking with REITs.

Just like bonds and stocks, be careful not to chase yields when deciding which REITs to buy. If you do buy REITs, try and diversify. Hold a variety of REITs that hold a variety of different types of commercial property such as apartment buildings, industrial buildings, and retail buildings. Just like stocks and bonds, your best course of action is probably to purchase a variety of REITs using a low cost ETF.

Besides stocks, bonds, and real estate, it is also possible to achieve diversification by investing in other asset classes such as precious metals, commodities, or even rare artwork. I've often found, however, that many of these asset classes are too speculative for my taste. No matter which investments you choose to buy, always try to remain an investor and not a speculator.

How many different investments should you hold in each asset class? There is some debate on this, but generally speaking, it is thought that fifteen to twenty stocks in different industries would be appropriate for the portion of your portfolio invested in stocks. You would also want to have the same level of diversity for the bond section of your portfolio and any other sections as well.

If buying all those individual financial securities seems like a lot of work, consider making all your purchases using low cost ETFs or mutual funds. In fact, my favorite way to invest in bonds, REITs, and international stocks, is to do just that. I purchase ETFs that hold a variety of these types of investments, all at a low cost.

MPT in Action

The table on the next page offers an example of how MPT is able to get you the best return for the least amount of risk. This table shows the historical returns and the historical risk for of a number of different asset classes and for a portfolio of investments that holds a mix of these asset classes (40% stocks, 30% bonds, and 30% REITs). Risk is expressed in terms of the number of years the asset class or the diversified portfolio lost money.

The data for the table, taken from the Federal Reserve database in St. Louis and the website REIT.com, shows the historical performance of the S&P 500 (stocks), U.S. T-Bonds with a ten year yield (bonds), and the FTSE NAREIT U.S. Real Estate Index (REITs), from 1972-2015. This is the longest time frame for which the REIT Index information is available. Risk is expressed in terms of the number of years over the dataset (forty-four years) in which an asset class would have lost any money and the number of years in which an asset class would have lost more than 5% of its total value. Returns are expressed as the average annual returns over the dataset.

Return and Risk of Various Asset Classes (1972-2015)

	Stocks	Bonds	REITs	Portfolio*
Average Annual Return	11.7%	7.5%	11.9%	10.5%
Number of years lost money	9	7	10	7
Number of years lost more than 5%	7	4	8	3

* Portfolio is made up of 40% stocks, 30% bonds, and 30% REITs.

Referring to the table above, it can be seen that the highest returns were generated by stocks and REITs, (11.7% and 11.9%, respectively). Bonds, with an average annual return of 7.5%, offered the lowest returns.

As expected, the higher returns offered by stocks and REITs came with higher risks. Over the forty-four years examined, both stocks and REITs lost money in more years than bonds did. REITs lost money in ten of the forty-four years examined and stocks lost money in nine of the forty-four years examined. In contrast, bonds only lost money in seven of the forty-four years examined. As well, stocks and REITs lost more than 5% of their value in more years than bonds did.

In fact, while bonds lost more than 5% of their value in only four of the forty-four years evaluated, stocks and REITs lost more than 5% of their value in seven years and eight years, respectively. This means you would have been almost twice as likely to lose more than 5% of your investment in any given year if you had invested all your money in either stocks or REITs, compared to if you had invested all your money in bonds alone.

Now let's consider the return and risk properties of the portfolio of asset classes. The portfolio contains a mix of all three asset classes, weighted with 40% stocks, 30% bonds, and 30% REITs.

Over the forty-four years examined, the portfolio offered an average annual return of 10.5%. This average return is much higher than the average return generated by the bonds and only slightly lower than the returns generated by stocks or real estate.

As well, this return came with the lowest risk of any of the asset classes examined. The portfolio lost money in seven of the forty-four years evaluated, the same as bonds, and only lost more than 5% of its value in three of the forty-four years evaluated, the lowest of any asset class. Just like MPT predicts, a portfolio of different asset classes offered the best risk-adjusted return.

Let's now shift gears away from MPT and turn our attention to three other important investment strategies that will help lower risk and increase expected returns. These three strategies are: (1) compounding, (2) dollar-cost averaging, and (3) rebalancing.

Compounding

Compounding has been described by many as one of the most important financial strategies around. It is easy to implement and **given enough time, compounding will make you rich.**

Compounding is the ability to generate more and more earnings from your previous earnings. You invest $100 at an annual growth rate of 7% and a year later, it is worth $107. If you do nothing else but reinvest your interest and your dividends, you will now not only have $100 working for you, you will have $107 working for you. The magic of compounding has begun. This might not sound all that impressive at first, but consider the following example.

Let's assume that the day a child is born his or her loving parents invest $10,000 in a low cost index fund that mirrors the S&P 500 index. The thoughtful parents then do nothing else except leave this $10,000 to experience the magic of compounding. Later, they arrange to have the total savings this investment generates gifted to their child on his or her 65th birthday.

Sure, $10,000 is a lot of money, but these parents are financially wise. They realize that the power of time will be on their newborn son or daughter's side and that time, combined with the power of compounding, will result in their son or daughter eventually achieving great wealth.

They also realize that if they live below their means for a year or two before their baby is born, they will be able to offer their child this wonderful gift.

They reason that even if their child saves nothing his or her whole life, this gift will ensure that he or she can retire comfortably. In their infinite wisdom, the parents cancel their all-inclusive two week vacation to Mexico and invest these savings instead. They have been to Mexico before and they will go again, but this year they decide to save their money. They brown bag it to work, make their coffee at home, and only eat out once a week for the next year. By the end of the year, the account is opened and the $10,000 is deposited. As if by divine intervention, a baby girl is born the next day.

Decades pass, and then on her 65th birthday, a woman hears a knock at her door. A smiling man presents the woman with a cheque along with a note that reads, "From your loving parents." How much do you think this cheque is worth?

If the S&P 500 were to realize a CAGR of 8%, this cheque would be worth roughly $1.5 million. If the S&P 500 were to realize a CAGR of 11.3%, its average over the 30 year period between Jan 1, 1985 - Jan 1, 2015, this cheque would be worth roughly $10.5 million. If this were to be the case, that year of frugal living that took place sixty-five years ago could, theoretically, result in intergenerational wealth for decades to come.

This example doesn't include the effects of inflation or taxes; nonetheless, it shows just how powerful compound interest can be. One of the best ways to get wealthy is to simply harness the power of compound interest and time.

If you haven't started taking advantage of the power of compound interest, then start doing so today. Invest some money wisely, make sure to reinvest your interest and your dividends (see below), and start building your wealth.

Who knows, maybe decades from now your son or daughter might be rewarded with a magic knock at their door.

Reinvest Your Dividends

To realize the power of compounding, you need to try to never dig into your principal and try to always reinvest all the dividends and income your investments generate. **Don't take your dividends; reinvest them so that you can make even more money.**

The graph at the top of the next page shows the return of the S&P 500 over a twenty year period, both with and without the reinvestment of dividends. The graph assumes an investment of $10,000 per year in an S&P 500 index fund over the twenty year period between Jan 1, 1995 to Dec 31 2014. The solid line assumes that dividends get reinvested, while the dashed line assumes that dividends get removed from the portfolio as soon as they are received.

Effect of Dividend Reinvestment on Savings
(Investment of $10,000 per year in an S&P 500 Index Fund)

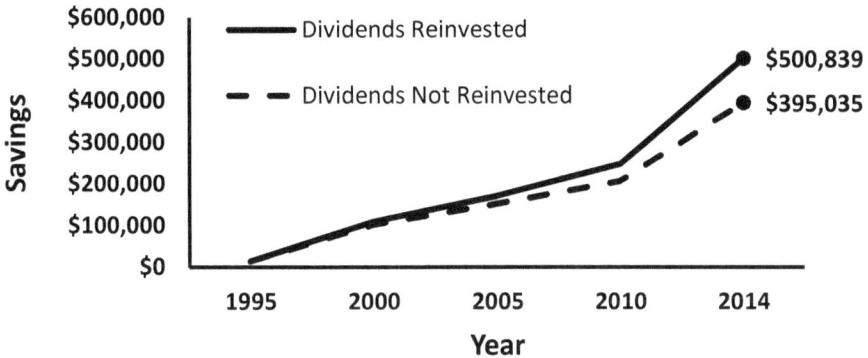

The graph above shows that by the end of the twenty year period, the portfolio that had its dividends continually reinvested ends up with just over $500,000. By comparison, the portfolio that did not have its dividends reinvested ends up with only $395,000.

This means that the portfolio that had its dividends continually reinvested ends up with total savings that are approximately 27% higher than the portfolio that did not have its dividends continually reinvested.

One of the easiest ways to reinvest your dividends is to simply sign up for a dividend reinvestment plan (DRIP). This can be done with your managed funds provider or your online broker. In many cases, companies offer a small discount of between 2-5% when purchasing shares through a DRIP. Moreover, many companies will waive the commission charges involved with the dividend reinvestment.

The other advantages of signing up to a DRIP are; forced saving, paying yourself first, and dollar-cost averaging. We have already discussed the benefits of forced saving and paying yourself first, so let's now consider the benefits of dollar-cost averaging.

Dollar-Cost Averaging

Dollar-cost averaging is a technique that involves buying a fixed dollar amount of a certain investment at regular periodic intervals.

Assuming the price of the investment fluctuates, sometimes going up and sometimes going down, the benefit of dollar-cost averaging is that you end up buying more of the investment when prices are low and less of the investment when prices are high.

Dollar-cost averaging will result in the cost of your purchases being averaged out over time. This tends to smooth out the price fluctuations of your purchases, which can help to lower risk. Dollar-cost averaging also offers the benefit of buying more of a good long-term investment when prices are depressed, which can lead to greater returns.

For example, if an investment costs $10 per share at the beginning of the year, and you invest $100 in this investment, you will end up purchasing 10 shares. If this investment drops to $5 per share by the end of the year, and you invest another $100 into it, you will now end up adding an additional 20 shares to your total, (not just 10). If the investment then returns back to $10 per share by the end of the second year, you will have 30 shares valued at $10 a share, for a total value of $300. As your total cost was only $200, you have a profit of $100 and have realized a return of 50%.

In contrast, if you had invested all of your $200 in the middle of the first year, when the share price was between $10 and $5, then, assuming a price of $7.50 per share, you would have only purchased 27 shares, not 30 shares. This, in turn, would mean that by the end of the second year, when the investment returned to a price of $10 per share, your portfolio would have been valued at only $270 and not $300. Under this scenario, with a profit of only $70, your return would have only been 35%.

In this example, dollar-cost averaging resulted in a higher profit compared to investing all your money in one lump sum. It is important to realize, however, that dollar-cost averaging is not infallible. Moreover, under some situations, it might be considered reasonable to just invest everything you have in one fell swoop.

If you are only able to make periodic investments, perhaps after getting paid every two weeks, then you can't help but use a strategy of dollar-cost averaging. It doesn't really matter whether you want to use this strategy or not. However, what if you suddenly receive a large lump sum of money? What if your parents decide that, rather than waiting until they are dead, they will help you out today and they suddenly give you $100,000 to invest.

In this situation, unlike the one involving your biweekly paycheque, you now have a choice. Should you invest this $100,000 in one lump sum or should you use a strategy of dollar-cost averaging, break the $100,000 up into a series of smaller investments, and invest it gradually over time?

In truth, many studies have shown that you are more likely to make a greater amount of money in the long-run if you just invest the whole sum right now. This is because dollar-cost averaging is most effective when it allows you to purchase investments at depressed prices. Most good investments, however, just keep going up in price. Therefore, if you don't invest the full amount right away, you just end up keeping some of your money on the sidelines to buy the same investments that are more expensive at a later date.

The downside to investing all your money all at once, however, is the risk that as soon as you invest it, your investments experience a sharp drop in price.

Is there a way to minimize this risk? In fact, the same research that shows a lump sum investment often delivers superior returns in the long-run, also suggests that **dollar-cost averaging is more likely to prevent a very large loss in the short-term.**

Experiencing a large loss immediately after investing a large sum of money would be an emotional nightmare. It is because of this potential nightmare that, if I have a large sum of money available to invest, I choose to follow a dollar-cost-averaging approach. Instead of investing it all at once, I break it up into a series of periodic investments and invest it over time. However, rather than spread these investments out over a period of years and risk missing out on more gains, I simply make these investments over a period of months.

If dollar-cost averaging works best when purchases are made at depressed prices, is there a way to ensure you reliably achieve this goal? Sometimes there is. And the best way to realize this benefit is by periodically rebalancing your portfolio.

Rebalancing

If you have properly diversified your portfolio, you will, more than likely, have a number of investments across a variety of asset classes.

This being this case, you will probably notice that in some years the stock portion of your portfolio outperforms, in some years the bond portion outperforms, and in some years the real estate portion outperforms. Sometimes, one of your asset classes will collapse, like the stock portion during a particularly nasty bear market, or the bond portion after a steep increase in interest rates. When something like this happens, it can cause your portfolio to lose its desired asset class weightings and, furthermore, can result in your risk-adjusted return being different from what you had originally planned.

The good news is that when asset class weightings get all out of whack, you can rebalance your portfolio and get your asset class weightings back to where you want them to be. Let's look at an example to illustrate how one can rebalance a certain portfolio to get its desired asset class weightings back after this portfolio undergoes a shift from its original asset class weightings.

Let's assume, for example, you have a simple portfolio of 50% stocks and 50% bonds. Let's also assume that by the end of the year, the stock portion of your portfolio falls by 20% while the bond portion of your portfolio climbs by 10%. Under this scenario, you would then have something closer to 42% of your total portfolio in stocks (40/95) and 58% of your total portfolio in bonds (55/95). How could you rebalance your portfolio to get it back to its ideal weightings of 50% stocks and 50% bonds?

To get your portfolio back to its ideal weightings, 50% stocks and 50% bonds, you need to sell some of your bonds and use the proceeds to buy some more stock. To accomplish this, you would need to sell 8% (50-42) of the value of your total portfolio, all in bonds, and then use these proceeds to repurchase some more stock.

Remember to always consider the costs involved in any rebalancing and, whenever possible, to simply rebalance your portfolio by using your future contributions. This way, you will save on the transaction costs involved with selling and buying your current investments and only pay the transaction costs associated with buying new investments.

Also, with transaction costs in mind, consider only rebalancing your portfolio once the weightings of your various asset classes have moved away from their targets by more than 5-10%.

Besides primarily managing risk, rebalancing your portfolio can also lead to increased returns. In fact, Gregg Fisher, writing for CFA Institute, showed that rebalancing a portfolio of U.S. and emerging market stocks, over the twenty year period ending in 2014, led to higher returns versus not rebalancing at all.

For this twenty year period, U.S. stocks and emerging market stocks each averaged a compounding return of 8% annually. However, if a portfolio were split evenly between the two and regularly rebalanced, the investor would have earned closer to 9%.

In terms of increased returns, rebalancing works best when asset classes have similar long-term rates of returns. Rebalancing your portfolio to buy more bonds, which have lower expected rates of return compared to stocks, might not necessarily lead to increased returns. It would, however, help to manage risk. That, in and of itself, is an important enough reason to do it.

Rebalancing, however, can only increase your expected returns so much. If you really want to go after higher returns, then your next best option might be the use of leverage.

While borrowing money to invest will no doubt involve more risk, the potential returns might be well worth it. Let's move onto the next chapter and consider this option now. Before doing so, however, let's leave this chapter with a cautionary tale of what can happen when investors fail to properly manage risk and end up putting all their eggs in one basket.

Retirement Dreams Shattered

Enron was a diversified energy, commodities, and services company that was ranked as one of the largest companies in the world in 2001. At its peak, Enron employed more than 20,000 people, and by the year 2000, it was claiming sales revenues in excess of $100 billion. What's more, Enron had recorded average sales growth of 57% a year, over the previous four years.

Sound like a good investment? For many of Enron's employees it did. In fact, many of Enron's employees decided that Enron was such good investment; they ended up transferring all of the money in their 401(k) retirement accounts into nothing but Enron Stock. Unfortunately for these investors, this lack of diversification would turn out to be a very costly mistake.

Enron's stock peaked at $90.75 in August 2000. By January 2002, it was worth 67 cents. It has been reported that some of the company's rank and file employees that were nearing retirement saw the value of their 401(k) retirement accounts fall from as high as $475,000 to as low as $2,200. In a little over one year, many people saw a lifetime of savings totally wiped out. Furthermore, they saw their retirement dreams shattered.

This story serves as a powerful reminder of the importance of proper diversification. It also shows just how quickly fortunes can be lost when investors fail to properly manage a portfolio's risk.

KEY POINTS FROM CHAPTER EIGHT

- You must ensure your financial freedom fund is never at risk of collapsing.

- There are three main risks that can affect your financial freedom fund; systematic risk, unsystematic risk, and currency risk.

- Selling all your holdings after a large market downturn rarely makes any sense.

- The best way to manage systematic risk is to invest in different asset classes and to stay invested for the long-term.

- Unsystematic risk can be greatly reduced by diversifying your holdings.

- Currency risk can be mitigated through currency hedging strategies (offered by many international ETFs and mutual funds).

- The best diversification offers the highest return for the least amount of risk.

- Holding investments whose returns differ over time (whose returns are not correlated), offers the best return for the lowest amount of risk.

- Most investors should hold a portfolio made up of stocks, bonds, and real estate.

- Given enough time, compound interest can make anyone a millionaire.

- Reinvesting your dividends is essential to realize the full power of compounding.

- Dollar-cost averaging can help reduce risk.

- Rebalancing your portfolio can help manage risk and can lead to increased returns.

CHAPTER NINE

The Power of Leverage

Have you ever seen the movie *21*? This movie is based on the true story of a group of students from MIT who were able to legally win large amounts of money from casinos world-wide while playing black-jack.

The MIT students used card counting techniques to determine when the odds of a big return outweighed the risks involved with placing a bet. When the students encountered large odds in their favour, they placed very large bets.

Their strategy, in essence a mathematical calculation involving risk and return, was an effective one and the students reputedly won millions of dollars over the course of the group's existence.

Normally I don't like comparing investing to gambling, as the most successful investors buy quality investments and hold them for the long-term, they don't gamble.

That being said, I do believe that financial markets sometimes overreact and present the individual investor with greater odds of a larger return.

Sometimes fear takes hold, investors sell all their investments in a panicked, irrational state, and good investments become undervalued.

When this happens, rational investors are suddenly rewarded with an opportunity to purchase good investments at depressed prices. And just like the MIT students playing black-jack, these rational investors are then presented with better odds for a larger return.

This point (that rational investors sometimes get to purchase good investments at depressed prices), was made by Warren Buffett in a letter to Berkshire Hathaway shareholders that summarized Berkshire's 2009 performance. In this letter, when describing some of the opportunities that occurred after the 2008 financial crisis, Warren Buffett had this to say, "Opportunities come infrequently. When it rains gold put out the bucket, not the thimble." I couldn't have agreed more.

It was the middle of 2009, the financial crisis had hit, and within a few short months it had wiped out close to half of our financial freedom fund. And even though we were disciplined enough to not sell all our investments, our financial freedom now seemed further away than ever.

It soon occurred to my wife and me, however, that this crisis may be a blessing in disguise. Whenever the S&P 500 has dropped by greater than 20% in a calendar year, in any of the last 81 years (1934-2015), the index has returned positive gains in the following year. Moreover, the index gains an average of 28% the year after a drop of greater than 20% and gains an average of 41% over the two year period after such a drop.

Even though there is no guarantee that history will continue to repeat itself, this is still a pretty reassuring statistic to have after a large drop in stock markets and a whole lot of nervous investors wondering if they should sell everything and run for the hills.

Even more promising, at this time, was the fact that interest rates had begun to drop to record lows. In fact, by the middle of 2009, the interest rate on our margin account (an investment account that lets you borrow money using your investments as collateral) was only 3.5%. The interest we paid on our HELOC was an unbelievably low 2.25%.

It didn't take long for us to use some financial acumen and figure out that incredibly low interest rates combined with a beaten-down stock market that could be expected to generate large short-term gains and generate long-term gains of approximately 7% a year, offered us a good chance to earn some high returns if we borrowed money to invest.

In fact, if one were ever to borrow money to invest, I'm not sure there was a better time than after the 2008 financial crisis. Even if dividend payments got cut in half (which they didn't), the dividend payments alone could have covered the interest on the money borrowed to invest and still paid out a profit.

Just like the students in the movie *21,* my wife and I calculated that the odds of a big return outweighed the risk. And just like the students in the movie, we decided to place a large bet.

We borrowed hundreds of thousands of dollars, using a HELOC and a margin account, and over the next few years we put all that borrowed money to work. We put it to work in real estate and we put it to work in stocks. And although we didn't know it at the time, this move would prove to be one of the largest reasons we were able to achieve financial freedom at such a young age.

Leverage

Even though debt is constantly frowned upon by most individuals, debt isn't always as bad as many people make it out to be.

The truth is that debt can do good things for governments, good things for corporations, and more importantly, debt can do good things for you. **The**

key is to use borrowed money to increase your wealth, not to squander it on money sucking maggots.

Countries that borrow money to build roads, to build bridges, and to invest in education, will likely see their economies grow. CEOs who borrow money so their companies can invest in projects that will increase the company's earnings will see the value of their companies increase. Finally, individual investors who borrow money when it makes sense to do so, manage their debt appropriately, and invest this money properly, should see their wealth increase, too.

The CEOs of almost every large, successful corporation borrow money to invest. In fact, by the end of 2013, the value of the U.S. corporate bond market was close to $10 trillion. That's $10 trillion being put to work to help these companies earn money.

What's more, the money these companies borrow to invest often represents a significant percentage of their total assets. In fact, it is not uncommon to see the debt levels of many large, successful corporations in the range of 30% of their total assets. Therefore, if a company has $100 million in assets, it would not be uncommon for this same company to have $30 million in debt, all helping it to earn even more money.

Just like the CEOs of these large, successful corporations, you should also consider using leverage to increase your wealth. Whether it is leveraging yourself to buy an investment property or leveraging yourself to invest in the stock market, borrowing to invest can be a powerful way to grow your wealth.

However, while borrowing to invest offers a greater opportunity to earn higher returns, it also comes with greater risks. You must be sure you are financially savvy enough to manage these risks appropriately.

If you use leverage to invest in the stock market, you must be sure that leveraging yourself makes sense in the first place (discussed below), that you leverage yourself in an appropriately diversified portfolio of solid long-term investments, and that you are disciplined enough to not sell your investments should they suffer a temporary short-term loss.

You must also be sure that you don't overleverage yourself. If you overleverage yourself, you will find it very difficult to manage your debt load. This, in turn, might force you to sell some of your investments at the worst possible time - after they have dropped in value and before they get a chance to climb back up.

Let's explore the topic of leverage in greater detail and examine; (1) why you might already be using a strategy of leverage, (2) when you should consider using leverage to invest in the stock market, (3) how you can leverage yourself using margin accounts, (4) how leverage affects your risk-adjusted return, (5) the advantage of using leverage after large drops in the stock market, (6) how leverage can affect your taxable income, and (7) the key success factors for using leverage.

You Have Probably Already Borrowed to Invest - You Just Didn't Know It

Still not convinced it might make sense to borrow money to invest? The truth is you have probably already borrowed to invest, you just didn't know it.

When students get loans to go to college or university, they are actually borrowing money to invest. Even though they are not investing in the stock market, they are investing in themselves. In doing so, they hope their investment in education leads to a better paying job.

Furthermore, anybody that has invested in real estate and rented out a property has also, quite likely, borrowed money to invest (assuming their property had a mortgage).

In both of these cases, this borrowed money can add up to hundreds of thousands of dollars.

All this being said, it is amazing to me the amount of people that think nothing of borrowing hundreds of thousands of dollars to buy an investment property, even if the rent doesn't cover all the expenses and receives no favourable tax advantages, and then think that borrowing money to invest in a portfolio of large, successful companies whose dividends do get taxed favourably and whose dividends rise every year, is too risky.

In the first scenario (buying the investment property), you have no diversification at all, and you also have a large amount of work to do in managing and maintaining the property. In the second scenario (investing in a portfolio of large, successful companies who increase their dividends every year), you are well diversified and have almost no work at all to do. The second scenario also provides you with dividend income that gets taxed more favourably than rental income (more on this in chapter 10).

Here's another example of borrowing to invest. We have all heard about the gruelling hours and high rates of failure involved in staring your own business. Yet, here again, many people would consider borrowing money to start their own business less risky than borrowing money to invest in a portfolio of large, financially-stable companies with a proven history of rising income and growing dividends.

It seems to me that keeping your day job and borrowing money to invest in a portfolio of large, financially stable companies with a proven history of rising income and growing dividends, is less risky and far less work than borrowing money to invest in and run a risky start up business.

When to Borrow Money to Invest in the Stock Market

If you believe it might make sense to borrow money to invest in the stock market, your next question should be, "When does it make sense to do so?"

The best case scenario for you to borrow money to invest in the stock market is when: (1) interest rates are low, (2) dividend yields on financially stable companies are high, and (3) stocks are undervalued.

The first two criteria (low interest rates and high dividend yields on financially stable companies) are easier to figure out than the third criterion. Usually, these first two criteria are met if you are able to find some large, financially stable companies that pay a dividend large enough to cover the interest expense on the money borrowed to invest.

Make sure, however, that you don't borrow money to invest in companies that are *not* financially stable. Don't borrow money to invest in companies that are not increasing their earnings or dividends, but are simply paying out an extraordinarily high dividend.

Normally, a dividend in the high single digits indicates a company is not financially stable, it's just more risky. A dividend yield in the range of 7-10% could reflect the fact that a dividend cut is on the horizon, especially if the payout ratio is over 100%. **When borrowing money to invest in the stock market, always make sure you act as an investor and not a speculator.**

It's far better to buy a wonderful company at a fair price, than a fair company at a wonderful price."
- Warren Buffett

The third criterion (borrowing money to invest when stocks are undervalued), is a bit more difficult to determine. That being said, history has shown that large market drops (greater than 20%) usually offer such opportunities. And even though historical performance is no guarantee of future performance, I would feel more comfortable borrowing money to invest in a company whose stock price has fallen by 20% and who is continually increasing its earnings and its dividend, compared to borrowing money to invest in a company that is not increasing its earnings or its dividend and is trading at its all-time high. As Warren Buffett says, "It's far better to buy a wonderful company at a fair price, than a fair company at a wonderful price".

Borrowing money at a good interest rate is also extremely important. Obviously, it makes sense to get the lowest interest rate you can find. In my experience, the lowest interest rates are usually offered through HELOCs or through margin accounts (margin accounts are offered at most brokerages).

Most people have heard of HELOCs, which are simply lines of credit secured against your primary residence, but many people may not be as familiar with margin accounts. Let's explore these types of accounts now.

Margin Accounts

A margin account is an account offered by brokerage firms that allows investors to borrow money to buy financial securities. Margin accounts work by allowing investors to borrow up to a certain percentage of the value of their holdings in their brokerage accounts. For this privilege, the broker of the account charges the investor interest on the borrowed money and uses the securities in the investor's account as collateral for the loan.

Typically, the amount of money you can borrow will depend on the value of the investments you possess and the amount of cash held in your account. However, because the value of the investments held in your account can fluctuate from day to day, the broker will usually calculate and update the amount that you are able to borrow (your margin) at the end of each trading day.

It is important to realize that if your investments decrease in value, so does your margin. Therefore, if you use up all your margin to buy investments and your investments then fall in value, the broker will ask you to deposit more money or more collateral into your account. This is what is referred to as a *margin call*.

If you get a margin call, you have exceeded the margin available to you and the broker needs you to deposit more collateral into your account to bring your margin back to within its allowable limits.

You are able to increase the collateral in your account by depositing more cash, by buying new investments (without borrowing money to do so), or by selling some of your investments for cash and leaving the proceeds in your account.

The problem with getting a margin call, assuming you have no more funds available to deposit money or to make additional purchases, is that a margin call forces you to sell some of your investments at depressed prices. This isn't something you ever want to be forced into doing.

If you use a margin account, do not overleverage yourself. Plan to never have to worry about getting a margin call. This is especially important if you don't think you could cover a margin call by buying more stock or depositing more money into your account.

In this regard, it might be prudent to only borrow up to the point that it would take a 50% drop in your holdings to trigger a margin call. Assuming you are properly diversified, a drop greater than 50% is very unlikely.

Different brokerages have different rules regarding when they will issue a margin call. Moreover, the math behind some of the calculations used to determine your margin can be a little complicated. With this in mind, it is important to make sure you take the time to understand how your broker calculates your margin and under what circumstances your broker will issue you a margin call. Furthermore, take the time to understand all of this before you start using the margin available in your account.

In addition to margin calls, brokers have other rules for margin accounts that are designed to ensure their loans to investors don't get too risky. For example, brokers will not allow investors to use all their margin to purchase only one or two stocks. This is just too risky. Hopefully, after reading the last chapter on risk, this is something you would never consider doing anyway, even if it was allowed.

Diversifying your holdings so that you are able to get the best return for the least amount of risk is paramount to investing success. Moreover, diversification becomes even more important when you use leverage. With this in mind, let's take a closer look at the relationship between leverage, risk, and return.

Leverage, Risk, and Return

Most investors who are looking to earn higher returns don't ever use a strategy involving leverage. Instead, they just buy riskier investments. This might be a mistake.

Despite the possibility for higher returns, these riskier investments often come with substantially higher risk. This means that investors who adopt this strategy might not be getting the best *risk-adjusted* return.

Let's examine why leveraging yourself with a diversified portfolio of less risky stocks might be a better way to go after a higher return. Before we do so, however, we will need to define the difference between high beta stocks and low beta stocks.

Stocks that experience price changes greater than the market as a whole are defined by academics and investment professionals as high beta stocks. These stocks, because of the higher variation of their returns, possess more risk than the market as a whole. Moreover, because of this risk, investors expect a higher return from these investments. Technology stocks would be an example of the type of stocks that often fall into this category.

In contrast, stocks whose prices are less sensitive to market ups and downs, when compared to the market as a whole, are said to be low beta stocks. As opposed to high beta stocks, investors are usually willing to accept a lower return for holding low beta stocks. This is due to the simple fact that low beta stocks are less risky. Large blue chip companies with reliable earnings would often fall into this category.

As mentioned above, many investors who seek out higher returns often chose to fill their portfolios with nothing but high beta stocks. If we were to ask Nobel Prize winner Harry Markowitz about this strategy, however, and examine his work around MPT, we might come to a different conclusion.

Assuming your cost of borrowing is less than your expected return, **MPT suggests that the best way to earn a high return for the lowest possible amount of risk is to buy a diversified portfolio of quality investments and then leverage yourself to buy even more of this diversified portfolio** (see appendix).

Moreover, a recent article in *The Economist* titled "The Secrets of Buffett's Success" indicates that research has recently confirmed that low beta stocks, such as large, financially stable blue-chip companies that pay regular dividends, have traditionally offered a higher risk-adjusted return compared to high beta stocks. According to this article, it should be possible to exploit this fact and earn a higher return by borrowing money to invest in a portfolio of low beta stocks.

Having said all of this, the truth is that any amount of leverage is more risky than no leverage at all. This is because, as previously discussed in chapter 6, not only does leverage have the effect of magnifying gains, it also has the effect of magnifying losses.

If you invest $20,000 to buy a $100,000 investment (effectively borrowing $80,000) and that investment increases in value to $105,000, then you haven't just gained 5% of your investment ($5,000 of $100,000), you have gained 25% ($5,000 of $20,000).

Conversely, if you invest $20,000 to buy a $100,000 investment and that investment falls to $95,000, then you haven't only lost 5% of your investment ($5,000 of $100,000), you have lost 25% ($5,000 of $20,000).

The risk of suffering larger losses means that **leverage is not for the faint of heart.** Nonetheless, if you are looking to retire sooner rather than later, you are disciplined enough to invest for the long-term, and you are controlled enough to manage your emotions and to not over-leverage yourself, then using a little bit of leverage might just be the best way to go after the higher returns you seek.

If, however, you can't sleep at night with this increased risk, you think you may sell all your investments after a short-term loss, you refuse to properly diversify, or you risk more than you can afford to lose, you should not leverage yourself at all.

The Advantage of Leverage After the 2008 Financial Crisis

My wife and I borrowed and invested hundreds of thousands of dollars in the stock market over the course of our wealth building years. The majority of that borrowing and investing started after the 2008 financial crisis.

"Opportunities come infrequently. When it rains gold put out the bucket, not the thimble."
- Warren Buffett

After the 2008 financial crisis, interest rates were low, dividend payments on financially stable stocks were high, some good companies were undervalued, and we believed the stock market would recover, just like it always does. As Warren Buffett advised, "Opportunities come infrequently. When it rains gold put out the bucket, not the thimble." We definitely put out the bucket.

Let's examine how an investor would have fared if they had used some leverage after the 2008 financial crisis and had borrowed some money to purchase an index fund mirroring the S&P 500 index.

Let's assume this investor was able to dramatically cut his or her costs and was able to invest $25,000 a year in employment income and $25,000 a year in borrowed money. We will also assume that this investor started investing at the beginning of 2009 and finished investing at the end of 2014. This means that this investor would have invested a total of $150,000 in borrowed money and a further $150,000 in employment income (not borrowed). Finally, let's assume that this investor paid an interest rate of 4% on any money borrowed to invest and that this investor was able to reinvest all of his or her dividends. Transaction costs, taxes on investments, and the costs associated with holding the funds are not included. The results of this analysis are shown in the table below.

The Power of Leverage

Year	Earned Income Invested	Borrowed Money Invested	Total Invested	Value of S&P 500 Index Fund (End of year)	Total Debt	Interest on Debt
2009	$25,000	$25,000	$50,000	$63,555	$25,000	$1,000
2010	$25,000	$25,000	$50,000	$130,441	$50,000	$2,000
2011	$25,000	$25,000	$50,000	$184,176	$75,000	$3,000
2012	$25,000	$25,000	$50,000	$271,363	$100,000	$4,000
2013	$25,000	$25,000	$50,000	$425,581	$125,000	$5,000
2014	$25,000	$25,000	$50,000	$541,211	$150,000	$6,000

Referring to the table above, it can be seen that had an investor adopted this strategy, this investor would have had a portfolio valued at $541,211 by the end of 2014. After only six years, this investor would have had a portfolio of investments valued at over half a million dollars. Furthermore, this investor would have only invested $150,000 in employment income to achieve this ($25,000 a year for six years).

It should be noted that the S&P 500 exhibited larger than average returns in the years following the 2008 financial crisis. The average growth rate in the years shown above (2009-2014), including dividends, was roughly 18% per year. However, even though these growth rates were higher than the S&P 500's long-term average, they were not uncommon for the years that follow large drops in the stock market of greater than 20%.

Even if this investor had stopped using leverage at the end of 2014 and paid back the $150,000 in debt, he or she would still be left with a portfolio valued at close to $400,000 (assuming all interest expenses had been paid along the way). And while the interest expenses involved in holding this debt might appear expensive at first glance, this investor would have been helped out by the fact that these interest expenses, more than likely, would have been tax-deductible.

Many times, investors are able to claim the interest expense on money borrowed to invest as a tax deduction when they file their income taxes (see chapter 10). Therefore, assuming this investor was in a 40% tax bracket (not uncommon for Canada), the interest on his or her debt would have only amounted to 60% of the $21,000 in total interest expenses.

This works out to roughly $12,600 in total and averages out to $2,100 a year. When you think about the fact that this investor only contributed $150,000 towards a portfolio that is now worth close to $400,000, $12,600 in interest expenses doesn't seem all that bad.

Leverage and Taxes

Besides the obvious reason of borrowing to invest when one can get a rate of return that is higher than the cost of borrowing, the CEOs of many companies also have a tax incentive to borrow money to invest.

Generally speaking, many companies are able to claim a tax deduction on the interest expenses they realize when they borrow money to invest. This tax deduction means that many companies are able to reduce their borrowing costs below the interest rate they are actually charged. Just like large corporations, individual investors are able to do the same.

At the time of writing this book, **individual investors in the U.S. and Canada are, under certain conditions, able to claim their interest expense as a tax deduction on any money borrowed to invest.** This tax deduction can result in substantial savings on interest expenses, especially if the investor is in a high tax bracket.

Assuming you are in a 40% tax bracket (again, something not uncommon in Canada), and you borrow money to invest in the stock market at an interest rate of 5%, your true cost of borrowing, after you claim your tax deduction, is only 3%.

Furthermore, even if investments are purchased with borrowed money, Canadian residents still receive the dividend tax credit and still pay only half of their marginal tax rate on all their capital gains (see chapter 10).

U.S. residents, however, are not allowed to claim the reduced tax rates on dividends or capital gains when investments are purchased with borrowed money (see chapter 10).

Always consult a tax specialist before you borrow any money to invest, and always be sure you comply with all the necessary rules that will enable you to claim your interest as a tax deduction.

Key Success Factors for Leverage

We have already established that borrowing money to invest makes sense if you believe you can earn a higher return on your investments than the cost of borrowing. We have also established that borrowing to invest in the stock market can be less risky than some of the other more common reasons people borrow money to invest, such as buying an investment property or starting their own business. As well, we have demonstrated that if you intend to seek out higher returns than what the stock market traditionally has to offer, then borrowing to invest in a well-diversified portfolio of less risky stocks is, very likely, a better option than not borrowing to invest and simply going after a higher return by purchasing more risky stocks.

However, even though all of this may be true, you still need to follow a disciplined plan when you adopt a strategy involving leverage. The last thing you want to do is to be reckless. Leverage requires discipline, patience, and an ability to control your emotions.

With this in mind, let's finish the chapter by listing some of the key success factors required for using leverage.

<u>Key Success Factors for Leverage</u>

- Get some investing experience and have a well thought-out investment strategy.
- Don't borrow more than you can afford to lose.
- Make sure you can cover the interest expense on the debt.
- Diversify your investments.
- Invest for the long-term.
- Consider investing after a large drop in the stock market, when stocks are beaten down, interest rates are low, and dividend yields are high.
- Pay attention to taxes.

Get Some Investing Experience and Have a Well Thought-Out Investment Strategy

Louis Pasteur, the brilliant scientist who, among other things, brought the world pasteurization and created the first vaccines for rabies and anthrax, once said, "Chance favors the prepared mind." He is absolutely correct. You can only successfully take advantage of an opportunity if you are prepared.

"Chance favors the prepared mind."

- Louis Pasteur

With regards to your financial freedom fund, if you have taken the time to build your investment knowledge and you have gained some investing experience using a proven strategy, you will be far better prepared to use leverage when the chance presents itself.

If you do not have much investment knowledge or experience investing in the stock market, you may want to refrain from using leverage until you are more confident in your investing abilities.

Ideally, you want to be able to build a properly diversified portfolio of good companies and not be prone to fits of anxiety, fear, or greed. All of these emotions can cause irrational decisions. As previously discussed, these types of irrational decisions will only magnify losses once leverage enters the equation.

My wife and I had accumulated more than a few years of investing experience before we used any leverage. When we did eventually use a strategy involving leverage, we were confident in our investing strategy and we were used to the fact that our investments sometimes went up and sometimes went down. We were also used to the fact that our investments could drop by thousands of dollars on any given day. We were comfortable with this fact because we knew we had chosen good companies and we knew that our investments would eventually recover in price.

Without having this previous investing experience, I'm not sure we would have been confident enough in our strategy or disciplined enough to stay invested when we started using leverage and initially suffered a large drop in the value of our portfolio.

If you want to use leverage, make sure that you have an investment strategy and make sure you have some investment experience.

Don't Borrow More Than You Can Afford to Lose

If you are going to model yourself after many of the CEOs of large, successful companies, you are going to want to make sure you don't get yourself into trouble by borrowing more than you can afford to lose.

Remember, most large, successful companies borrow around 30% of their total assets, they don't borrow 100%. One of the keys to using leverage is to never borrow so much that if you encounter a short-term drop in your investments, you are forced to sell.

The best strategy is to buy investments that you want to hold and live off of forever. If you are ever forced to sell your investments at a loss, before they can recover in price, you will end up putting a big dent in your financial freedom fund.

As previously discussed, a good rule of thumb is to make sure your portfolio can withstand a 50% loss in its value without the need to sell any of your investments. If you can withstand this type of loss without the need to liquidate any of your investments, and you are confident that you are able to remain invested for the long-term, you have probably not borrowed more than you can afford to lose.

If, however, you can't withstand a 50% loss, or for any reason you think you may be forced to liquidate some of your investments in the near future, then you may be borrowing too much.

Make Sure You Are Able to Cover the Interest Expense on the Debt

If you have leveraged yourself so much that you are having trouble covering the interest expense on the money you borrowed to invest, you are asking for trouble.

Not being able to make the required interest payment on your debt is a good sign that you might end up having to sell some of your investments before you would like. It is also a good sign that you should deleverage yourself to a level where you can make these interest payments.

A good way to ensure you can cover the interest expense on your debt is to buy quality investments that pay a dividend large enough to cover these expenses. However, even though this would ensure you could make the interest payments, the best case scenario would be to cover these interest payments through employment income alone. That way, you would be able to reinvest the dividends you receive and buy even more investments. You would be able to harness the power of leverage, compounding, and dollar-cost averaging, all in one fell swoop (see chapter 8).

Diversify Your Investments

If using your hard earned money to buy only one or two investments is a bad idea, then *borrowing* money and using it to buy only one or two investments is a downright awful idea.

All companies face risk. If something terrible happens to one of the companies in your financial freedom fund (remember the Enron story) and you only own two companies, then something terrible happens to half of your financial freedom fund. If you used leverage to buy these two companies, given the fact that leverage magnifies losses, something terrible has happened to your entire financial freedom fund.

In contrast, if you own twenty companies and something terrible happens to one of these companies, you might not even notice a loss. Ronald Reed, the $8 million janitor mentioned in chapter 8, owned shares in the now defunct bank Lehman Brothers. But because his portfolio was well diversified and he owned many good companies, it barely put a dent in his overall wealth.

Invest for the Long-Term

Remember; over the short-term stock markets have gone up and stock markets have gone down, but over the long-term they have eventually always gone up.

If you have invested in good companies that continue to increase their earnings and dividends every year, then the worst thing you could do after leveraging yourself would be to sell these companies if they suffer a temporary decrease in price. If these companies are still the same great companies they were when you bought them, stick with them and stick with your investment plan.

I realize that this might be easier said than done, especially when the stock market is falling. I can remember, all too well, the feelings my wife and I had after initially leveraging ourselves and suffering a large drop in the value of our stocks. However, we stuck with our strategy, bought more stocks, and ended up being better for it.

Investing in the stock market involves discipline and patience. Your first goal is to pick a proven long-term strategy, diversify, and make your investments. After that, your next order of business is to prevent yourself from letting fear, greed, and irrational behaviour, sabotage your returns.

Consider Using Leverage After a Large Drop in the Stock Market

One strategy for borrowing to invest in the stock market is to only consider using leverage after the stock market experiences a large drop.

As previously stated, large stock market drops of over 20% typically result in undervalued stocks, lower interest rates, and higher yields. All of these circumstances favour the use of leverage.

Moreover, even though I think that timing the market is difficult, I do believe that large market selloffs often result in undervalued companies and good buying opportunities.

Furthermore, if you were to leverage yourself with smaller periodic investments over a period of months, as opposed to leveraging yourself with one giant lump sum all at once, you could reduce your chances of a large initial loss even more (see chapter 8).

Contrast a strategy that uses leverage after a large market drop and enters the market with smaller periodic investments, to a strategy that uses leverage when stocks are trading at all-time highs and involves investing a large lump sum all at once, and it's easy to see how the former strategy would provide more peace of mind.

If stock markets have experienced large losses, interest rates are low, and dividend yields on quality stocks are high, then consider using leverage and getting into the market a little bit at a time. If stock markets are soaring, interest rates are high, and dividend yields are low, consider deleveraging.

If it's not a good time to use leverage in the stock market, perhaps an opportunity exists in the real estate market. If there are no opportunities to use leverage in the stock market or the real estate market, you will need to be patient. Focus instead on cutting costs, saving and investing, and building core competencies. That way, when an opportunity to use a strategy involving leverage presents itself, you will be in a better position to take advantage of it.

Pay Attention to Taxes

Investors would be wise to always pay close attention to the tax implications of all their investment decisions. However, this is especially true when adopting a strategy involving leverage.

If you are going to borrow money to invest, be sure that you follow all the rules necessary to make your interest payments tax-deductible. Depending on how much money you borrow, this could result in tens of thousands of dollars in savings.

On that note, let's move onto the next chapter and learn some more about taxes. More specifically, let's learn how you can save as much as possible on your taxes and get all those tax savings working for you. Before we leave this chapter, however, let's take a closer look at legendary investor Warren Buffett and examine one of the reasons his company, Berkshire Hathaway, has been so successful.

How Does Buffett Generate Such High Returns?

In February 2015, Berkshire Hathaway released its 2014 Annual report. The eagerly anticipated report marked Berkshire's 50 year anniversary and came complete with a gold cover to signify the event. In this report, the company summarized its performance over the last 50 years under the management of its CEO, Warren Buffett. So how did the company do?

According to its 2014 annual report, Berkshire managed to increase its stock price over the last half-century by 1,826,163 percent. This is equivalent to a compound annual gain of 21.6 percent. This compares to an overall return of 11,196% or compound annual gain of 9.9% for the S&P 500 (dividends included), over the same time frame.

Looking at these results, it is obvious that Berkshire's return over the last 50 years has exceeded that of the S&P 500 by mind-blowing proportions. To put this performance in perspective, a $10,000 investment in Berkshire

Hathaway in 1964, when Berkshire was first created, would have resulted in $180 million, fifty years later. A $10,000 investment in the S&P 500, over the same timeframe, would have resulted in only $1.1 million. How could Berkshire beat the market by such a staggering amount?

A 2012 paper titled "Buffett's Alpha," written by Andrea Frazzini, David Kabiller, and Lasse Pedersen, might have the answer. According to this paper, at least part of the reason for Berkshire's stellar performance is because of the company's use of leverage.

In fact, Frazzini, Kabiller, and Pedersen, highlight in their paper the fact that Berkshire Hathaway, on average, leveraged its capital by 60% between 1989 and 2009. Their conclusions were that this leverage significantly boosted the company's total return. Furthermore, the authors make the claim that it is the use of leverage combined with a focus on cheap, safe, quality stocks that is the secret to Buffett's success.

Take a page out of Warren Buffett's playbook. Buy quality stocks that are undervalued, and if it makes sense, consider going after higher returns by employing a strategy using leverage.

KEY POINTS FROM CHAPTER NINE

- Consider borrowing money to increase your wealth. Do not borrow money to buy money sucking maggots.

- If you use leverage to invest in the stock market, be sure that you understand all the risks involved and that you manage these risks appropriately.

- The best time to use leverage in the stock market is when interest rates are low, dividend payouts on good companies are high, and stocks are undervalued.

- When borrowing money to invest in the stock market, make sure you act as an investor and not as a speculator.

- If you use a margin account, do not overleverage yourself. Plan to never have to worry about getting a margin call.

- According to MPT, leveraging yourself to buy a properly diversified portfolio offers a better risk-adjusted return than simply buying riskier investments.

- Leverage is not for the faint of heart. It requires discipline, patience, and an ability to control your emotions.

- Under certain circumstances, investors are able to claim their interest expense as a tax deduction on money borrowed to invest.

- Get some investing experience and have a well thought-out investment strategy before attempting to use leverage in the stock market.

- Don't borrow more than you can afford to lose.

- Make sure you can cover the interest expense on the debt.

- Make sure you are well diversified and invest for the long-term.

CHAPTER TEN

Taxes

I hadn't felt this alive for as long as I could remember. It was a cool summer day in July 2012, and I was about to land an airplane.

"Cleared to land, runway one-nine," said the control tower.

My heart pounded with nervous excitement. It was the first time I had been all alone in an airplane and, after months of lessons, I was about to land the little airplane I was now sitting in all by myself.

I maneuvered the small airplane into one last turn and lined it up with the narrow runway ahead of me. I focused on keeping my landing spot fixed in my windshield and double checked my speed. The runway threshold was now getting to be so big in my windshield that I knew it was time to fix my eyes at the end of the runway, level out, and get ready for the touchdown. I focused at the end of the runway and concentrated on keeping the airplane over the centerline. At the same time, I slowly powered all the way back to idle. Using my peripheral vision, I could see the ground coming up quickly. I gently pulled back on the control column to slightly raise the nose. The single-engine airplane gently touched down on the main landing gear and I immediately started breaking so that I wouldn't use up any more of the very short runway I had just landed on. I had just landed an airplane and it felt absolutely amazing.

It had been four years since the financial crisis, and seven years since we had started our financial freedom fund. The disciplined saving, investing, and leverage, had all paid off. We were now financially free. We no longer had a mortgage on our primary residence, and we were now earning enough income in rent and from our investment portfolio that we no longer needed to work.

I had quit my job as a pharmaceutical sales representative in March 2012 and had enrolled as a student at a local flying school. I didn't *have* to work, but I *wanted* to.

I chose to pursue a career as a pilot. I was studying part-time, looking after our children part-time, and I was living the life I truly wanted. Going to school can be great, especially when you like what you're learning. And I loved it.

I also loved all the tax benefits we were getting. Becoming a pilot is an expensive endeavour; as a Canadian resident, however, a lot of my school expenses could be claimed as a tax credit.

Moreover, while I was going to school, I was also able to claim a tax deduction for our childcare costs. Last but not least, most of our dividend income was taxed at less than half the rate that our employment income had been taxed at. And if that wasn't enough, the interest on the money we had borrowed to invest was also eligible for a tax deduction.

Making use of all the tax advantages available to you is critical if you ever want to achieve any sort of financial freedom at a young age. In many cases, it could make the difference between retiring early and not retiring at all.

My wife and I have always taken advantage of every tax deduction, tax credit, tax-deferral, and tax-lowering strategy available to us. In the process, we have probably saved hundreds of thousands of dollars over the course of our lives.

Lower Your Taxes

Taxes can be complicated. Moreover, tax laws change all the time. This being the case, some of the strategies discussed below might not be applicable by the time you read this.

Before you adopt any of the strategies discussed below, make sure you verify that these strategies still make sense and that the tax laws surrounding these strategies have not changed. The best course of action would be to verify any tax strategy you are thinking of implementing with a tax professional before you adopt it. Even if this involves a little bit of work, it will be well worth the effort.

CEOs do everything in their power to lower the taxes their companies pay. They set up their businesses in locations that have low tax rates, they minimize their taxable income, they maximize their tax deductions and tax credits, and they control the timing of their income and deductions so that their taxes are kept to a minimum. They hire tax specialists and they hire smart accountants. In short, they make sure they legally reduce their tax bills as much as possible. You need to do the same.

In fact, the online newspaper *Business Insider* reported in 2013 that Apple avoids paying roughly $17 million dollars in taxes every day through various tax avoidance schemes. **Tax avoidance is the practice of reducing your taxes through legal methods. Tax evasion, in contrast, is the illegal evasion of taxes.**

One can argue whether or not some tax avoidance practices are morally right, but if it is tax avoidance, as opposed to tax evasion, then it is legally justifiable. I'm not sure anyone can be blamed for wanting to legally reduce their taxes, especially given the amount of taxes some of us pay each year.

One metric used to determine the amount of taxes the average family pays each year is *Tax Freedom Day*. Tax Freedom Day is measured every year in

Canada by the Fraser Institute. It is measured every year in the U.S. by the Tax Foundation.

Tax Freedom Day is the first day of the year that the average family has theoretically earned enough money to pay for all of its taxes for that year (assuming all income up until that point were to go towards paying their taxes for the year). The calculation includes local taxes, income taxes, payroll taxes, property taxes, sales taxes, and any other type of taxes paid.

In Canada, according to the Fraser Institute, the average family celebrated tax freedom day on June 7th, for the 2016 tax year. This means that if the average family in Canada had devoted every dollar they started earning as of Jan 1, 2016 towards paying their annual tax burden for the year, they would have only finished paying all of their taxes by June 7th, 2016. According to this calculation, **the average family in Canada is paying approximately 43% of their annual income in taxes.**

In the United States, according to the Tax Foundation, Tax Freedom Day occurred on April 24, for the 2016 tax year. Even though this is a little better than Canada, it still means that **the average family in the United States is paying roughly 31% of its income in taxes.**

Just like the CEOs of successful companies, you need to do as much as you can to minimize your taxes through legal methods.

Do not lie to the taxman, and do not commit tax evasion. Despite the obvious fact that this is immoral, the consequences of such behaviour could be severely detrimental to your financial freedom fund and, even worse, could land you in jail.

<u>**To Legally Minimize Your Taxes You Need to Consider All of the Following:**</u>

- The best place to live and work.
- How to minimize taxable income.
- How to maximize tax credits and tax deductions.
- How to best control the timing of income and deductions.

Where to Live and Work

One of the biggest factors CEOs take into consideration, when deciding where to set up their business, is their tax burden.

For example, it isn't just coincidence that Google and many other large corporations have their European headquarters located in Ireland and that Ireland has one of the lowest corporate tax rates in all of Europe.

If you have the ability to live and work in many different places, taking tax rates into consideration wouldn't be a bad idea. It's amazing how different some tax rates can be, even among different cities in the same country.

Obviously, tax rates are not the only thing worth considering when debating a move. Quality of life, cost of living, and employment opportunities (just to name a few), would also all play into the decision.

Nonetheless, let's assume you are able to choose where you can live and work and look at how this decision could affect your finances from a tax point of view.

Let's assume you have the choice of living in the fictional locations of either City A or City B. Let's also assume that you could get a job earning you roughly $60,000 a year in either of these two cities. With this in mind, let's compare the income tax burden of living in either of these two fictional cities and determine how this might affect your financial freedom fund.

The table below shows the total income tax burden on $60,000 of employment income in both City A and City B.

Income Tax Burden for a Single Person in Two Fictional Cities

Employment Income	City A	City B
$60,000	$14,841	$19,004

Looking at the table above, it can be seen that if you earned $60,000 and lived in City B, your total income tax bill would be approximately $19,004. However, if you earned $60,000 and lived in City A, your total income tax bill would be only $14,841. It would, therefore, cost you an additional $4,163 dollars in income taxes (close to 30% more) to live in City B versus City A.

Now let's see what these savings could mean to your financial freedom fund, assuming both you and your significant other were to live in City A instead of City B and were to invest your combined savings of $8,326 into a tax-free retirement savings account (discussed below), starting at the age of twenty-five years-old. The results of this analysis are displayed in the graph at the top of the next page.

Growth of Tax Free Savings Account

(Assumes $8,326 contribution per year and 7% CAGR)

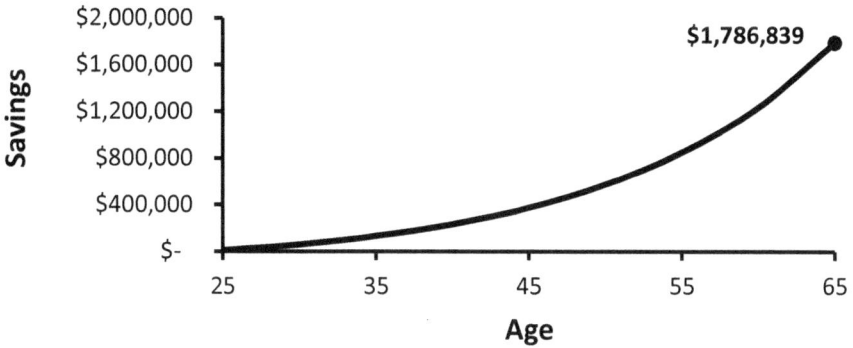

The results of this analysis are shocking. If you and your significant other were to live in City A instead of City B and do nothing else but invest the income tax savings you both realized into a tax-free retirement savings account, by the time you reached the age of 65, you and your significant other would have accumulated a combined total of close to $1.8 million (assumes a CAGR of 7%).

This simple analysis is a powerful incentive to act like the CEOs of large, successful companies and, if possible, move to a location that offers a lower tax burden.

Furthermore, the above analysis once again demonstrates how cutting costs and making periodic investments into your financial freedom fund, whether it is through moving to a location with lower taxes or by living more frugally, can result in great wealth.

Minimize Taxable Income

Besides moving to a location that offers lower taxes, good CEOs also focus on minimizing their company's taxable income. This doesn't mean that they minimize their company's total income; it means they minimize their company's *taxable* income.

Minimizing taxable income is all about finding ways to avoid paying taxes on part of your total income. How are the CEOs of large, successful companies able to do this? They do this by taking advantage of government incentives that allow certain investments to be made tax-free or allow certain investments to defer tax. You need to do the same.

For many individuals, **the most powerful way to minimize taxable income is to invest in tax-advantaged retirement savings accounts.**

In Canada, these tax-advantaged retirement savings accounts are usually registered retirement saving plans (RRSPs) and tax-free savings accounts (TFSAs).

In the United States, the most common tax-advantaged retirement savings accounts are 401(k)s, Roth 401(k)s, individual retirement accounts (IRAs), and Roth IRAs.

It almost always makes sense to maximize your investments in these types of tax-advantaged retirement savings plans before investing outside of these plans. Moreover, if you are lucky enough to work for an employer who will match your contributions to one of these retirement plans, then you absolutely need to take advantage of this. Not doing so is saying no to free money!

In the U.S. and Canada, broadly speaking, tax-advantaged retirement savings accounts can be divided into two different groups:

Types of Tax-Advantaged Retirement Savings Accounts:

- Tax-*deferred* retirement savings accounts.
- Tax-*free* retirement savings accounts.

Let's take a closer look at these two different types of accounts right now, starting with tax-deferred retirement savings accounts.

Tax-Deferred Retirement Savings Accounts

Tax-deferred retirement savings accounts allow their owners to defer the income tax owed on all their contributions to these plans until these contributions get withdrawn at a later date. Furthermore, they allow these contributions to grow tax-free until they are withdrawn. Income tax is, nonetheless, due upon withdrawal.

In Canada, the most common type of tax-deferred retirement savings account is an RRSP. In the U.S., the most common type of tax-deferred retirement savings accounts are 401(k)s and IRAs.

A big advantage of tax-deferred retirement savings accounts is that you have the opportunity to invest the tax savings you realize by making the contribution in the first place, (assuming you are disciplined enough to not spend these tax savings).

For example, if you are in a 30% tax bracket and invest $10,000 into a tax-deferred retirement savings account, you can get all of this $10,000 working for you. If you invest this $10,000 outside of a tax-deferred retirement savings account, then, at some point during the year, the taxman will take $3,000 of this $10,000 in the form of income taxes. This means, no matter how you slice it, if you keep this $10,000 outside of the tax-deferred retirement savings account, you will wind up with $3,000 less to invest.

The benefit of investing the tax savings you receive by making contributions to any tax-deferred retirement savings account, along with the benefit of the tax-free growth realized inside these types of accounts, cannot be overstated.

To illustrate how powerful these tax-deferred retirement savings accounts can be, let's look at the growth in savings realized by two investors, both in a 30% tax bracket and both with $10,000 left over to invest each year (before taxes).

We will assume that both investors have $10,000 left over to invest each year for the duration of their working lives (age 25-65). We will also assume that these investors disagree on the effectiveness of tax-deferred retirement savings accounts.

One investor chooses to invest all of his or her money inside a tax-deferred retirement savings account, while the other investor chooses to invest all of his or her money outside a tax-deferred retirement savings account. Finally, let's also assume that all investments realize a CAGR of 7% and that returns get taxed as income when these returns are made outside of a tax-deferred retirement savings account.

The results of this analysis are illustrated in the graph at the top of the next page. The investor that invests all of his or her money inside a tax-deferred retirement savings account, starting at age twenty-five, can expect to have roughly 2.1 million inside of his or her savings account by the time he or she reaches the age of sixty-five. By contrast, the investor that invests all of his or her money outside of a tax-deferred retirement saving account can expect to have only about $873,000 in his or her savings account by the time he or she reaches age sixty-five.

The Power of Tax Deferred Compound Growth
($10,000 contribution per year, 7% CAGR, and 30% tax bracket)

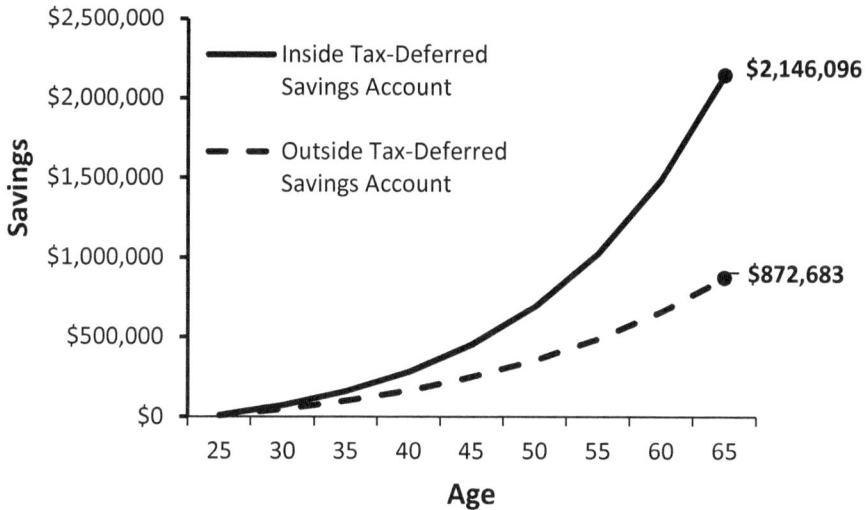

Of course, the $2.1 million inside the tax-deferred retirement savings account will owe taxes when it is withdrawn. This is the reason these types of accounts are called *tax-deferred* savings accounts. The tax is deferred until the money is withdrawn from the account. Nonetheless, if the money is withdrawn a little at a time and the investor remains in the same 30% tax bracket, then this investor will still end up significantly ahead.

The table at the bottom of the next page shows the total amount in savings, in five year intervals, for the investments made in the example above. This table shows the total savings for the tax-deferred retirement savings account before and after the funds are withdrawn and compares these savings to the savings accumulated outside of a tax-deferred retirement savings account. This analysis does not include penalties that might be incurred as a result of an early withdrawal.

Once again, this analysis assumes that taxes are due every year on the gains made outside the tax-deferred retirement savings account and that these gains get taxed as ordinary income. It also assumes that income taxes are due on the original sum invested. Therefore, an investor in a 30% tax bracket with $10,000 left over to invest before taxes, really only has $7,000 left over to invest when this investment is made outside of a tax-deferred retirement savings account.

In contrast, no initial taxes are due on any of the funds contributed to a tax-deferred retirement savings account, and all the gains inside a tax-deferred retirement savings account are allowed to compound tax-free. As previously mentioned, funds in a tax-deferred retirement savings account are only taxed upon withdrawal.

The Power of Tax-Deferred Compound Growth

(Assumes $10,000 contribution per year, 7% CAGR, and 30% tax bracket)

Age	Before Withdrawn from Tax-Deferred Savings Account	After Withdrawn from Tax-Deferred Savings Account	Ordinary Savings Account
25	$10,000	$7,000	$7,000
30	$71,533	$50,073	$47,494
35	$157,836	$110,485	$98,930
40	$278,881	$195,216	$164,264
45	$448,652	$314,056	$247,253
50	$686,765	$480,735	$352,667
55	$1,020,730	$714,511	$486,565
60	$1,489,135	$1,042,394	$656,645
65	$2,146,096	$1,502,267	$872,683

The table at the bottom of the previous page shows that by the time both investors reach sixty-five years-old, the investor who invested all of his or her money inside the tax-deferred retirement savings account will end up with roughly $1.5 million (assuming savings are withdrawn to maintain a 30% tax rate). The investor who invested all of his or her savings outside the tax-deferred savings account, however, will only end up with about $870,000. As well, notice that the longer the money stays inside the tax-deferred retirement saving account, the greater the advantage.

Besides the disadvantage of losing out on tax-free compounding, early withdrawals from tax-deferred retirement savings accounts could also lead to penalties (penalties are not included in this table).

Let's move on from tax-deferred retirement savings accounts to tax-free retirement savings accounts and consider the merits of these types of tax-advantaged accounts as well.

Tax-Free Retirement Savings Accounts

Unlike tax-deferred retirement savings accounts, tax-free retirement savings accounts do not save their contributors any taxes on their initial contributions. They do, however, offer other tax advantages.

Even though income taxes are still owed on the initial contributions made to tax-free retirement savings accounts, once these contributions are inside the tax-free retirement savings account they not only get to grow tax-free, they also get to be withdrawn tax-free as well.

Just like tax-deferred retirement savings accounts, tax-free retirement savings accounts are powerful savings vehicles that should be taken full advantage of.

In Canada, the most common type of tax-free retirement savings account is a TFSA.

In the U.S., the most common types of tax-free retirement savings accounts are Roth 401(k)s and Roth IRAs.

The table below shows the amount of savings realized after making a series of investments each year, over the course of an individual's working life (age 25-65), either inside a tax-free retirement savings account or outside of a tax-free retirement savings account. The table assumes an investor has $10,000 left over to invest each year (before taxes).

Furthermore, the table also compares the resultant savings in five year intervals. We will again assume a marginal tax rate of 30%, a CAGR of 7%, and that investment gains made outside of the tax-free retirement savings account get taxed as ordinary income each year.

The Power of Tax-Free Compound Growth

(Assumes $10,000 contribution per year, 7% CAGR, and 30% tax bracket)

Age	Before Withdrawn from Tax-Free Savings Account	After Withdrawn from Tax-Free Savings Account	Ordinary Savings Account
25	$7,000	$7,000	$7,000
30	$50,073	$50,073	$47,494
35	$110,485	$110,485	$98,930
40	$195,216	$195,216	$164,264
45	$314,056	$314,056	$247,253
50	$480,735	$480,735	$352,667
55	$714,511	$714,511	$486,565
60	$1,042,394	$1,042,394	$656,645
65	$1,502,267	$1,502,267	$872,683

Given you still owe income taxes on any initial contributions, if you have $10,000 of earned income to invest each year (before taxes), it really only amounts to $7,000 after we account for the $3,000 in taxes (30% of $10,000). The benefit of the tax-free retirement savings account, however, is that no taxes are due on any gains or on any withdrawals.

This being the case, your total savings are identical - both before and after you withdraw them from the tax-free retirement savings account. Referring to the table above, it can also be seen that the amounts withdrawn from the tax-*free* retirement savings account at the various time intervals are identical to the amounts withdrawn from the tax-*deferred* retirement savings account at the same time intervals.

This relationship holds true as long as the marginal tax rates stay the same for both types of tax-advantaged retirement savings accounts, both when contributions are made and when funds are withdrawn.

Just like the tax-deferred retirement savings account, the tax-free retirement savings account results in roughly $1,500,000 in savings by the time you reach age sixty-five, while the account with no tax advantages results in only $872,683.

Tax-Deferred Savings Account or Tax-Free Savings Account?

You should try to maximize your contributions to every tax-advantaged retirement savings account you can. However, if you can only choose one, which tax-advantaged retirement savings account is the better option, a tax-deferred savings account or a tax-free savings account?

One way to answer this question would be to determine what you think your tax rate will be when you eventually withdraw your money from either type of account. If you expect your future tax rate to be lower than the tax rate you face at the time of the initial contribution, you might be better off with a tax-deferred retirement savings account. This is because a tax-deferred retirement savings account would allow you to defer paying taxes at a higher tax rate and allow you to pay them at a lower rate later on.

If, however, you expect your future tax rate will be higher than your current tax rate, chances are, you are better off with a tax-free retirement savings account. With a tax-free retirement savings account, you would pay a lower tax rate upfront and be able to save on paying a higher tax rate later on.

Unfortunately, as David Chilton points out in *The Wealthy Barber Returns*, it's not quite that simple. The other thing to consider when you compare these two types of accounts is whether or not you have the discipline to invest the initial tax savings you generate, should you choose to go with the tax-deferred retirement savings account.

If you have a certain fixed sum of money in your bank account, let's say $5,000, and you choose to invest your money in a tax-deferred retirement savings account instead of a tax-free retirement savings account, but you don't invest the tax refund, you would have probably been better off sticking that $5,000 in the tax-free retirement savings account.

Think about it. If you invest $5,000 into a tax-deferred retirement savings account (and don't invest the initial tax savings) and you invest $5,000 into a tax-free retirement savings account, and both types of account generate the same return, then many years later you'll have a large identical sum in both of these accounts. The tax-deferred retirement savings account, however, will owe a whole whack of taxes, while the tax-free retirement savings account won't!

If you have a fixed sum of after tax dollars available to invest, the only way to make sure the tax-deferred retirement savings account can compete with the tax-free retirement savings account is to also invest the tax-savings your contributions to the tax-deferred retirement savings account generate in the first place.

Additional Benefits of TFSAs (Residents of Canada Only)

In Canada, TFSAs also offer the additional benefit of allowing their owners to withdraw their money from these types of retirement savings accounts at any time without taxes or penalties. Moreover, you are also allowed to put this money back into the TFSA at a later date. RRSPs do not offer either of these benefits.

As well, in Canada, investing in TFSAs could also reduce the chances of clawbacks in your retirement years. Depending on their income, Canadian seniors sometimes see clawbacks of their guaranteed income supplement, old age security pension, and age amount tax credit.

As opposed to the income withdrawn from RRSPs, the income withdrawn from TFSAs does not count towards determining these clawbacks.

Income Splitting (Residents of Canada)

If you are a resident of the United States, you are already able to take advantage of splitting income with your spouse. You are able to achieve this by filing a joint tax return. If you are a resident of Canada, however, you don't have this option.

Income splitting is a strategy that involves shifting income away from a spouse in a higher tax bracket to a spouse in a lower tax bracket. In the U.S., couples can elect to combine their income and file a single joint tax return. This allows U.S. couples to split their income.

In Canada, however, no such election is possible. Furthermore, Canada has rules that are designed to prevent couples from saving taxes by shifting income between themselves (*attribution rules*). **Despite the attribution rules, Canadians can still take advantage of a number of legitimate tax-planning strategies to effectively redistribute income in a family unit.**

The simplest way to split income with a spouse would be to contribute to a spousal RRSP so that you and your spouse can have similar income levels once you are financially free.

If you are over sixty-five years-old, the Canadian government, at the time of writing this, allows you to split most pension income with your spouse. If you want to retire much earlier, however, you might be out of luck. If you are under sixty-five years of age, eligible pension income available for income splitting purposes only appears to include lifetime annuity payments under a registered pension plan (RPP).

Consider a scenario where a couple have both reached the age of fifty years-old. One spouse has accumulated RRSP savings of $1.5 million dollars, while the other spouse, however, has no retirement savings at all. If this couple chooses to retire early and withdraw 5% of the $1.5 million each year, then $75,000 would be taxed each year in the hands of just one spouse.

Assuming the couple lived in Ontario, this would result in roughly $15,850 a year in taxes. This would reduce the amount of income that the couple had to live off of to approximately $59,150.

If, however, the couple were able to split this $75,000 in income or had tax-deferred retirement savings accounts of $750,000 each, then the total tax they owed each year would drop to only $10,600 ($5,300 each). The couple would be able to save $5,250 a year in taxes by splitting their income. Over the course of 15 years, this would result in tax savings of approximately $78,750.

This example highlights the importance of Canadians trying to split as much income as possible during their working years and planning to split as much income as possible once they are financially free, especially if they plan to retire before the age of sixty-five.

If all your savings are in tax-free savings accounts (TFSAs), you wouldn't have to worry about splitting income. TFSAs pay no tax when the money is withdrawn. Therefore, if all your savings are in TFSAs, no tax is owed at all.

Another advantage of TFSAs is that one spouse can contribute to another spouse's TFSA and not have to worry about the attribution rules. Because all money in a TFSA grows tax-free and can be withdrawn tax-free, there would be no tax to attribute back.

Besides spousal RRSPs, other opportunities also exist to split income, especially if you own your own business. I will leave it to you to investigate these opportunities on your own. Be aware, however, that depending on the situation and the difference in marginal tax brackets between spouses, some Canadians may be able to save thousands of dollars by taking advantage of some of the legitimate income splitting techniques available to them.

Saving for Your Children's Education

As I write this, I have received close to $10,000 in free money from the Canadian government to help save for my two children's post-secondary education. What's more, my children are still only six and eight years-old. I will be able to receive thousands more in free government money to help with their education in the years to come.

Education is expensive, and it only gets more expensive every year. **If the government is willing to help you save for your children's education, take advantage of it.**

In Canada, you should explore the benefits of registered education savings plans (RESPs).

In the U.S., you should explore the benefits of 529 Savings Plans and Coverdell Education Savings Accounts.

Many of the tax-advantaged savings accounts that are designed to help save for a child's education do not offer an immediate tax-deferral on contributions. They do, however, usually allow contributions to grow tax-free.

Moreover, other advantages, such as matching of contributions, can also exist. It goes without saying that whenever you can get free money to save for your child's education, you should do all you can to take advantage of it.

In Canada, as I write this, each child is able to get up to $500 a year from the Canada Education Savings Grant (CESG) when you open up a registered education savings plan (RESP). The basic CESG provides 20 cents on every dollar you contribute, up to a maximum of $500 on an annual contribution of $2,500. The maximum lifetime grant (for 2016) the Government of Canada can give your child through the CESG is $7,200.

On top of the CESG, many provinces in Canada also provide grants to help save for a child's education. Provinces like Saskatchewan, Alberta, and British Columbia, all offer additional educational savings grants.

In the U.S., some states will match up to a certain amount of the contributions made to 529 Savings Plans. This matching is often dependent on total family income. As well, many states will also provide state income tax deductions on all or part of the contributions.

In the U.S., qualified withdrawals from these types of education savings plans are usually tax-free.

In Canada, qualified withdrawals usually get taxed in the hands of the beneficiary. Assuming the beneficiary is going to school, these contributions will, more than likely, get taxed at a much lower rate than the rate that would have been required by the individuals making the contributions.

Be sure to pay close attention to the rules outlined in any education savings plan. If the funds in these savings plans don't get used according to the rules outlined in the plans, or the child named in the plan chooses not to pursue higher education, the funds will likely be subject to further taxes and possibly penalties.

Given the large differences in employment income that accompany higher levels of education (see chapter 3), it makes sense to do all you can to encourage your children to aspire to higher education and to help them attain it.

Consider the Tax Advantages of Dividend Paying Stocks

If you have been a diligent saver and have saved so much that you have maxed out your contributions to all the tax-advantaged retirement savings accounts available to you, give yourself a pat on the back. Not many people are able to accomplish this level of saving and investing.

Next, for all the additional investments made outside of your tax-advantaged retirement savings accounts, consider the tax advantages of investments that pay dividends and the tax advantages of investments that lead to capital gains.

Generally speaking, there are three types of investment income, and each type of investment income can get taxed differently.

Types of Investment Income

1. Income from interest payments.
2. Income from dividend payments.
3. Income from capital gains.

Interest income is typically received from bonds, savings accounts, and other forms of fixed income securities. It is usually taxed at your marginal tax rate in the same way that your employment income is taxed. There are, however, sometimes exceptions to this rule. For example, at the time of writing this, municipal bonds in the U.S. are usually free from U.S. federal income taxes.

Dividend income, as previously discussed, is normally given out to the owners of a company's common or preferred shares. Unlike interest income, dividend income can sometimes get taxed at a lower tax rate compared to normal employment income or interest income.

In the U.S., at the time of writing this, dividends typically qualify for a lower than ordinary tax rate if they are received from U.S. corporations and they meet the holding period requirements.

In Canada, eligible dividends received from Canadian corporations also get preferential tax treatment.

Dividends received from foreign corporations, more often than not, do not receive any type of preferential tax treatment in either Canada or the U.S.

The tax savings offered by dividend income, in both Canada and the U.S., can be substantial. At the time of writing this, it would be possible for an individual investor to earn up to $40,000 a year in eligible dividends and pay virtually no tax at all in many Canadian provinces, assuming this was that investor's only source of income.

In the U.S., again at the time of writing this, it would possible for an individual investor to earn up to $37,650 in qualified dividends or for a couple to earn up to $75,300 in qualified dividends and also pay virtually no federal tax at all on this dividend income. This scenario would again assume that these dividends were the only source of income.

Dividend tax savings are usually only available for investments made outside of any tax-advantaged retirement savings account. Moreover, the income distributed by REITs is typically not eligible for any type of dividend tax savings.

Consider the Tax Advantages of Capital Gains

A capital gain arises when an investor sells investments such as stocks, bonds, or real estate, for a profit. In contrast, a capital loss arises when an investor sells these investments at a loss.

For example, if you bought 100 shares of company xyz at a price of $10 per share, your initial investment would be $1,000. If you then sold your 100 shares of company xyz, a few years later, at a price of $15 per share, you would receive $1,500 from the sale of your shares and realize a capital gain of $500 ($1,500 - $1,000).

In contrast, if you had sold your 100 shares of xyz, a few years later, at a price of $9 per share, you would have received $900 from the sale of your shares and would have realized a capital loss of $100 ($900 - $1,000).

Just like dividends, capital gains that get realized outside of any tax-advantaged retirement savings account often get taxed at lower tax rates compared to either employment income or interest income. This is true for both Canada and the U.S.

In Canada, at the time of writing this, capital gains tax is only one-half the level of the normal marginal tax rate applied to employment income and interest income. Again, this is the tax rate that gets applied to capital gains realized outside of any tax-advantaged retirement savings accounts.

In the U.S., we need to distinguish between what the government considers a short-term capital gain and what the government considers a long-term capital gain. In the U.S., capital gains that result from the sale of investments that were held for less than one-year are classified as short-term capital gains. Short-term capital gains get taxed at an investor's ordinary income tax rate. Capital gains that result from the sale of investments that were held for greater than one year are classified as long-term capital gains. Long-term capital gains get taxed at a lower rate than an investor's ordinary income tax rate.

In the U.S., at the time of writing this, long-term capital gains tax is zero for the first two marginal tax brackets applied to ordinary income (10% and 15%). Long-term capital gains tax is approximately one-half the ordinary income tax rate for the remaining tax brackets. Once again, this is the capital gains tax that gets applied to investments outside of any tax-advantaged retirement savings accounts.

The tables shown on the following two pages show the 2016 marginal tax rates for different types of income in both the U.S. and Canada.

These tables highlight the tax advantages associated with receiving investment income in the form of qualified dividends and long-term capital gains in the US, and the tax advantages associated with receiving investment income in the form of eligible Canadian dividends and capital gains in Canada.

Notice again how one is able to earn up to $37,650 in qualified dividends and long-term capital gains in the U.S. and pay 0% in federal income tax (assuming this is an investor's only income).

As well, notice how one is able to earn up to $45,282 in eligible Canadian dividends as a resident of Ontario and pay no tax at all if this is an investor's only income.

Combined U.S. Tax Brackets and Tax Rates

2016 Single Taxable Income	Ordinary Income Tax Rate	Qualified Dividend Tax Rate	Long-term Capital Gains Tax Rate
$0 – $9,275	10%	0%	0%
$9,276 – $37,650	15%	0%	0%
$37,651 – $91,150	25%	15%	15%
$91,151 – $190,150	28%	15%	15%
$190,151 – $413,350	33%	15%	15%
$413,351 – $415,050	35%	15%	15%
$415,051+	40%	20%	20%

Combined Canada and Ontario Tax Brackets and Tax Rates

2016 Taxable Income	Other Income	Eligible Canadian Dividends	Capital Gains
first $41,536	20.05%	-6.86%	10.03%
over $41,536 up to $45,282	24.15%	-1.20%	12.08%
over $45,282 up to $73,145	29.65%	6.39%	14.83%
over $73,145 up to $83,075	31.48%	8.92%	15.74%
over $83,075 up to $86,176	33.89%	12.24%	16.95%
over $86,176 up to $90,563	37.91%	17.79%	18.95%
over $90,563 up to $140,388	43.41%	25.38%	21.70%
over $140,388 up to $150,000	46.41%	29.52%	23.20%
over $150,000 up to $200,000	47.97%	31.67%	23.98%
over $200,000 up to $220,000	51.97%	37.19%	25.98%
over $220,000	53.53%	39.34%	26.76%

Maximize Tax Credits and Tax Deductions

By taking advantage of tax credits and tax deductions, CEOs probably save large corporations billions of dollars each year.

Good CEOs make it a priority to know all the tax credits and tax deductions available to them. Whether it's a tax credit or a tax deduction, these CEOs use tax deductions and tax credits to lower their companies' taxes and to save their companies money. Then, they put these tax savings to work to earn these companies even more money. You need to do the same.

If you want to see more of your hard earned money devoted to your financial freedom fund and less of it given away to the tax man, you too need to **make it a priority to take advantage of all the tax credits and tax deductions available to you.**

I can't tell you how many people I've spoken to that have no idea about the dividend tax credit available to all Canadians. Many are also not aware of the fact that they are often able to claim a tax deduction on any money they borrow to invest. In addition, many people don't know the difference between a tax credit and a tax deduction.

The difference between a tax credit and a tax deduction is that a tax credit reduces your tax - dollar for dollar, while a tax deduction reduces your tax by your marginal tax rate.

This means a $1,000 tax credit saves you $1,000 in taxes. However, $1,000 in tax deductions doesn't save you $1,000 in taxes; it only lowers your taxable income by $1,000. If you are in a 25% tax bracket, for example, and your taxable income gets reduced by $1,000, then $1,000 in tax deductions saves you $250 in taxes. Tax credits and tax deductions can go a long way to saving you money. It's unfortunate that many people miss out on many of these savings.

In 2014, H&R Block ran an ad campaign in the U.S. claiming that U.S. taxpayers who do their own taxes end up leaving $1 billion in tax savings on the table. This is, presumably, because these taxpayers miss out on all the potential tax credits and tax deductions they are entitled to.

It is beyond the scope of this book to go into all the possible tax credits and tax deductions out there, but you should definitely spend some time ensuring you are aware of as many of these tax credits and tax deductions as possible. More importantly, make sure you claim all the ones you are entitled to.

To illustrate just how many tax credits and tax deductions are out there, take a look at the results of a google search querying tax credits and tax deductions pertaining to Canadians with children (queried in 2016).

Google Search Results for "Tax Credits and Tax Deductions for Canadians with Children"

1. Child tax credit.
2. Children's fitness credit.
3. Children's arts tax credit.
4. Child care deduction.
5. Universal child care benefit.
6. Canada child tax benefit.
7. National child benefit supplement.
8. Child disability benefit.
9. Adoption expenses.
10. Transit pass cost.
11. Tuition.
12. Education and textbook amount.
13. Student loan interest.

That's quite a list of tax credits and tax deductions, and we haven't even looked at the lists of credits or deductions related to healthcare, working, education, being a homeowner, or investing.

Even though we aren't going to cover all the tax credits and tax deductions that might be available to you, we will take a look at the tax deduction available for the interest charged on money borrowed to invest. If you plan on using leverage, this will certainly be an important one for you to know about.

Claim a Tax Deduction on the Interest Charged on Money Borrowed to Invest

Just like large corporations, individual investors in both the U.S. and Canada are able to receive a tax deduction on the interest charged on money borrowed to invest.

This tax deduction can be a powerful incentive, given the right circumstances, to use the power of leverage to grow your financial freedom fund.

Let's look at this tax deduction a little more closely and consider the following example of a well-paid professional who has relentlessly cut her costs, maxed out all her tax-advantaged retirement savings accounts, and is interested in investing more.

Let's assume this well-paid professional is a diligent saver. She has aggressively paid down her mortgage over the last five years and, as a result, has built up a large amount of equity in her home. She decides she will tap into this equity by taking advantage of a HELOC. Then she uses the proceeds of this line of credit to invest in the stock market. She does not squander the proceeds from her line of credit on money sucking maggots. She borrows in a low interest rate environment, invests for the long-term in good dividend paying companies, and ensures that she has not overleveraged herself.

If this well-paid professional is in a 40% tax bracket, she will receive 40% of her interest expenses back (in the form of tax savings). Not only that, if she is a resident of Canada and invests in Canadian dividend paying stocks, her investments will be eligible for the Canadian dividend tax credit. She claims this tax credit and pays a tax rate on her dividend income that is only one-half of the tax rate she pays on her employment income.

Cutting your borrowing costs by 40% and then using this borrowed money to generate dividend income that gets taxed far lower than your marginal tax rate is a powerful incentive to borrow money to invest, especially under the right circumstances (see chapter 9).

Sure there are times when borrowing to invest doesn't make sense, but a large tax deduction on money borrowed to invest, combined with low interest rates, can certainly make a strong case for it. If you can borrow money at 3.5% and get 40% of the interest expenses back in the form of tax savings, your cost of borrowing is really only 2.1%. This low cost, combined with a CAGR of 8% for the S&P 500 index over the last ten years (2004-2014), makes a good case for using a strategy involving leverage.

In fact, the higher your marginal tax bracket is, the more this strategy might make sense. If you are a higher earning Canadian, then you might be paying 50% or more of your earned income in income taxes alone.

With an income tax rate of 50%, even if your borrowing cost was 10%, it could still be profitable to borrow money to invest. If you are in a 50% tax bracket and the cost of borrowing money is 10%, your real borrowing cost is only 5% once you have claimed the tax deduction.

If you are a resident of the U.S., there is a cap on deductibility that is equal to your net investment income. Any leftover interest expense, however, can be carried over for future use without expiration. Moreover, if you are a resident of the U.S., qualified dividends and long-term capital gains get taxed at your ordinary tax rate and not the reduced rate if you elect to treat them as investment income when you use borrowed money to buy these investments.

Finally, in both Canada and the U.S, you are not allowed to claim investment interest on money borrowed to invest when you use this borrowed money to purchase investments in any sort of tax-advantaged retirement savings account.

U.S. investors that borrow money and invest it in tax-free municipal bonds are also not allowed to claim their interest expense as a tax deduction.

Furthermore, both Canada and the U.S. have rules regarding how you are able to claim a tax deduction on the interest charged on money borrowed to invest. Be sure to familiarize yourself with these rules and to talk to a tax specialist regarding these rules before you borrow any money to invest.

Control the Timing of Income and Deductions

Controlling the timing of your income and your tax deductions for tax purposes is referred to as income smoothing. And savvy investors that make use of this strategy can sometimes save themselves tens of thousands of dollars.

Income smoothing is all about realizing your income and claiming your tax deductions so that you can save the most tax. Sometimes it is not possible to time when you take your deductions or when you realize your income. If you get paid every two weeks, it will be hard not to realize this income every two weeks. Sometimes, however, it is possible to control how much taxable income you realize and to smooth out your income in order to pay less tax.

To some extent, you use an income smoothing strategy when you invest in a tax-deferred retirement savings account. Tax-deferred retirement savings accounts allow you to shelter your income from taxes in your higher earning years and, hopefully, result in these earnings being taxed at a lower rate in your lower earning years (when you are retired).

For example, if you are in a 30% tax bracket in your higher earning years, when you make all your contributions to your tax-deferred retirement savings account, and you end up in a 20% tax bracket when you make all your withdrawals, you will end up saving 10% in taxes. This is in addition to all the savings you will have realized thanks to tax-deferred compound growth.

Besides tax-deferred retirement savings accounts, there may be other opportunities to control when you realize income and when you claim deductions.

Control the Timing of Capital Gains and Capital Losses

If you are planning to sell some of your investments and these investments will result in a capital gain, then, if possible, attempt to sell these investments in a lower earning year when you are in a lower tax bracket.

Perhaps you are nearing retirement or are planning on taking a year off work. Maybe you have just been laid off. In any of these situations, you would be wise to try and register any capital gains you are considering taking in the year you are making less income. Depending on the size of the capital gain and the change in your marginal tax bracket, this strategy could result in tax savings of tens of thousands of dollars.

For example, if you plan to take a year off work to travel the world, and you plan on selling an investment property you own to fund this adventure, plan to sell this property in the year you are not earning any income.

Assuming you are living in Canada and you register a capital gain of $100,000 on the sale of this investment property, then, for the 2016 tax year, you would pay income taxes of approximately $8,400 (if you lived in the province of Ontario and earned no other income during the year).

In contrast, if you registered this $100,000 capital gain in the same year that you earned $90,000 in employment income, the taxes you would owe on the sale of this property would be about $21,670. Moreover, this $21,670 would be on top of the $20,900 in taxes you would owe for your employment income.

This means the sale of the property would cost you an additional $13,270 in taxes if you sold it in the year you were working.

By this same logic, if you have registered a capital gain on some of your financial securities and are debating selling some of your underperforming investments, then perhaps it makes sense to sell your underperforming investments in the same year that you have registered a capital gain. That way, assuming you register a capital loss, you could use the capital loss to offset the capital gain.

It would also make sense, assuming you remain in the same tax bracket or end up in a lower one, to postpone taking a capital gain at the very end of the year and, if possible, take this capital gain at the beginning of the next year instead. By doing so, you would avoid paying taxes on this capital gain until the following tax year.

Control the Timing of Any Severance Package

If you are in the unfortunate position of having been laid off from work near the end of the year and you are being offered a severance package, then see if this severance package can be paid out to you at the start of the following year. Assuming you don't work as much in the following year and end up in a lower tax bracket, you would likely save a bundle in taxes.

Control the Timing of Any Deduction

If you have the option, it's always better to take a tax deduction in a year that you are in a higher tax bracket versus taking it in a year when you are in a lower tax bracket.

For example, in Canada, at the time of writing this, one is allowed to claim moving expenses when relocating for a new job. Moreover, one has a two-year window to claim these expenses. If one were to expect a higher salary after a relocation to a new job and, therefore, expect to be in a higher marginal tax bracket, then one should claim these moving expenses in the year when one is in the higher marginal tax bracket.

It's also worth noting that Canadians moving to a province with lower income tax rates would do well to make this move before the end of the year. That way, they could take advantage of these lower income tax rates for that entire year.

For example, if you earned $60,000 in employment income for 2015, and you moved from Quebec to Ontario in the middle of December 2015, then you would pay your income taxes for 2015 as a resident of Ontario and would owe approximately $14,841 in income taxes. If, however, you moved to Ontario a few weeks later, at the beginning of January 2016, then you would pay your 2015 income taxes as a resident of Quebec and owe $19,004 in income taxes. This two week delay would cost you more than $4,000 in income taxes!

Don't Lose Sight of the Big Picture

These are just some of the strategies that can add up to substantial tax savings over the course of an investor's lifetime. Further research and consultation with a tax specialist may be well worth it for those seeking more advanced tax strategies.

It would also be a good idea to find an easy to read book, offering up a variety of tax tips, and read it before you file your next tax return.

When implementing any tax strategy, make sure you don't lose sight of the big picture. **There's no use implementing a tax strategy that saves a small amount in taxes but costs a large amount in overall returns.**

With all this in mind, let's move onto the next chapter and see just how quickly one can grow his or her financial freedom fund if he or she implements not only the tax strategies discussed above, but all the strategies discussed so far that have been used by the most successful CEOs and business leaders of the last 200 years.

Let's see just how much you can grow your financial freedom fund if you think like a CEO and adopt a range of strategies that include business planning, concentrating on core competencies, ruthless cost-cutting, building financial acumen, proper investing, risk management, leverage, and tax avoidance. Before we leave this chapter, however, let's look at the story of Ingvar Kamprad, business magnate and founder of IKEA, the world's largest furniture retailer.

IKEA used to run an ad campaign that would say, "IKEA is Swedish for common sense." And even though this is not a correct translation, it is obvious that IKEA's founder, Ingvar Kamprad, possesses an abundance of common sense.

The Common Sense of Ingvar Kamprad

Ingvar Kamprad grew up on a farm in Sweden near the small village of Agunnaryd. Before the age of ten, he developed a business selling matches to neighbours from his bicycle. By 2012, according to the Bloomberg Billionaires Index, Kamprad was ranked the fifth richest person in the world and the second richest person in all of Europe. How did Kamprad achieve this great success?

Even as a young boy, Kamprad had a desire to grow his wealth. He started off selling matches and quickly realized that by reinvesting all his earnings back into his business he could make even more profits. From matches, he soon branched out to selling fish, seeds, and Christmas tree decorations. Then in 1943, when he was 17 years-old, Kamprad founded IKEA at his uncle Ernst's kitchen table (the name IKEA is an acronym derived from Kamprad's initials and his hometown). By 2015, the IKEA Group employed more than 155,000 people in 43 countries and had sales of approximately $35 billion.

It wasn't just desire and constant reinvestment that led to IKEA's success. A 2011 article titled "The Secret of IKEA's success" published in *The Economist* highlights the fact that the company owes a great deal of its success to its thrifty cost cutting culture and shrewd tax planning. Kamprad adopts the same strategies himself.

In his memoir, *Testament of a Furniture Dealer*, Kamprad writes, "We don't need flashy cars, impressive titles, uniforms or other status symbols. We rely on our strength and our will!" Kamprad is so frugal he reportedly stocks his closet with second hand clothes. One year he arrived at a gala to receive a Businessman of the Year award and was initially refused entry because he arrived on a bus.

In terms of saving on taxes, Kamprad left his native Sweden in 1973 and relocated to Switzerland in order to avoid paying high taxes. In the 1970's, Sweden's tax on wealthy individuals reached as high as 85%, while in Switzerland, federal income tax does not exceed 11.5% and wealth tax hovers around 1%.

In 2015, Kamprad returned to Sweden and paid taxes in his native country for the first time in 40 years. However, he still paid a relatively low amount of personal income tax because the Swedish tax authorities had abolished the wealth tax and because the billionaire had transferred his stake in IKEA to charitable foundations outside of Sweden.

Follow Ingvar Kamprad's lead. Have desire, reinvest your earnings, cut costs, and do whatever you can to save on taxes.

KEY POINTS FROM CHAPTER TEN

- Tax avoidance is the practice of reducing your taxes through legal methods. Tax evasion is the illegal evasion of taxes.

- In 2016, the average Canadian family paid 43% of its annual income in taxes. The average U.S. family paid 31% of its annual income in taxes.

- Consider all of the following to legally minimize your taxes; the best place to live and work, how to minimize taxable income, how to maximize tax credits and tax deductions, and how best to control the timing of income and deductions.

- If you have the ability to live and work in many different places, then take tax rates into consideration.

- Minimize taxable income by taking advantage of tax-advantaged retirement saving accounts.

- If you aren't going to invest the initial tax savings realized on contributions to a tax-deferred savings account, consider investing in a tax-free savings account instead.

- If you are a resident of Canada, consider income splitting strategies.

- Take advantage of programs that help save for a child's education.

- The tax savings offered by dividend income and capital gains, in both Canada and the U.S., can be substantial.

- Take advantage of all tax credits and tax deductions possible.

- Try to smooth out your taxable income so that you pay less tax.

- Don't implement a tax strategy that saves a small amount in taxes but costs a large amount in overall returns.

CHAPTER ELEVEN

Putting It All Together

The view from the top was amazing. My wife and I took our seats in a small coffee shop that was perched precariously high on the edge of a rocky cliff, overlooking the Mediterranean Sea, and soaked it all in.

We were sitting outside on a tiny balcony in one of the many restaurants lining the coast of a small Spanish fishing village named Nerja.

The charm and beauty of Nerja is difficult to overstate. The white washed village with its cobblestone streets and spectacular beaches offers a perfect combination of old world charm and natural beauty.

On this particular day, the sun was shining, a gentle sea breeze was blowing, and the vista we were treated to was especially picturesque.

"I can't believe we are actually here," I said to my wife. In fact, I had said this to my wife many times in the months that had followed our move to the sunny southern coast of Spain known as "The Costa del Sol."

It was December 2014, and after achieving financial freedom two years earlier, my wife and I had decided to take a break from our busy lives in Vancouver and take the whole family on an adventure in Spain.

The name "Costa del Sol" translates into English to "Sunshine Coast," and from the moment we arrived, the Costa del Sol had lived up to its reputation. We had traded in 170 days a year of rain for 330 days a year of sunshine. And even though it was the middle of December, I was sitting outside in a t-shirt, basking in the warm Mediterranean sun.

It wasn't just the rainy weather that we had traded in. We had also traded in the hectic lifestyles we had lived back home in Canada. Now, here in Nerja, all the stress of that past life seemed to melt away. It all seemed so surreal. Could we actually live like this?

In Canada, we had always seemed so busy. In fact, despite having been financially free for about two years, my wife and I had continued working and commuting for ten to twelve hours a day. And when we weren't working, we were taking the kids to some sort of after-school activity each night.

There's a popular saying that advises people should work to live, not live to work. Unfortunately, for most of us in North America, it seems that, far too often, we end up living to work.

Even though my wife and I could work less, we didn't. And even though the children didn't really want to be enrolled in some sort of activity every single night, they were. Everybody else did it, so we did it too. We all ran around like a bunch of headless chickens and just accepted that this was the only way to live.

Spain was different. Life was slower and more family centered. We spent much more time together as a family and much less time running around. And we loved it. Back home, we always seemed tired and full of stress, but here in Spain, we always seemed happy and energetic.

We had managed our financial freedom fund like the CEO of a successful company and it had paid off. We had grown our financial freedom fund to the point that we could now live the lives we truly wanted to live, and we were doing just that.

Putting It All Together

CEOs and famous business leaders don't just become wealthy by chance; they become wealthy by strategic thinking, careful planning, and hard-work. CEOs constantly look for ways to cut costs and they constantly look for ways to grow income and minimize taxes. They invest their money to make more money, and they take full advantage of borrowing money to invest when it can lead to increased profits. If you copy this way of thinking, you will become wealthy, too.

Let's look at an example detailing one couple's journey to an early retirement and see how thinking and acting like a CEO led to financial freedom at a young age.

In this example, we will follow the journey to financial freedom of a fictional couple whom we will call Jack and Jill.

We will also compare Jack and Jill's journey to financial freedom to the financial journey of another fictional couple whom we will call Frick and Frack.

This example will show how Jack and Jill, by thinking like a CEO, are able to achieve financial freedom at a young age. It will also show that, by thinking like "the herd," Frick and Frack are not.

Jack and Jill's Journey to Financial Freedom

Jack and Jill are both twenty-five years-old and start their journey to financial freedom off well.

They have both gotten some post-secondary education and are both climbing their respective career ladders. Jack earns about $50,000 a year, and Jill earns about $55,000 a year, for a combined total income of $105,000 a year.

Jack and Jill have been saving up and now have $40,000 to use as a down-payment for their first home. They don't have any other savings, but they do have good jobs that provide reliable income.

They have concentrated on building their core competencies and are eager to use them to achieve financial freedom. They are tired of their day jobs and tired of the rat-race. Furthermore, they have a crazy plan to live life to its fullest and to travel the world while they are still young, healthy, and full of energy.

With all this in mind, Jack and Jill plan to live a frugal lifestyle and save and invest as much money as possible so that one day they can realize their dream of financial freedom at a young age.

Jack and Jill, in many ways, are a lot like Frick and Frack. Frick and Frack are the same age as Jack and Jill and also make a combined total of $105,000 a year. As well, Frick and Frack do not have any debt.

Frick and Frack, however, don't really think too much about saving for the future or for their retirement. And even though they have no debt, Frick and Frack have not managed to save up any sort of down payment for the purchase of their first home.

Unlike Jack and Jill, Frick and Frack decide that the time to enjoy themselves is right now. They have no plans to live frugally, to save for the future, or to invest any money at all.

Buying Their First Home and Avoiding the Trap of a Big Mortgage

Jack and Jill start looking for their first home in the city where they work and quickly discover that house prices are way more expensive than they realized. They decide to scale back their expectations and look to buy a smaller house a little further out from the city.

They also decide to look for a house with a rental suite. This way, they will be able to generate some rental income to help pay down their mortgage.

They end up buying a house for much less than they can afford and spend a total of $400,000 on their new home. Moreover, the house they buy comes with a rental suite that can earn them $1,000 a month in rental income. They put down their $40,000 and get a twenty year mortgage for $360,000 that comes with a fixed interest rate of 4%. This mortgage results in mortgage costs of roughly $2,200 per month.

Meanwhile, Frick and Frack decide that they don't want the inconvenience of moving to a home outside the city and are not willing to settle for a house smaller than the maximum they can afford. They decide to buy a home in the city for $600,000. They aren't able to make any sort of down-payment on this house, but they are able to afford the monthly mortgage payments by getting a mortgage with a large amortization period of forty years.

Like Jack and Jill, Frick and Frack also end up with a mortgage rate of 4%. Despite their much larger mortgage, however, because of their forty year amortization period, Frick and Frack's monthly mortgage payments work out to be just slightly higher than Jack and Jill's. These mortgage payments end up costing Frick and Frack $2,500 a month.

Controlling Expenses and Cutting Costs

Jack and Jill have a combined pre-tax income of $105,000, but their after tax income is closer to $86,000 (not including their rental income).

They commit to only live off of one person's salary, roughly $43,000 a year (after taxes), and commit to use the other $43,000 a year to purchase investments or to pay down their mortgage.

Even though the house they bought is a little dated, and many of their friends say the kitchen and the bathrooms could use some renovations, everything in their house works just fine. Jack and Jill decide that they would rather save for their retirement than spend out on costly renovations, therefore, they leave everything the way it is.

As well, even though they are both driving older cars, their cars also work just fine. Therefore, Jack and Jill decide not to purchase any new vehicles either. They don't have any car loans and they want to keep it that way.

Jack and Jill also commit to only eat out one night a week and to not take any extravagant vacations over the next couple of years. They bring their lunch to work, make their morning coffee at home, and try their best not to splurge.

Thanks to their rental income of $1,000 a month, Jack and Jill's mortgage really only costs them $1,200 a month or $14,400 a year. This leaves Jack and Jill with about $28,600 a year for the rest of their expenses. They look at all these expenses and believe that spending roughly $2,400 a month, after paying for their mortgage, is doable. They know it will be difficult, but they also know plenty of people who live on less than this after they pay for their housing.

Jack and Jill appreciate the time value of money and know that if they can sacrifice for a number of years now, they will be able to retire much earlier than most. They constantly make a concerted effort to cut costs and to save and invest as much money as possible.

Frick and Frack also have after tax income of $86,000, but because they don't have a rental suite, they end up using $30,000 a year of this after tax income on their mortgage (more than twice as much as Jack and Jill).

Frick and Frack also decide that even though everything works, their house is in *desperate* need of renovations. They decide that this year will be the kitchen, next year the bathrooms, and the year after that, the backyard. They plan to spend roughly $10,000 a year on these renovations.

They also decide that they can't be seen driving around in older cars. They both buy expensive new cars and end up with monthly car loan payments of $500 each, for a total of an additional $12,000 a year.

Frick and Frack eat practically all of their meals out and are constantly buying coffees to go. As a result of these frivolous purchases, they end up spending $1,000 more on food a month than Jack and Jill.

Frick and Frack also like to go on expensive vacations and to take lots of weekend getaways. Frick and Frack devote another $7,000 a year for these trips. They don't make any concentrated effort to save anything and after all their expenses, they usually have nothing left over to save for retirement.

The choices Frick and Frack make mean they will certainly enjoy themselves now, but these choices also mean it will be very difficult for Frick and Frack to achieve financial freedom until much later in life, if at all.

Business Planning

Jack and Jill know that it is easy to procrastinate saving for their financial freedom. They also know that the cost of procrastination is dear (see chapter 2). In order to keep their plan of financial freedom on track, they decide to make a detailed business plan that maps out their path towards financial freedom.

They know that most people retire in their sixties, usually after working for forty or fifty years, but Jack and Jill put together an audacious plan to be able to retire in the next ten years.

They have decided to contribute $43,000 a year to their financial freedom fund (one person's entire salary) and decide that this money will come directly from Jack's paycheque. They make sure this paycheque gets automatically deposited into their financial freedom fund every two weeks. They know that having a plan and having a strategy of paying themselves first will prevent them from spending all their money before they can invest it.

Jack and Jill build up their investing knowledge and realize that they need to diversify in order to be successful. They decide to invest 20% of their portfolio in bonds, 20% in real estate, and 60% in stocks. Furthermore, they plan to use low cost ETFs for all of their purchases and also plan to be properly diversified within each asset class.

Frick and Frack do not have any plan at all to achieve financial freedom and never dream of paying themselves first. Every year, they say that they will save some money, but because they don't have any plan to do so, and because they never arrange to pay themselves first, they never do.

Financial Acumen

Jack and Jill continue to build up their investment knowledge by reading books and by reading the investment section of a reputable newspaper (just like Ronald Reed, the $8million janitor mentioned in chapter 7). They also make it a point to pay close attention to all their financial decisions. They have quickly built up their financial acumen and exercise it regularly by making smart choices that will enable them to retire early.

Jack and Jill maximize their contributions to all their tax-advantaged retirement savings accounts and always invest their money inside their tax-advantaged savings accounts before they invest any money outside of these accounts. They know that, over the course of their lives, this simple strategy alone could result in hundreds of thousands of dollars in extra savings (see chapter 10).

Given that they are residents of Canada, Jack and Jill also embark on a strategy to make the interest on their mortgage tax-deductible. They aggressively pay down their mortgage and, given they believe it makes sense to leverage themselves (see chapter 9), they borrow this money back against their home and use it to invest. They reason that this strategy makes more sense than a strategy of not paying down their mortgage and simply investing their money. They believe this because paying down their mortgage and then borrowing the money back to invest enables them to have an investment portfolio *and* to convert their non-tax-deductible mortgage interest

(Canadian residents) into tax-deductible interest (see chapter 5). Once again, this strategy is not applicable to U.S. residents. Unlike residents of Canada, U.S. residents already have the ability to claim their mortgage interest as a tax deduction.

Shortly after creating their financial freedom fund, Jack gets asked by his parents, who have just retired, if he would be the executor of their will. Jack's parents tell Jack that they plan to leave him and his brother a large sum of money upon their deaths and that they are keeping this money safe in a bank account that they never plan to use.

Jack tells his parents that this money would help him out more now, as opposed to later. He explains to his parents that this money could be used to help him payoff some of his large mortgage debt or could be used to help him pay the tuition for a part-time MBA.

He also explains to his parents that the money they are saving for him in the bank account, after factoring in inflation, is probably decreasing in value. Jack's parents realize that Jack is financially responsible and decide to gift Jack some of this money right away. They tell Jack that they will pay for his part-time MBA, and they make a $50,000 payment toward his mortgage.

Frick and Frack never think much about any of their financial decisions. As a result, they have very little investment knowledge and no financial acumen. They believe that it is impossible to make money in the financial markets unless you are some sort of fancy stock broker on Wall Street and that investing in stocks is a recipe for disaster.

Keeping Their Day Job and Investing in Themselves

Jack keeps his day job and invests in himself. He registers for an MBA and plans to complete it on a part-time basis. Jack already has an accounting designation and believes an MBA will help him build on these core competencies and allow him to get an even higher paying job. He has done some research and knows that he can get some course exemptions due to his accounting designation. He has also done some research around what type of benefits an MBA can provide and knows that an MBA will provide him with more job opportunities and will, very likely, lead to a higher salary.

Two years later, Jack finishes his MBA and is offered a managerial position with a salary of $70,000 a year. He and Jill continue to live off of Jill's salary alone. Given Jack's higher salary, Jack and Jill now have an extra $14,000 a year (after income taxes) to invest. They invest a total of $57,000 a year into their financial freedom fund, from this point on.

Frick, on the other hand, has grown to hate his job. At the same time that Jack moves into a managerial position, Frick decides that he will quit his job and try to go into business for himself.

Unfortunately, the move ends up costing Frick and Frack a lot of money. They lose the guaranteed income of Frick's previous job and also end up with a large unpaid loan to try and start the business. Frick spends a year trying to start his business, but in the end he admits defeat and goes back to a job similar to the one he had before he quit. Frick and Frack still have no money to invest and still have no plan to start saving for retirement anytime soon.

Despite the fact that Jack and Jill saw their income rise and Frick and Frack saw their income fall, you wouldn't know it by looking at the two couples. While Jack and Jill continue to live a frugal life, Frick and Frack continue to take expensive vacations, drive expensive new cars, and eat out most nights. Despite all this spending, Frick and Frack don't really seem any happier than Jack and Jill.

Jack and Jill seem content. And even though they would like to have nice things, they still manage to live a happy life living below their means. They have no stress related to money and are excited to see their savings increase every year.

Jack and Jill are confident that they will obtain financial freedom much quicker than originally thought and have no interest in *keeping up with the Joneses* if it means postponing their financial freedom by decades. Unlike

Frick and Frack, Jack and Jill see a way out of the rat-race and this has put a spring in their step.

Investing in Real Estate

As opposed to Frick and Frack, who had borrowed against their home in a failed attempt to start a business, Jack and Jill decide to borrow against their home to purchase an investment property.

Jack and Jill had been patiently looking for an investment property for a while, but it had taken a few years to find one that met all their criteria. These criteria included the rent being able to cover all the expenses and the property yielding a yearly cash flow of at least 7% of their down payment.

Jack and Jill buy a detached house in an area with low vacancy rates. They also buy their detached house in an area that they believe will show above average appreciation over time. They purchase this property for $200,000 and put $50,000 down as a down payment. Thanks to a CFROI of just over 7%, they are able to realize additional free cash flow of $3,600 a year.

Frick and Frack have no money to invest and are unable to mortgage themselves any further, even if they wanted to buy an investment property. They got the largest mortgage they could afford to buy their primary residence and, therefore, would be unable to qualify for another mortgage on an investment property.

Investing in the Stock Market and Getting the Best Return for the Lowest Risk

As Jack and Jill's investment knowledge grows, they become more confident in their investing abilities. They decide to invest part of their portfolio in a diversified group of large, blue chip, dividend paying stocks. They accomplish this by purchasing an ETF that focuses on companies that have increased their dividend payouts for at least twenty consecutive years.

Jack and Jill also focus on getting the best return for the lowest amount of risk. They invest in multiple asset classes and make sure that they are well diversified within each of these asset classes. They use REITs to beef up their real estate holdings and low cost ETFs for the bond portion of their portfolio. They also use low cost ETFs for all their international stock holdings and make sure these ETFs adopt a currency hedging strategy.

With all their investments, Jack and Jill concentrate on keeping their transaction costs and management fees low. They also don't take part in any type of speculative behaviour and make sure they invest for the long-term. Furthermore, they don't buy anything that they don't fully understand.

For the first time in years, Frick and Frack find themselves with some money to invest. They decide to invest it all in the shares of some small technology company that has gone up 200% over the last two years. They don't diversify, and even though the company doesn't have any earnings or pay out any dividends, Frick and Frack believe they are guaranteed to make big money.

Not too long after Frick and Frack make their investment, the stock market crashes. The stock market falls by 20%, but their risky stock falls by 40%. Frick and Frack immediately sell all their shares and pull out. They swear they will never invest any money in the stock market again.

Meanwhile, even though the stock market has fallen by 20%, Jack and Jill's diversified portfolio is only down by 15%. Moreover, their dividend payments keep growing every year and keep getting distributed on a regular basis. Jack and Jill use these dividend payments to purchase even more shares at depressed prices. They realize that the market has ups and downs but in the long-run, history has proven that it eventually always goes up. They stay invested and think about investing more.

Leverage

With the stock market down 20%, interest rates low, and companies undervalued, Jack and Jill decide to borrow some money to invest. They commit to not overleveraging themselves and also commit to pay the loan interest with their employment income.

Given that their house had increased in value by 20% over the last four years, and that they had reduced their mortgage principal by $50,000 with their regular mortgage payments (not including any prepayments), Jack and Jill have an extra $130,000 of home equity available to them to borrow against and invest ($80,000 + $50,000). They invest an extra $100,000 in a portfolio of dividend paying stocks (held outside of their tax-advantaged retirement savings accounts) and claim the loan interest as a tax deduction.

Frick and Frack decide that they won't invest in the stock market anymore. They believe it is just a way to lose money. This doesn't really matter, however, as Frick and Frack don't have any money to invest anyway.

They also have no way to borrow against their home. Frick and Frack hadn't made any prepayments on their mortgage and had already borrowed everything they could against their home in a failed attempt to start a business.

Moreover, the large amortization period on Frick and Frack's mortgage had resulted in their monthly mortgage payments barely putting a dent in their mortgage principal. Instead, almost all of their monthly payments had gone to paying mortgage interest.

In fact, over the first four years of mortgage payments, Frick and Frack's $600,000 mortgage, with its forty year amortization period, had experienced a reduction in mortgage principal of only $26,600 and had cost Frick and Frack a whopping $93,200 in interest payments alone.

On the other hand, Jack and Jill's $360,000 mortgage, with its twenty year amortization period, had experienced a reduction in mortgage principal of $51,150 (almost twice as much as Frick and Frack's) and had generated an additional $48,000 in rental income. Moreover, compared to the $93,200 in interest payments paid by Frick and Frack, Jack and Jill's interest payments had amounted to only $53,260.

Taking into consideration the reduction in principal, the rent collected, and the interest paid over the first four years of their mortgages, Jack and Jill were approximately $112,550 wealthier than Frick and Frack. This extra $112,550 was due entirely to Jack and Jill's choice of mortgage amortization period and type of housing. Jack and Jill invested all this extra money, got it working for them, and made even more money.

The total interest on Jack and Jill's mortgage, over the course of its twenty year life, can be expected to amount to approximately $162,000. In contrast, the total interest on Frick and Frack's mortgage, over the course of its forty year life, can be expected to amount to a staggering $600,000.

Furthermore, Jack and Jill aggressively pay down their mortgage and change their non-tax-deductible mortgage interest into tax-deductible mortgage interest (Canadian residents). Given this, Jack and Jill will pay even less than $162,000 in interest.

In fact, all of Jack and Jill's prepayments result in their mortgage being completely paid off in just seven years. This reduces their total interest payments to only $56,000.

This means Frick and Frack will spend over $544,000 more in interest payments compared to Jack and Jill, over the life of their mortgage. And unlike Jack and Jill, they will receive absolutely no rental income to show for these extra mortgage costs. Moreover, none of Frick and Frack's mortgage interest will be tax-deductible.

Taxes

Jack and Jill claim the interest on all the money they borrow to invest as a tax deduction and, furthermore, realize tax savings on all the dividends they receive from the eligible shares they hold outside of their tax-advantaged retirement savings accounts.

As they previously planned, Jack and Jill always invest all they can inside their tax-advantaged retirement savings accounts before they invest outside of these accounts. They also make sure that they are aware of and claim all the tax deductions and tax credits they are entitled to.

All these tax deductions and tax credits result in a combined tax refund each year of about $8,000. Jack and Jill immediately invest this $8,000 as soon as it is received. Most of their tax refund is due to their strategy of investing in their tax-deferred retirement savings accounts; however, they always invest all they can in both their tax-deferred and their tax-free retirement savings accounts.

Frick and Frack never contribute anything to their tax-advantaged retirement savings accounts. As a result, they miss out on hundreds of thousands of dollars in tax savings over the course of their lives (see chapter 10).

The Results

Before claiming any tax credits or tax deductions, Jack and Jill were able to invest $43,000 a year for the first two years and, after Jack's raise, were able to invest $57,000 every year after that.

After claiming all their tax credits and tax deductions, the bulk of which came from investing in their tax-deferred retirement savings accounts, Jack and Jill ended up getting a combined tax refund of $8,000 a year, every year.

In total, with this yearly tax refund of $8,000, Jack and Jill invested $51,000 a year in year one and year two and $65,000 a year in the years after that. From these sums, Jack and Jill subtracted the interest payments they incurred each year by borrowing to invest.

With everything taken into consideration, Jack and Jill invested roughly $30,000 a year into tax-advantaged savings accounts and $21,000 a year into a nonregistered account, for the first two years of their plan. They invested roughly $35,000 a year into tax-advantaged savings accounts and $30,000 a year into a nonregistered account for all the years after that.

Their investments in their nonregistered account were made by paying down their mortgage and then borrowing this money back against their home (using a HELOC) to invest.

In year three, they took a $50,000 gift from Jack's parents and used it to pay down their mortgage even further. They then immediately borrowed this amount back against their house and used it to buy an investment property. This investment property generated an additional $300 a month in cash flow.

In year four, they borrowed against their home, which had increased in value by 20%, and invested an additional $100,000 in the stock market. They did this after the stock market experienced a 20% drop in value and they believed stocks were undervalued.

Seven years after developing their financial freedom fund, Jack and Jill managed to completely pay off the mortgage on their primary residence.

After the mortgage on their primary residence was completely paid off, Jack and Jill were able to invest directly into their nonregistered investment account without first prepaying their mortgage and then borrowing these funds back.

The table at the top of the next page summarizes Jack and Jill's payments towards their mortgage. In years one and two, Jack and Jill made extra prepayments of $21,000 a year. In year three, Jack and Jill made a $30,000 prepayment as well as a $50,000 prepayment (thanks to a $50,000 gift from Jack's dad), for a total prepayment of $80,000. In years four, five, and six, they made prepayments of $30,000 a year. In year seven, Jack and Jill only needed to make a prepayment of $21,360 to have their entire mortgage paid off.

MORTGAGE TABLE

Year	Annual Payment	Total Extra Payments	Total Payments	Interest	Principal	Ending Balance
1	$26,103	$21,000	$47,103	$14,064	$33,039	$326,961
2	$26,103	$21,000	$47,103	$12,729	$34,374	$292,586
3	$26,103	$80,000	$106,103	$11,341	$94,763	$197,824
4	$26,103	$30,000	$56,103	$7,512	$48,591	$149,232
5	$26,103	$30,000	$56,103	$5,549	$50,554	$98,678
6	$26,103	$30,000	$56,103	$3,507	$52,597	$46,081
7	$26,103	$21,360	$47,463	$1,382	$46,081	$0

Ten Years Later

Ten years after starting their financial freedom fund, all the planning, saving and investing pays off. At the age of thirty-five years-old, Jack and Jill become financially free.

Real Estate Holdings

Ten years after developing their financial freedom fund, Jack and Jill determine that their home has appreciated by just over 4% a year and is now worth $600,000.

Jack and Jill have raised the rent in their rental suite to $1,200 a month, and they now generate $400 a month in free cash flow from their other investment property. These two property rentals now provide them with total rental income of $1,600 a month or $19,200 a year.

Furthermore, Jack and Jill's investment property has also appreciated in value and is now worth $300,000. Jack and Jill now own roughly $900,000 in real estate holdings alone. The only mortgage they have left is the one on their investment property and it is only $90,000.

Investments in the Stock Market

At the same time that Jack and Jill were paying down their mortgage, they were also maxing out their tax-advantaged retirement savings accounts and borrowing back against their primary residence to invest even more money in a non-registered account. It was a strategy that paid off.

Their investment portfolio went up by 7% a year for years one and two and then fell 15% by the end of year three (when the stock market collapsed by 20%). At the beginning of year four, believing stocks were undervalued, Jack and Jill borrowed against their home and added an additional $100,000 to their normal investment contributions. Their portfolio then went up 20% a year in years four and five, as the stock market recovered, and went up by 7% a year in the years after that. By the end of year ten, their investment portfolio was worth approximately $1,055,000.

The results of all of Jack and Jill's investing are shown in the table at the top of the next page.

VALUE OF INVESTMENT PORTFOLIO

Year	Available to Invest	Amount Invested After Subtracting Interest on HELOC	Total Portfolio	Growth	Total Savings at End of Year
1	$51,000	$50,412	$50,412	7%	$53,941
2	$51,000	$49,824	$103,765	7%	$111,028
3	$65,000	$61,584	$172,612	-15%	$146,721
4	$165,000	$157,944	$304,665	20%	$365,597
5	$65,000	$57,104	$422,701	20%	$507,242
6	$65,000	$56,264	$563,506	7%	$602,951
7	$65,000	$55,666	$658,617	7%	$704,720
8	$65,000	$55,666	$760,386	7%	$813,613
9	$65,000	$55,666	$869,279	7%	$930,129
10	$65,000	$55,666	$985,795	7%	$1,054,800

Money Borrowed to Invest

The total debt in their HELOC went up by $21,000 a year in the first two years after they started their financial freedom fund and went up by $30,000 a year in each of the following years. As explained above, this is because Jack and Jill would use some of their income to pay down their mortgage and then borrow this money back to invest.

The debt in their HELOC went up by an additional $50,000 in year three when they received this money as a gift from Jack's dad, used it to pay down their mortgage, borrowed it back, and then purchased their investment property. This means the debt in their HELOC increased by $80,000 in year three ($50,000 + $30,000).

The debt in their HELOC also went up by an additional $100,000 in year four when they tapped into the increased value of their home and borrowed $100,000 against it to invest in the stock market. This means the debt in their HELOC increased by $130,000 in year four ($100,000 + $30,000).

After Jack and Jill paid $21,360 to finish paying off their mortgage in year seven, they no longer accumulated any other debt in their HELOC. In total, their HELOC contained roughly $333,360 in borrowed money by the end of year seven and cost Jack and Jill roughly $9,334 a year in annual interest payments (see table below).

TOTAL DEBT IN HELOC

Year	Yearly Debt Incurred	Total Debt	Interest Rate	Total Interest	Total Interest After Tax Deduction (Assumes a 30% Tax Bracket)
1	$21,000	$21,000	4%	$840	$588
2	$21,000	$42,000	4%	$1,680	$1,176
3	$80,000	$122,000	4%	$4,880	$3,416
4	$130,000	$252,000	4%	$10,080	$7,056
5	$30,000	$282,000	4%	$11,280	$7,896
6	$30,000	$312,000	4%	$12,480	$8,736
7	$21,360	$333,360	4%	$13,334	$9,334

Net Worth

With a primary residence valued at $600,000 and an investment property valued at $300,000, Jack and Jill own $900,000 in real estate. They also have an investment portfolio worth just over $1 million. When all these holdings are combined, it adds up to total assets of just under $2 million. Jack and Jill have paid off the mortgage on their primary residence and have a $90,000 mortgage left on their investment property. They also have a HELOC totaling $333,360. All told, Jack and Jill have total liabilities of $423,360. When these liabilities get subtracted from their total assets, Jack and Jill have accumulated a net worth of roughly $1.5 million.

NET WORTH STATEMENT

ASSETS

Primary Residence	$600,000
Rental Property	$300,000
Investments	$1,054,800
Total Assets	**$1,954,800**

LIABILITIES

Mortgage on Primary Residence	$0
Mortgage on Rental Property	$90,000
HELOC	$333,360
Total Liabilities	**$423,360**

NET WORTH	**$1,531,440**

Living off Their Investment Income

Besides the fact that they are millionaires, Jack and Jill also benefit from the ability to earn roughly $37,000 a year in income from their investments in the financial markets (assumes a 3.5% yield). This income works out to roughly $27,600 a year, after the interest on the HELOC is subtracted. Additionally, when Jack and Jill take into consideration the rent from their lower suite and the net rent from their rental property, Jack and Jill also generate roughly $19,200 a year in rental income. All of this income can be earned from anywhere in the world.

This works out to total investment and rental income of roughly $46,800 a year or $3,900 a month (see table below). This income is earned without the need to sell any of their investments or dig into their principal.

INCOME FROM INVESTMENTS

INVESTMENT PORTFOLIO

Dividends and Investment Income	$36,918
HELOC interest	-$9,334
Total Investment Income	**$27,584**

REAL ESTATE

Net Income Rental Suite	$14,400
Net Income Investment Property	$4,800
Total Rental Income	**$19,200**

Total Income (Real Estate and Investments)	**$46,784**

Given that Jack and Jill have been living off of $43,000 a year for the last number of years, this yearly income of $46,800 now means that they have managed to create a source of investment income that they can live off of. In fact, given that they no longer have any more mortgage payments on their primary residence, Jack and Jill will have an additional $1,200 a month available to them that they didn't have before.

With no more mortgage payments and income of roughly $3,900 a month that gets taxed much more favourably than their employment income, Jack and Jill believe they are able to take a break from work. They have achieved financial freedom. They now have a choice. They can choose to work or they can choose to take a break from work and realize their dream of traveling the world.

A Break From Work

Jack and Jill manage to negotiate a year off of work and decide to spend this year living in another country. They have achieved a level of financial freedom few people their age ever obtain.

They rent out the upper level of their home for an additional $1,500 per month and add this income to the $3,900 a month they were already receiving. They also make a promise to themselves to never dig into their investment principal, a move that could result in them losing their financial freedom. Jack and Jill plan to live off of the income produced by their investments, not the investments themselves.

Jack and Jill find that because they are in such a low tax bracket and because a lot of their income is tax advantaged (thanks to dividends and tax-free savings accounts), they pay far less tax than they used to.

With the extra $1,500 a month they get from renting out the upper level of their home, Jack and Jill get a combined total of $5,400 a month in income from their investment portfolio and their real estate holdings.

They determine that even after paying taxes, they will still have roughly $5,000 a month to fund their adventure of living in another country.

They find a long-term rental in sunny Southern Spain, which is only a fifteen minute walk to the beach, for only $750 a month. This leaves them $4,250 a month to play with. They spend their days taking tennis lessons, learning Spanish, and exploring all the little towns and villages that dot the southern coast of Spain.

Frick and Frack wonder how on earth Jack and Jill were able to leave their jobs and move to Spain at such a young age. They figure Jack and Jill must have either inherited a bunch of money or won the lottery.

Frick and Frack are now ten years into a forty year mortgage, and unlike Jack and Jill, they still have mortgage payments of $2,500 a month for the next thirty years. They are absolutely dependent on their jobs to pay for their mortgage and to support their extravagant lifestyles.

Moreover, Frick and Frack haven't been able to save up any large amount of money, and what they have saved up is sitting in a bank account earning them little to no interest. They haven't taken any risk by investing in stocks or by borrowing money to invest in either stocks or real estate and, therefore, have very little opportunity to earn any type of income outside of their jobs. They still have no plan to obtain financial freedom and continue to spend everything they earn.

Early Withdrawals From Tax-Advantaged Retirement Savings Accounts

Note, if you are a U.S. resident and are withdrawing money from your tax-advantaged retirement savings accounts before 59 1/2 years-old, you will want to speak with a professional to determine if this can be done without a penalty for early withdrawal. There are some options available, and these options should definitely be explored.

In Canada, at the time of writing this, there are currently no early withdrawal penalties for RRSPs or TFSA, but there are withholding taxes on withdrawals made from RRSPs when these withdrawals are made before you retire.

The best strategy, if at all possible, is to leave as much money as you can in your tax-advantaged retirement savings accounts so it can continue to grow tax-free.

Conclusions

In the above example, both couples had similar employment income, however, Jack and Jill had a strong desire to achieve financial freedom and Frick and Frack did not. As well, Jack and Jill were willing to sacrifice and live below their means in order to realize their dream of achieving financial freedom in a much shorter time frame. Furthermore, Jack and Jill were also willing to increase their investment knowledge and strengthen their financial acumen while Frick and Frack were not.

Frick and Frack were not willing to live below their means, were mostly indifferent to achieving financial freedom, and had no interest at all in increasing their investing knowledge or their financial acumen. As a result, Jack and Jill became financially free in only ten years and Frick and Frack did not.

Besides having the desire to become financially free, Jack and Jill also had a well thought-out plan and made sure to use a proven strategy that involved investing in proven wealth generating vehicles such as real estate and the financial markets. Jack and Jill also made smart investments, managed their risk appropriately, used the power of leverage, and minimized their taxes.

In summary, Jack and Jill thought like a successful CEO and were able to achieve financial freedom much earlier than traditionally thought possible.

It isn't possible for everyone to achieve financial freedom as quickly as Jack and Jill did. If you don't have a good paying job, aren't able to use leverage, or the stock market generates returns that are lower than its traditional average, it will prove more difficult to achieve financial freedom quickly.

Nonetheless, the fictional story of Jack and Jill is a good example of how two people with relatively good paying jobs can achieve a certain degree of financial freedom in a relatively quick time frame when they think like a CEO.

Just like the CEOs mentioned throughout this book, Jack and Jill employed all of the strategies mentioned in the previous chapters to achieve financial success.

Strategies Used by Jack and Jill to Achieve Financial Freedom

- Having a business plan.
- Concentrating on core competencies.
- Relentlessly cutting costs and controlling expenses.
- Strengthening financial acumen.
- Investing their money in proven wealth building vehicles such as stocks, bonds, and real estate.
- Managing risk appropriately.
- Using the power of leverage.
- Minimizing taxes.

If Jack and Jill would have had even higher paying jobs, would have been able to safely leverage themselves even more, or would have been willing to live even more frugally, they might have been able to achieve financial freedom even quicker.

Even if you aren't in the same situation as Jack and Jill, there's no doubt that thinking like a CEO will greatly accelerate your time to financial freedom.

No matter what your situation is, if you are able to employ all or even some of the strategies discussed above, you will end up achieving financial freedom much quicker than what you would have by not employing these strategies at all.

In addition, employing some of the strategies mentioned above will also allow you to start feeling more confident about your financial future. Maybe it will take you longer than ten years to achieve financial freedom, but I guarantee you that if you start using some of the strategies mentioned throughout this book right now, you will achieve financial freedom quicker than you could have by not using them at all.

Many people aren't fortunate enough to have the knowledge that Jack and Jill had. Simply put, they don't know what they don't know. They never learn anything about investing in school or from their parents, and they never read about investing or take any courses on it.

Most people just follow society's norms of working harder and harder, spending more and more, and never trying to get any of their money working for them.

Unlike most of these people, you are now fortunate enough to have the knowledge to obtain financial freedom. With this knowledge you now have a choice. You can choose to spend everything you earn or you can choose to think like a CEO and achieve financial freedom much quicker than most.

The Story of Sir John Templeton

Perhaps more than any other business leader or CEO previously mentioned, Sir John Templeton epitomizes many of the strategies outlined in this book.

Sir John Templeton was born in 1912 to a poor Tennessee family in the small town of Winchester. He would later become a billionaire by pioneering the use of globally diversified mutual funds and would be described by *Money Magazine* as "arguably the greatest global stock picker of the century."

At an early age, Sir John realized the importance of an education and developing some useful core competencies, at an early age. He graduated top of his class in high school and was one of the first in his town to go to university. He went on to graduate from Yale University with a degree in economics, graduating among the top in the class. He was then named a Rhodes Scholar to Balliol College at Oxford, from which he graduated with an MA degree in law. On top of all of this, he also became a chartered financial analyst, a designation that would serve him well throughout his investment career.

Not only did Sir John develop some useful skills, he also got his money working for him at a young age. He started working on Wall St in 1937, the same year that he married his first wife, and although he had the means to spend his money, he didn't. Sir John and his wife made a pledge to save 50% of their income and furnished their apartment with only $25 worth of furniture. And what furniture he couldn't buy cheap at auctions, he made himself out of wooden boxes. Like so many of the successful business leaders mentioned throughout this book, Sir John embraced thrift.

Sir John also believed in taking calculated risks. In 1939, when stocks were battered because of the Depression and the looming prospect of war, Sir John borrowed $10,000 (the equivalent of $175,000 in 2016 dollars) and bought everything that was trading for less than $1 on the NYSE. He would go on to make this money back many times over.

By 1940, Sir John had opened his own fund management company. He would later go on to create some of the largest and most successful international investment funds in the world. He was known for his philosophy of buying after step selloffs, what he described as buying at the time of "maximum pessimism." He liked unglamorous dependable stocks and disliked speculation. Moreover, he held onto his investments for the long-term. His mantra was "search for companies around the world that offer low prices and an excellent long-term outlook." He pioneered portfolio diversification, and when he started his Templeton Growth Fund in 1954, it was one of the first funds to start buying stocks outside the U.S.

Then in the 1960's, Sir John made the controversial decision to renounce his U.S. citizenship and move to the Bahamas, a country that charges no income tax and no investment tax. As a result of tax-free compounding, Sir John Templeton was worth several billion dollars when he passed. Although not necessarily advising people to renounce their citizenship, Sir John strongly advised individuals to take full advantage of tax-advantaged retirement savings accounts.

Upon his death in 2008, Sir John had become one of the world's great philanthropists and had contributed a sizable amount of his assets to his philanthropic endeavours. His philanthropy lives on through the work done by the foundation he created in his name, The John Templeton Foundation.

KEY POINTS FROM CHAPTER ELEVEN

- If you think like a CEO, you will be able to achieve financial freedom much quicker than most.

- Many people are not fortunate enough to possess the knowledge of how to achieve financial freedom. It is not taught in school and it is rarely learned from parents.

- With the knowledge of how to obtain financial freedom, you now have a choice. You can chose to spend everything you earn, or you can chose to think like a CEO and retire earlier than most.

CHAPTER TWELVE

Manage Your Finances and Live the Life You Truly Want

It was August 2015, and after spending a year in Spain, we had decided to return back to Canada. The thing we had missed most about Canada was the family and friends we had left behind, and it was great to be reunited with them again.

The thing we hadn't missed, however, was the hectic life we had experienced in Canada in the years leading up to our trip to Spain. And even though we were no longer in Spain, we were determined to continue to live the more relaxed lifestyle we had enjoyed so much in the Costa del Sol.

I hadn't yet returned to my job as a flight instructor and had chosen to write this book instead. I was exercising every day, was flying for fun, and was continuing to spend more time than before with my wife and children.

My wife had also made some changes. Instead of going back to work full-time, she started a new job, doing something she was interested in, that was part-time. She didn't have to work, but she wanted to. She went to work part-time, started taking violin lessons, and also continued to spend more time with our children and me. All of this would not have been possible without some sort of financial freedom.

I'm sure that many people are happy without much wealth, and that many people are wealthy without much happiness, but my guess is, more often than not, the two are related. Wealth offers possibilities that a lack of wealth cannot.

My wife and I now had more choices with regards to work and lifestyle than we had before we had achieved financial freedom. What's more, because we weren't dependent on our jobs, we had more freedom to choose where we wanted to live and what we wanted to do with our time (like become a pilot or write a book).

We could go back to school, continue to work, or just drop everything and take off to another country for a year. We had achieved financial freedom and were better able to live the life we truly wanted. Now our challenge is to make sure it stays that way.

Now, more than ever, we are careful to manage all the risks faced by our financial freedom fund. And we are careful to not spend more than we earn from our investments. The last thing we want to happen, now that we have achieved financial freedom, is to lose it.

When you do achieve financial freedom, your next task is to make sure you continue to properly manage your financial freedom fund, protect your wealth, and use this wealth to live a happier life.

Even better, use your wealth to live a happier life and then pass your wealth on to your children so that they can do the same.

Manage Your Finances and Protect Your Wealth

Whether you decide to quit work altogether, or you decide to get a part-time job doing something you actually would like, **you need to make absolutely sure that you are managing your financial freedom fund appropriately.**

The world is full of stories about people who at some point in their lives had vast amounts of wealth and then somehow ended up losing it all. You need to make sure that this does not happen to you.

Don't be like the lottery winner or the celebrity you hear about on the news that had it all and then somehow lost everything. Be like a great CEO, like Henry Ford, who enables his company to stand the test of time and, furthermore, enables it to live on for generation after generation.

There are basically three risks to your financial freedom fund, and you must do everything in your power to manage these risks appropriately.

Risks to Your Financial Freedom Fund

- Mismanagement of your financial freedom fund.
- Catastrophic events.
- Lawsuits.

Good CEOs have strategies in place to manage all these risks. You need to do the same. You need to ensure you have strategies in place to mitigate the risk of any one of these events from derailing your financial freedom and from draining your financial freedom fund.

Moreover, you are better off setting up strategies to guard against these three risks right now, as opposed to waiting until you have already achieved financial freedom. The truth is that without protection any one of these risks could result in you never even achieving financial freedom.

Mismanagement of Your Financial Freedom Fund

The large corporations run by many successful CEOs have several layers of protection when it comes to guarding against financial mismanagement. Managers oversee employees, and executives oversee managers. If this weren't enough, they also have a board of directors, elected by their shareholders, who are directly responsible for overseeing executives and protecting shareholder's interests. Finally, financial statements, meticulously detailing the company's finances, are continually prepared, audited, and distributed to shareholders, as a further layer of protection and transparency.

When it comes to protecting your financial freedom fund against financial mismanagement, you need to be just as vigilant. You need to continue to check, on a regular basis, that you are living within your means, continue to manage your risk appropriately, and continue to review your portfolio's performance to make sure you are getting the best return for the lowest risk. And you need to do these things often.

You hear it all the time, wealthy families with vast fortunes somehow end up losing all their money through a series of bad financial decisions. Bad decisions that involve not investing properly, not managing risk appropriately, not diversifying, or not keeping track of debt, can all lead to serious financial repercussions.

The most common way to lose one's wealth, however, is to live an extravagant lifestyle that is above one's means. Make sure you do not do this. Live at your means or, even better, live a little below your means.

Living below your means doesn't necessarily mean you have to live a life of poverty. If you have achieved financial freedom, in all likelihood, you have replaced an average level of employment income with an equivalent amount of income from investments. Furthermore, it is also likely that you have no debt to worry about.

Under this scenario, you should be able to live a fairly comfortable life indeed. You would enjoy all the privileges of the average working person without the need to pay a mortgage or to go to work.

Sure, you might not own your own yacht, but you wouldn't exactly be living on *Poverty Street*. Moreover, if you were to work part-time doing something you actually like, you'd fair even better.

However, if you have some big, expensive plans after you achieve financial freedom, like going back to school or traveling the world, you will definitely want to make sure that you will be able to fund these new adventures without starting a cascade of events that will slowly deplete your financial freedom fund.

If this is a scenario you think you might face, your best strategy would be to make sure you are comfortably able to fund these new adventures before you decide to leave the working world. If this means one or two more years of work, so be it.

If you spend a large chunk of your financial freedom fund as soon as you escape the rat-race, you will put your future financial freedom at risk. Digging into your principal will force you to sell some of your cash cows. And once you start selling your cash cows, you won't get any more money from them. You will kill the goose that lays the golden egg.

Even worse, you might start a cascade of events that will result in you continuing to sell more and more of your cash cows in order to meet more and more of your short-term financial needs. Such a cascade would inevitably cost you your financial freedom.

A far better strategy would be to play it safe and spend a little less than the total income generated by your portfolio. This way, you could continue to invest some of your income and continue to grow your financial freedom fund.

Once you leave work, you must also be sure that you are still appropriately managing your risk. Once you give up a perpetual stream of guaranteed income, you may need to re-evaluate you risk tolerance.

If you ever think you may be forced to sell some of your investments when they have dropped in value, you may need to hold a higher percent of your portfolio in less risky investments such as bonds.

If you still continue to use leverage when you are no longer working, make absolutely sure there is no way that a significant drop in the financial markets could force you to sell at a loss. Without a guaranteed employment income coming in, it would, more than likely, be wise to reduce any leverage you have.

Remember, more leverage equals more risk. And if a big drop in the markets were to occur and you didn't have the guaranteed steady income provided by a job, you might not have the resources to shore up any losses or be able to meet the demands of a margin call (see chapter 9).

Furthermore, working or not working, you also need to make sure a strategy involving leverage still makes sense. If interest rates are rising, stock markets are trading at all-time highs, and dividend yields are falling, then a more appropriate strategy might be to deleverage.

The biggest thing, however, is to not to let your new found wealth go to your head. Remain grounded and remain humble. Don't let the thought that you are wealthy result in a cascade of overindulgent spending and reckless behaviour.

Most of all, don't falsely believe your fortune can't all disappear with a small series of bad decisions. It absolutely can.

Catastrophic Events

The second way you can lose your financial freedom is through some sort of catastrophic event. Even though you might not know it, the CEOs of many large, successful companies take risks such as catastrophic events and lawsuits so seriously they have created their very own private insurance companies to manage these risks.

A *captive* is an insurance company that only offers insurance to the company that created it. Captives enable businesses to better insure themselves against a variety of risks. They also allow companies to insure themselves more effectively than a traditional insurance company could. A captive's sole purpose is to insure its creator against as much risk as possible. Take a page from these CEOs' playbooks and **make sure you have enough insurance to protect you, your family, and your financial freedom fund, from any sort of catastrophic event.**

Catastrophic events that severely damage property or severely affect health can happen to anyone. Events such as fire, floods, and earthquakes, could all result in the total destruction of your property. Illnesses that severely affect your health are even worse. In fact, a 2013 study from *Nerdwallet Health* indicates that medical bills are the single largest cause of bankruptcies in the United States.

The best way to protect yourself against these types of catastrophic events is by having proper insurance. Having proper insurance, both during your wealth building years and after you achieve financial freedom, is essential.

Furthermore, having adequate insurance won't only help to ensure you maintain your wealth, it will also help to ensure your wealth is protected and available to pass on to future generations.

Home Insurance

Be sure you protect your home and any other properties you own with a comprehensive home insurance policy. Moreover, be sure to read the fine print in any home insurance policy that you purchase and make sure your coverage includes as many catastrophic events that might befall your property as possible.

Life Insurance, Disability Insurance, and Health Insurance

In terms of serious illnesses, there are a variety of insurance products that you will need to consider and become familiar with.

If you are still in your wealth building years, not only will you be depending on your employment income to build your financial freedom fund, you will also be depending on it to pay your living expenses and to take care of your family.

Under these circumstances, you will absolutely need life insurance, long-term disability insurance, and short-term disability insurance. Moreover, no matter what your situation is, you will need adequate health insurance.

Adequate life insurance will ensure your loved ones are taken care of in the event of an untimely death. It will ensure that they can continue to pay their living expenses and, assuming you have the right amount, it will ensure that they are able to cover any other large expenses, such as a mortgage or a university education, which would have otherwise been paid for by your employment income. Disability insurance will ensure the same thing for you and your family if you ever become disabled and unable to work for either the short-term or the long-term.

While it is debatable as to whether or not you need life or disability insurance once you are financially free, you will always need proper health insurance.

With regards to life insurance and disability insurance, if your investments already provide a stream of income that could be used to take care of your family and to cover your family's future expenses in the event of your untimely death or disability, then you are likely better off avoiding any sort of insurance premium and just investing the money instead. It is not debatable, however, that you have proper health insurance.

If you live in Canada, you more than likely have adequate health insurance provided to you by the province you live in. However, you could still consider buying more insurance to cover events such as critical illnesses, long term hospital stays, or other treatments that may not be covered by provincial plans. I've heard of more than one example, in Canada, where critical illnesses have wiped out an individual's entire life savings and then that individual goes on to live for many more years in poverty.

If you live in the U.S., then there is a chance you don't have any health insurance at all. Even if you do have health insurance, there is still a good chance your health insurance is not adequate. Do yourself a favour and do the best you can to plan for and manage the potentially disastrous consequences that severe health problems could have on your financial well-being.

Remember to also have adequate health insurance when you travel to different countries. If this means purchasing additional travel insurance, then do it. I remember my dad, one time, leaving Canada for a week to visit my brother in the United States. Unfortunately, my dad ended up in a hospital in Seattle for a few days. The total cost for this hospital visit was close to $20,000. Case and point - have appropriate travel insurance.

Long-Term Care Insurance

Long-term care insurance is also something that is well worth looking into. It is well known in the health care industry that the last few years of a person's life can end up costing hundreds of thousands of dollars in health care costs.

If your last few years of life are spent in a long-term care facility, it will definitely end up costing you or your family a lot of money.

It's also worth noting that living in Canada doesn't necessarily mean the government will shield you from these expenses. My dad lives in Canada, and he currently pays over $3,200 a month for his long-term care, all out of his own pocket.

Moreover, he has been paying this expense for many years and could, quite likely, continue paying it for many years to come. It is not hard to see how these expenses can add up to hundreds of thousands of dollars.

It would be well worth your time to seek professional advice on how to plan for this possibility so that you can better protect your estate and your loved ones from this type of financial burden.

Health Care Directives and Wills

It goes without saying that you should have health care directives in place such as a living will or an advanced care plan that outline your wishes. Health care directives detail your choices with regards to advanced treatment decisions and/or the financial management of your accounts in the event that you are too sick to make these types of decisions yourself. Finally, also make sure that you have an updated will that lets your estate be distributed the way you see fit.

Lawsuits

Besides financial mismanagement and catastrophic events, getting sued is another risk that can put a big dent in anyone's wealth and financial freedom. In this regard, just like the previous section, your best defense is adequate insurance.

If you work in a profession that puts you at risk for being sued, like physician, child care worker, or business owner (just to name a few), then ensure that you have adequate personal liability insurance to protect you from work-related lawsuits.

Auto Insurance and Liability Insurance

I can remember, one day, driving in stop-and-go traffic while at the same time looking for an address at the side of the road. Quite suddenly, traffic ahead of me came to an abrupt stop and I bumped the car in front of me at a speed that can best be described as a crawl. I got out of the car to see if there was any damage and noticed a small scratch on my front bumper. As best as I could determine, there was no damage at all to the rear bumper of the car I hit. A few seconds later, I saw the driver of the car I hit calling for an ambulance.

To provide some background, everybody in the Canadian province where I live, British Columbia, has their auto insurance provided through a provincial crown corporation called the Insurance Corporation of British Columbia (ICBC), and it wasn't long before ICBC gave me a call. ICBC informed me that the person whose car I had hit was trying to claim some sort of injury compensation and that ICBC needed me to bring my car into one of their testing centres so, as part of their investigation into the claim, they could examine the damage it had sustained.

The results of ICBC's tests determined that I had hit the car in front of me at less than 5 mph. As far as ICBC was concerned, this impact could not have resulted in any sort of compensable injury. After the tests were complete, the insurance agent explained to me that, given ICBC would not be giving this claimant any sort of compensation for her alleged injury, the claimant's next course of action, if she desired, would be to sue me personally for up to $100,000.

In the end, the claimant chose not to sue me. This event, however, certainly opened my eyes to how easy it is for someone to sue you. Accidents happen, and if this small accident could have possibly cost me $100,000, then you better believe there's a chance for far worse. With this in mind, be sure you have adequate auto insurance coverage.

Umbrella Insurance

One option that some individuals may want to consider is purchasing some sort of umbrella insurance. Umbrella insurance is a type of insurance that offers additional protection, typically in million dollar increments, above the other types of insurance coverage that you have.

Umbrella insurance, therefore, would be able to help pay for any claims you might have to pay out in the event that your other sources of insurance coverage became exhausted.

Whether or not you purchase this type of extra insurance coverage will likely depend on how much you have to lose. However, even if you aren't worth millions just yet, if you work in a well-paying profession that has a high propensity of being sued, umbrella insurance might be something you want to look into.

This is because, by making a claim on your future earnings, someone might be able to sue you as if you were already worth millions. In these types of cases, the extra insurance provided by umbrella insurance may well be worth the additional cost.

Divorce

Finally, I would be remiss if I didn't mention the financial risk involved with getting a costly divorce.

Despite not really falling into the category of lawsuits, the risk of a divorce severely impacting your financial freedom is probably higher than any of the previous lawsuits mentioned.

You don't have to think too hard to come up with a few celebrities whose fortunes have been severely impacted by various divorces. Moreover, I've spoken to more than a few individuals who have told me that there is no way they can retire early because of the impact of a previous divorce.

Not only can divorce settlements result in a loss of your current assets, just like some of the lawsuits mentioned above, they can also result in a claim on your future earnings. This means that divorces can potentially impact your financial wellbeing well into the future.

Obviously, it's harder to insure yourself against this type of risk than it is to insure yourself against some of the other types of risk that we have already discussed, not unless you want to get a prenuptial agreement. Nonetheless, given the fact that about half of all marriages in Canada and the U.S. end in divorce, it may, unfortunately, be something that you might want to consider.

Passing Your Financial Freedom to Future Generations

The CEOs of many successful corporations, such as IBM, The Coca-Cola Company, and Johnson and Johnson, have ensured that these businesses have been around for over a hundred years. Some successful corporations, like Colgate, are over 200 years-old. The CEOs of these companies don't plan to use up all the company's money and have the company go bankrupt after one CEO finishes his or her tenure. Neither should you.

Not only do the CEOs of large, successful corporations properly manage their finances and protect their companies from risks, they also ensure that they groom future managers and future CEOs to do the same.

No respectable CEO would, all of a sudden, put someone in charge of their business if that person had absolutely no knowledge or experience about running this business (not unless that business wished for financial disaster). Neither should you.

You owe it to your children to ensure they have the knowledge to not only take over and run your financial freedom fund, but the knowledge, discipline, and courage, to create and manage their own financial freedom fund.

Just like CEOs groom future managers and future CEOs, you need to groom your children to create and manage their own financial freedom funds.

Moreover, just like a successful corporation gets passed on to future CEOs, you want to pass your financial freedom fund on to future generations. Ideally, you want each generation to benefit from your financial freedom fund, grow it, and then pass it on for future generations to do the same.

Financially free or not, frank discussions about wealth will help your children to learn the value of money, the importance of saving and investing, and the importance of starting these habits early.

Without these frank discussions, they will end up like the majority of society - saving very little, investing nothing, and living from paycheque to paycheque.

My parents were not financially free, but they instilled the merits of saving and investing in me at a young age. Looking back on this today, I cannot thank them enough.

My hope is that my wife and I can live a happy life, continue to grow our financial freedom fund, and then pass these investments on to our children one day. Moreover, it is also my hope that my children can then do the same for their children.

This will be a difficult task. According to Williams Group Wealth Consultancy, 70% of wealthy families lose their wealth by the second generation. An incredible 90% of wealthy families lose their wealth by the third generation.

In fact, there is a popular saying among wealth advisors that the first generation makes it, the second generation spends it, and the third generation blows it.

One strategy that some CEOs have adopted, in order to ensure their company's future success and longevity, is to have a type of roadmap for future generations to follow. This road map is meant to be used as a guide, in good times and in bad. When it comes to passing your financial freedom fund on to your children, this type of idea might be something well worth considering.

An example of such a guide in the corporate world is the credo created by Johnson and Johnson Inc. This credo is a one page document that lays out the company's values and guides the company's future investment decisions.

Every employee at Johnson and Johnson is expected to know the credo and refer to it when faced with difficult business decisions. The credo has been around since 1943, and it is still used by all levels of management in the company today. Its importance is underlined by the fact that it is chiselled into the wall of the company's New Jersey headquarters.

Just like Johnson and Johnson talks to all its employees about the credo, **you need to talk to your children about money. And you need to have these talks early in their lives and have them often.**

Unlike so many parents out there, help groom your children to achieve financial freedom. Help them to see that happiness comes more from spending time with family and friends and less from the accumulation of stuff. Encourage them to develop good saving and investing habits early on in their lives and help them to realize that achieving financial freedom is an important goal that should be aggressively pursued.

If your children are already adults and are not financially free, then consider leaving them a type of roadmap to manage your financial freedom fund when you are gone. This roadmap shouldn't be complicated, but it should pass on strategies for building wealth and for protecting it. It should emphasize the importance of saving money, not living beyond one's means, proper investing strategies, and the time value of money.

If you can instill some of these tried and true strategies for wealth building in your children, then perhaps you can become one of the lucky 10% of wealthy families out there that are able to achieve intergenerational wealth, and not one of the 90% of wealthy families out there that has one generation's wealth squandered by the next.

As a parent, I am constantly teaching my children to be kind and to be a force of good in this world. I teach them to respect and to take care of others and to respect and take care of themselves. I tell them that with hard-work and effort, they can be anything they want in life. I make sure they believe this. I teach them about the importance of patience, discipline, and caring. I love them unconditionally and, last but not least, I teach them about money sucking maggots.

The Story of the Vanderbilt Family

In 1794, Cornelius Vanderbilt was born into a poor family on Staten Island, New York. At the age of 16, Cornelius (also known as "Commodore Vanderbilt") started his own ferry service. By 1840, Cornelius owned a fleet of 100 steamboats and employed more people than any company in America. It was around this time that Cornelius started branching out into the railway business as well, and in 1847, he took over the presidency of New York, Providence, and Boston Railway. It was the first of many railways he would head.

In addition to steamships and railways, Cornelius operated many other businesses during his lifetime and also bought large amounts of real estate in Manhattan and Staten Island. In 1877, when he died, Commodore Vanderbilt was worth well over $100 billion (in terms of inflation adjusted 2007 US dollars).

At the time of his death, Cornelius Vanderbilt was survived by his wife and twelve of his thirteen children. Cornelius, however, left over 90% of his estate to only one of these children, William Henry Vanderbilt. William had been carefully groomed by Cornelius to manage the family's business and wealth, and he was the only child that Cornelius felt comfortable leaving his fortune to. His decision would prove to be correct. William would go on to expand the family's railroad empire and increase the family's fortune to an astonishing $231 billion (2007 inflation adjusted US dollars.) At the time of his death in 1885, William was the richest man in the world. From this point on, however, the Vanderbilt fortune would start to decline.

While Cornelius Vanderbilt had built his fortune with legendary frugality and hard work, many of his decedents were anything but frugal. The Commodore's descendants would go on to spend much of the family's fortune on extravagant lifestyles, great country estates, and opulent Fifth Avenue mansions, while doing little to expand on the family's business ventures.

According to the book *Fortune's Children: The Fall of the House of Vanderbilt*, written by Arthur T Vanderbilt II, much of the family's fortune is now lost. Arthur T Vanderbilt writes that by 1947, seventy years after the Commodore's death, all of the ornate Vanderbilt mansions had been broken to rubble and much of their contents auctioned off. He also writes that when 120 of the Commodore's descendants gathered at Vanderbilt University in 1973 for the first family reunion, there was not a millionaire among them.

If a fortune as large as the Vanderbilt's can be lost, then you better believe yours can be lost too. Talk to your children about money and talk to them about how to build and preserve wealth.

Live the Life You Truly Want

For this last section of the book, arguably the most important, let's skip any talk about CEOs or large, successful companies and, instead, talk about one of my personal mentors.

Upon returning from Spain, I quickly found myself back at the flying school where I had done all of my flight training.

I had gone back to the school to take an airplane up for a short sightseeing flight and to go out to lunch with my old boss, Dave Parry. I felt the excitement build as I stepped back into the airplane. Excitement, adventure, and seeing the world from a whole new perspective, was why I loved to fly. Flying, however, wasn't the only thing I was excited about that day. I was also excited to see my old boss and mentor, Dave.

Not only is Dave the best pilot I know, he is also the best teacher and the best boss I've ever had. He is warm, generous, and fun to be around. Most importantly, he is genuinely happy. What's more, his happiness is infectious. After you spend time with Dave, you usually end up leaving the school in a better mood than when you first came in. I have often reflected on what makes Dave so happy. Here's what I've come up with:

What Makes Dave so Happy?

1. He does what he loves.
2. He doesn't sweat the small stuff. We could be plummeting towards the ground together in a small plane that has entered a spiral dive and he'll be looking out the window saying something like, "Wow, look at those two eagles over there."
3. He's healthy. He bikes everywhere and makes an effort to take care of himself.
4. He is giving. He gives out compliments, he donates his time, and he donates his money. All this giving not only makes others happy, it makes him happy as well.
5. He makes time for what is important to him. He regularly makes time for his family and his friends, and he makes time for himself.

Maybe you get your financial freedom at a young age, maybe you don't. Whether you are wealthy or not, it is important to realize that financial freedom by itself will not necessarily bring happiness.

Whether you have already achieved financial freedom, or whether you are still working towards it, take a cue from Dave and start doing some of the things mentioned above so that you can start feeling happier right now.

Make some time to take care of yourself and make some time to start doing a few of the things you love. Don't sweat the small stuff, be more giving, and make time for friends and family. And when you do get your financial freedom, do more of these things.

"Every life is a story - make yours a best seller."

\- Unknown

Achieving financially freedom shouldn't be an end, it should be a beginning. It's a big, wonderful world out there. Try something new, live somewhere else, or start a new job. Whatever you end up doing, I hope you end up living the life you truly want and that you pursue that life with drive and vigour. As some wise soul somewhere once wrote, "Every life is a story – make yours a best seller!"

Final Conclusions

You now have all the knowledge you need to achieve financial freedom and start living the life you truly want. Now go back to the business planning section in chapter 2 and get started!

"Risk more than others think safe. Dream more than others think practical. Expect more than others think possible. Care more than others think wise."
- Howard Schultz (CEO of Starbucks)

Follow the lead of some of the most successful CEOs and business magnates the world has ever seen. Set some big audacious goals and go after them like John D. Rockefeller, cut costs like Sam Walton (and many of the other famous business leaders mentioned here), build up your financial acumen and innovate like Henry Ford, take advantage of opportunities like Ray Kroc, diversify and manage risk like Sir John Templeton, think about using some leverage like Warren Buffett, and minimize taxes like Ingvar Kamprad. Think like these famous CEOs and get rich.

KEY POINTS FROM CHAPTER TWELVE

- You must be sure to manage your financial freedom fund appropriately.

- The three big risks to your financial freedom are: (1) mismanagement of your wealth, (2) catastrophic events, and (3) lawsuits.

- The most common way to lose one's wealth is to live an extravagant lifestyle that is beyond one's means.

- Make sure you have enough insurance to protect you, your family, and your financial freedom fund, from any sort of catastrophic event.

- Ensure your children possess the knowledge to achieve financial freedom.

- Talk to your children about money early in their lives and have these conversations often.

- Make time for the things that make you happy. Spend time with family and friends, be healthier, be more giving, and don't sweat the small stuff.

- Go after the life you truly want.

Appendix: Modern Portfolio Theory

The risk-reward relationship obtained by holding a portfolio of individual investments is examined in the figure below.

Expected Return Vs Risk

(The Efficient Frontier)

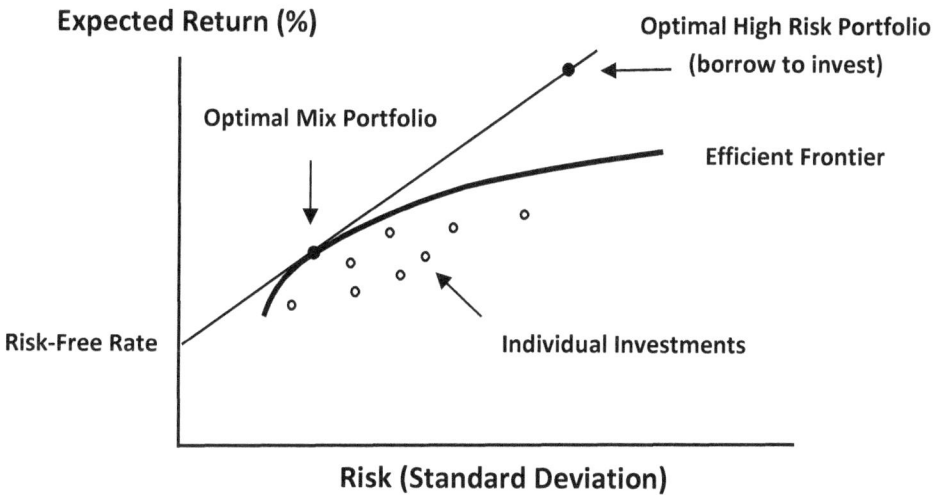

Expected Return (%)

Optimal High Risk Portfolio
(borrow to invest)

Optimal Mix Portfolio

Efficient Frontier

Risk-Free Rate

Individual Investments

Risk (Standard Deviation)

Expected return is expressed on the vertical axis. It is given as the percent return you would expect to generate by holding a given portfolio of individual investments.

The risk associated with this portfolio of investments is expressed on the horizontal axis and is given in terms of the variation of these expected returns.

Variation provides a gauge as to how much your actual return may differ from your expected return. For example, you may expect a portfolio of investments to generate an average return of 7% a year, over the long-term, however, this could mean 7% each and every year (in which case there is a low variation of returns and, therefore, low risk), or it could mean a return of positive 6% one year, negative 20% the following year, and positive 35% the year after that (in which case, even though the average return over the three year period is still 7%, the variation in returns is much higher and, therefore, so is the risk).

The risk-free rate is the point on the graph that represents the expected return from an investment offering almost no risk. It is always on the vertical axis and typically represents the return available on short-term government debt such as U.S. T-bills.

All other individual investments, such as stocks, bonds, and REITs, would be expected to possess more risk and would, therefore, be positioned to the right of the vertical axis.

The graph shows that for any given level of risk or conversely for any given expected return, there is an optimum portfolio of risky assets that lies on the *efficient frontier*.

Portfolios on the efficient frontier offer the highest return for a given level of risk (or the lowest risk for a given return).

The graph also shows that there is one portfolio, the *optimal mix portfolio*, which offers the highest expected return for the lowest amount of risk. The optimal portfolio, therefore, offers the highest risk-adjusted return.

Furthermore, the graph shows that the *optimal high risk portfolio* is created by borrowing money to invest in the optimal mix portfolio. This suggests that the least risky way to seek out higher investment returns is to borrow money and invest it in a portfolio of diversified investments that offers the highest risk-adjusted return.

The Efficient Frontier

Holding a mix of investments whose investment returns are not correlated over time, results in investment portfolios that lie on or close to the efficient frontier. The efficient frontier is shown as the bold curve on the graph above.

Portfolios of individual investments that are on or close to the efficient frontier offer the best expected return for the lowest amount of risk. That is why the efficient frontier lies above all the individual investments shown on the graph. By diversifying and holding a variety of investments, you move closer to the efficient frontier and get a better return for the risk you take on.

Portfolios that offer higher expected returns lie higher up and more to the right along the efficient frontier. Portfolios that offer lower expected returns lie lower down and more to the left along the efficient frontier.

Notice that whenever you desire a higher return, you are forced to take on more risk, even when moving along the efficient frontier.

The Optimal Mix Portfolio

The optimal mix portfolio offers the best risk-adjusted return. This portfolio lies on a line tangent to the efficient frontier that passes through the vertical axis at the risk-free rate. It is the point on the graph where the diagonal tangent line just touches the efficient frontier curve.

The optimal mix portfolio would contain a range of investments in a variety of asset classes. These investments would contain different levels of risk and offer different expected returns.

Higher expected return portfolios on the efficient frontier lie to the right of the optimal mix portfolio and are higher along the curve. These portfolios would offer higher expected returns, but would only do so at a greater than proportionate amount of risk. These portfolios might, for example, be portfolios that are diversified with a mix of tech stocks and higher risk corporate bonds.

Lower risk portfolios on the efficiency frontier lie to the left of the optimal mix portfolio and are lower down on the efficient frontier curve. These types of portfolios would offer lower risk, but would only do so at a greater than proportionate decrease in expected returns. These types of portfolios, for example, might be diversified with the stocks of utility companies and less risky short-term government bonds.

The best bang for your buck, however, would be the optimal mix portfolio. If you want less risk, then you need to accept a greater than proportionate decrease in expected returns. If you want higher returns, then you need to assume a greater than proportionate increase in risk.

The Optimal High Risk Portfolio

The optimal high risk portfolio offers the highest expected return for the lowest possible risk. It is the point on the graph located higher up on the tangent line.

The optimal high risk portfolio is created by investing in the optimal mix portfolio and then borrowing money at the risk-free rate and investing more in this portfolio.

According to MPT, investors that are willing to go after higher returns face the least amount of risk for the higher returns they seek when they borrow money and invest it in the optimal mix portfolio. This strategy would make sense when their expected return is higher than the risk-free rate.

About the Author

Tyrone Shephard has an MBA in finance and has had an interest in personal finance his whole life. Before attaining financial freedom, he worked in a variety of positions in the banking and the pharmaceutical industries.

At the age of thirty-six, after applying the business principles he learned at school and at work to his personal finances, Tyrone achieved financial freedom. He left the rat-race and never looked back. At the age of thirty-eight he had become a commercial pilot and a flight instructor. Shortly after, he and his wife threw caution to the wind, quit their jobs, and spent a year living off their investment income in the south coast of Spain.

Tyrone lives with his wife, Analia, and his two young children, Daniella and Alexander, in Coquitlam, British Columbia, where he is currently working on his second book, planning his next adventure overseas, and living the life he truly wants.

Please visit his website at www.moneysuckingmaggots.com